Francis Ellingwood Abbot, William J. (William James) Potter

Lectures and Sermons

Francis Ellingwood Abbot, William J. (William James) Potter

Lectures and Sermons

ISBN/EAN: 9783337158774

Printed in Europe, USA, Canada, Australia, Japan

Cover: Foto ©Lupo / pixelio.de

More available books at **www.hansebooks.com**

LECTURES AND SERMONS

BY

WILLIAM J. POTTER

With a Biographical Sketch

BY

FRANCIS ELLINGWOOD ABBOT, PH.D.

BOSTON
GEO. H. ELLIS, 141 FRANKLIN STREET
1895

CONTENTS.

	PAGE
PREFATORY NOTE	iii
BIOGRAPHICAL SKETCH .	v
LIST OF PUBLICATIONS	lxxix

RELIGIOUS SENTIMENT IN THE LIGHT OF SCIENCE	1
THE TWENTY-THIRD PSALM IN THE NINETEENTH CENTURY:	
I. The Eternal our Shepherd .	25
II. Green Pastures and Still Waters .	46
III. Paths of Safety	65
IV. The Valley of Shadows	89
V. The Overflowing Bounty	111
VI. The Eternal Goodness and Human Destiny	130
THE TRINITY OF EVOLUTION	153
RELIGION AS THE AFFIRMATION OF GOD IN HUMAN NATURE	167
RATIONAL GROUNDS FOR WORSHIP .	182
THE WORLD'S PARLIAMENT OF RELIGIONS . .	201
SEALED ORDERS	232

CONTENTS

WHEAT AND TARES	246
COURAGE OF CONVICTIONS	263
HEROISMS IN DAILY LIFE	276
THE SAVING POWER OF TRUTH	289
THE VOICE OF THE DRAFT	306
THE DRAMATIC ELEMENT IN THE CAREER OF LINCOLN	324
THE HIGHER PATRIOTISM	354

PREFATORY NOTE.

The sermons included in this volume extend over the greater part of Mr. Potter's ministry,—from 1863, the date of "The Voice of the Draft," to 1893, when "The World's Parliament of Religions" was written. Nearly all of them were preached many times, and subject to such constant revision that the final form, as here printed, often differs materially from the original. For this reason I have not assigned a date to each sermon. The series of lectures on the Twenty-third Psalm, which he delivered in Boston and Worcester in the fall of 1893, had originally been given in part as sermons in New Bedford in 1892. These lectures it was my father's expressed intention to publish. In the selection of the sermons I have been guided partly by the frequency with which he preached them, thus following somewhat his own judgment; and, also, by suggestions kindly made by his friends and parishioners in New Bedford. It is interesting to note that in many cases his own choice and that of his hearers seems to coincide. Many of these sermons, it may also be added, he carried with him and preached on his journey to the West in 1893.

ALFRED C. POTTER.

CAMBRIDGE, MASS., Dec. 10, 1894.

BIOGRAPHICAL SKETCH.

BY FRANCIS ELLINGWOOD ABBOT.

To be noble in character is the supreme service which one man can render to his fellows. It is greater than any particular achievement, however splendid, because it is itself the achievement of achievements, the most useful and the most difficult of deeds. Single actions may easily command more gratitude and more praise, since they tax less the average man's faculties of imagination, comprehension, and appreciation. But to be from birth to death one long activity devoted to the highest ends, disinterested and lofty and pure, is to be more than a doer of dramatic exploits, however brilliant, because, while this is possible to few, that is to exemplify and encourage what is possible to all. When asked what improvement he could suggest in the actual constitution of the universe, a pessimist replied: "I would make health as catching as disease." In this reply there was more wit than wisdom; for such is the actual order of things that, in the spiritual sphere at least, the contagiousness of good is even greater than that of evil. If it were not so, the world would scarcely hold together. And that it is so has been made clear to all, with the powerful persuasiveness of an example as beautiful as it is rare, in the life of William James Potter.

The story of this life is simple and short. Little is found for the recorder of it to tell. Its events were not such as to attract wide attention or to furnish the materials of an exciting tale. But its quality was such as to command the reverence and win the love of an ever increasing circle of those whose judgment is the judgment of the universal conscience. From beginning to end it was the self-consecration of a pure spirit to universal aims — the devotion of large intellectual powers, great practical wisdom, a strong but never aggressive will, and shy but tender sympathies, to the highest welfare of all. To have lived such a life, in luminous contrast and superiority to the melancholy self-seeking so common among mankind, is to have won the truest and grandest success which can crown any human career.

I.

William J. Potter was born at North Dartmouth, Massachusetts, youngest of the nine children of William and Anna (Aiken) Potter. A curious doubt in his own mind hung over the year of his birth. On February 1, 1848, he wrote in his journal: "Once more has time brought around my birthday — the first day of my twentieth year." On February 1, 1850, he wrote: "My twenty-first birthday — I am now *legally* a *man*, a *free*-man." These two entries fix the date of his birth as February 1, 1829.

Yet in later times he habitually thought and wrote of the year of his birth as 1830. It does not appear on the town records, but in the records of the Friends at Dartmouth it is recorded as "2 mo. 1st, 1829." Examination of these records, however, shows that they are not original, but were written at some subsequent time; and, as their source is unknown, they cannot be considered final. The reader, therefore, is left to draw his own inference from the facts.

The original emigrant-ancestor of the Potter family, from whom William was descended in the seventh generation, was Nathaniel Potter, who came from England to Rhode Island, and died there prior to 1644. His son, Nathaniel Potter (1637-1704), who married Elizabeth Stokes, was born at Portsmouth, Rhode Island, but removed to Dartmouth, Massachusetts. In the third generation, Samuel Potter (1675-1748) married Mary Benton and lived at Dartmouth. In the fourth generation, Benjamin Potter, of Dartmouth, married Ruth Brownell in 1736. In the fifth generation, William Halladay Potter, of Dartmouth, who married Patience Thurston, was born in 1748 and died in 1814. In the sixth generation, William Potter (1784-1870) married Anna Aiken in 1812; and their ninth child, William James, was born, as just shown, on February 1, 1829.

Other lineal ancestors were Adam Mott, of Cambridge, England, whose son, Adam Mott, born in England, came over to Newport in 1634, and was a prominent member of the society of Friends; John Williams, who came from England to Scituate in

1632; Captain Michael Pierce, who was born in England, lived at Hingham and Scituate, and was killed by the Indians in King Philip's War, 1676; Thomas Holbrook, of England, who lived successively at Weymouth, Dorchester, and Medfield, and died in 1677; Matthew Gannett, who was born in England in 1618, settled at Hingham, was at Scituate in 1651, and died in 1695; Anthony Dodson, who was at Scituate in 1650. All these were ancestors on the father's side, while among those on the mother's side are found the names of Aiken, Howland, Perry, and Hathaway. It appears, therefore, that William J. Potter came of good old New England stock, including original Quakers, and at least one Indian-fighter who laid down his life in defence of the colony. But no clergyman or minister has been thus far discovered among his ancestors.

II.

The materials from which this sketch of Mr. Potter's life is drawn are extremely meagre. Four manuscript journals covering portions of the period from 1847 to 1858, a few miscellaneous memoranda of his own, a few notes by his son, and a few pamphlets and newspaper cuttings,— these are the only data which have been supplied to me. Out of these scanty materials it is impossible to construct a connected story, or even to outline the course of development which, beginning with the Quaker boy on an old New England farm, ended in one of the wisest and best of men and one of the foremost religious reformers of our generation. Outwardly so peaceful and noiseless, inwardly so bold in thought and so rich in thought's results, his spiritual life flowed on like a river amidst the beautiful scenery of an old cultivated plain, yet brought down among the haunts of men an illimitable wealth of golden grains from the mountain fastnesses of his own being. All who knew him must rejoice that he lived long enough to concentrate this wealth in so beautiful a form as that of the series of lectures in Boston in which his life as religious teacher came to a memorable culmination. And multitudes who knew him not will now discover that, when he died, they had been "entertaining an angel unawares."

The brief story of his outward career is easily told.

Born and brought up on his father's farm, Potter was educated in the district schools of Dartmouth and the Friends' school at Providence, Rhode Island. His home life was happy, and during his vacations he cheerfully helped his father in doing the farm work. In fact, it was his father's strong desire to see him make farming his life-work and carry on the old place as his ancestors had done, But William felt the stirrings of higher aspirations and capacities than could be satisfied by agriculture as a permanent occupation, and felt constrained to take up teaching as opening a field for their better development. In the end his father reluctantly consented that he should go to the Normal School at Bridgewater and fit himself for the life of a teacher. This school he entered, December 2, 1847, and during his second term got some practical experience by instructing the entering class. On November 25, 1848, he began to teach a school at Kingston, and remained there till March 25, 1849; but he did not feel satisfied with his own success. While in Kingston, earlier desires to go to college were rekindled. May 1, however, finds him beginning a new school at Sandwich, with fifty scholars between the ages of twelve and seventeen. His stay was short; the school committee were not satisfied with the discipline maintained, and he returned home, May 26, to fit himself for college without a teacher. This difficult labor he pursued with more or less success till October 5, when he received a letter from Henry B. Wheelwright, preceptor of the Bristol Academy in Taunton, offering him a situation there. The salary was small, but he was to have Mr. Wheelwright's assistance in fitting for college. The offer was accepted, and he remained teaching at Taunton till May 15, 1850, when he returned home to resume his studies more uninterruptedly in preparing for the college examination. After some quite heroic work, he passed the examination successfully, and was admitted as a member of the freshman class at Harvard College, July 16, without conditions. The result was very creditable to him under his difficult circumstances. In August he joined his class in Cambridge.

Under date of September 19, 1850, only about three weeks after he began his college work, I find his first mention of the ministry, as follows: —

"For several months my mind has been quite unsettled again as to what is to be the business of my life, owing partly to my disappointment in teaching, and partly to a kind of *mental attraction* which I have for some time experienced towards the ministry. Of course, I feel my entire unfitness, both in talents and in depth of religious character, for such a work; yet I cannot blind myself to the very obvious inclining of my mind towards it. What is the motive of the movement is not so easily perceived. I have not yet been able to fully analyze this tendency of my feelings, so as to discover whence it springs, how composed, and how much attention it is worthy to receive. About all I can say is that it exists, and *has* existed for nearly a year, but that previously the bias of my mind was rather against the ministry as a profession for myself. Is it the voice of duty or of inclination? Is it the natural, legitimate product of my own soul, to be heeded and observed, or is it a mere fluttering of fancy sent to try my judgment, and which is to be expelled as a hostile intruder? These questions, though important, I cannot yet answer. When I look forward to such a work, I see numerous obstructions rising up in the way of my ever becoming engaged in it, and some of them apparently insurmountable; yet the *feeling* haunts me still, and reason sets to work with imagination to devise means for clearing the path of all hindrances. Besides deficiency of talents and religious character, which alone seems sufficient to debar me from a profession now suffering from this very cause, there are other hindrances, arising out of the circumstances of my past life and the nature of my present sentiments, peculiar to myself. I have not yet outlived the influence of the Quaker element in my education. My mind still has a kind of repugnance to *learning* to be a minister, though my *reason* finds nothing objectionable in it. Again, I can scarcely reconcile the idea of my becoming a clergyman with my present views of theology, churches, religious rites, &c. And what society or sect must I go with, believing with none? What creed should I preach, possessing none? I have in my mind, it is true, an *ideal* minister different from any *real* one whom it was ever my lot to know. But have I any reason to hope I could approach more nearly my ideal of a minister than I have approached my ideal of a teacher? Thus the matter comes to my mind, presenting arguments pro and con, and receiving replies; but as yet there is no decision. In the meantime let me do *present* duty, and the future in due season will develop itself. More light will be afforded, as I use correctly present supplies."

During his freshman vacation, from December 1, 1850, to February 28, 1851, Potter kept school in Medfield, succeeding somewhat better than formerly in meeting the demands of his own exacting ideal. Probably he taught school more or less in the winter vacations of his later college years; but no journal has been found which gives a record of his college life beyond the end of his sophomore year. He was appointed "orator" by "our class society" (Institute of 1770), and gave his oration to universal satisfaction at the close of that year. He became a member of the Alpha Delta Phi and the Phi Beta Kappa societies, and was graduated in the class of 1854.

III.

On June 1, not long before his graduation, Potter received the appointment of "Hopkins classical teacher" in the Cambridge High School, being the first to hold this position, and continued to discharge its duties till 1856, when he resigned it. During the year 1856–1857, he was a student in the Harvard Divinity School, but was never graduated there.

On August 9, 1857, he started from New York for Europe in the "Louis Napoleon," a German sailing-vessel, together with Gerald Fitzgerald (Divinity School, 1859) and Henry W. Brown (Harvard College, 1852, and Divinity School, 1857). Arriving at Hamburg on September 14, he immediately proceeded to Berlin, and on the 19th was matriculated as a student of philosophy at the University, engaging lessons in German at the same time from a private teacher. When the term began, October 22, he listened to lectures by Haupt on the Satires of Horace and Trendelenburg on the history of philosophy; but he writes, "I scarcely understood a dozen words of both of them." Later in November, he heard lectures by Wuttke on the history of Christian dogma and on Hegel's philosophy and its relation to Christianity — by Michelet on the philosophy of modern history since 1775, — by Vatke on some metaphysical questions, — and by Althaus on Goethe's

"Faust;" and now, he writes, "I begin to discover a little progress in understanding the lectures." He remained at Berlin, studying, visiting the art-galleries, and observing German life, till March 1, 1858, when he went to Dresden. Here he stayed about a month, devoting much of his time to the picture galleries; then, passing rapidly through Leipzig, Bamberg, Nuremberg, Munich, Ulm, and Stuttgart, he repaired to Tübingen, April 13, where he remained to study, rooming with Mr. Brown. Here he heard Baur on an uninteresting subject, and Fichte on the history of modern philosophy ("the students here call him 'der wortreiche Sohn des geistreichen Vaters'"); but the lecture courses were not sufficiently attractive to induce him to matriculate. On May 10, he writes: "Concluded to give up attending lectures and devote myself to study in my room. Still read Baur and his school of theology with great pleasure." On July 1: "To-day we are packing for Switzerland. Our Tübingen race is run. Though we make it a short term, I feel that I have got much from it — much from my reading. I now see what Baur and his school have done, and am better able to give a scientific reason for my disbelief in the old-school theology than I was before." And on July 2: "Left Tübingen at 12 o'clock in company with Brown and Brooks for Switzerland, by way of Baden and Freiburg."

The itinerary of the Swiss-Italian journey, which occupied about six weeks, can be made out to have been as follows: —

July 2. Tübingen, Wildbad.
" 3. Baden-Baden.
" 5. Freiburg.
" 6. Schaffhausen.
" 7. Dachsen and the Rhine Falls.
" 8. Zürich.
" 9. Horgen, Zug, Arth, Mt. Rigi.
" 10. Wäggis, Küssnacht, Lucerne.
" 11. Fluelen, Amstag, Gothard Pass, Hospenthal.
" 12. Furka Pass, Grimsel.
" 13. Guttanen, Reichenbach.
" 14. Greater Scheideck, Faulhorn.
" 15. Grindelwald.
" 16. Wengern Alp, Lauterbrunnen, Interlaken.
" 17. Lake Brienz, Giessbach Falls.
" 18. Neuhaus, Thun, Berne.
" 19. Freiburg.
" 20. Vevay, Chillon.
" 21. Geneva.
" 23. Chamonix.
" 25. Martigny, *via* Tête Noire.
" 26. St. Bernard Pass.
" 27. Aosta, Chatillon.
" 28. St. Théodule Pass, Breuil.
" 29. Görner Grat.
" 30. Zermatt, Vispnach.
" 31. Simplon Pass.
August 1. Isella, Domo d' Ossola.
" 2. Pallanza, Lake Maggiore.
" 3. Magadino, Luvino, Lugano.

August 4. Carpolago, Milan.
" 6. Sondrio.
" 7. Bormio.
" 8. Stelvio Pass, Mals.
" 9. Finstermüng Pass, Landeck.
" 10. Innsbrück.
" 11. Kufstein, Rosenheim.
" 12. Stock, Traunstein, Reichenhall.
" 13. Berchtesgaden.
" 14. Hallein, Salzburg.
" 15. Munich.

From Munich, where he stayed a few days, Potter went to Heidelberg on August 22, made a five-days excursion to Mannheim, Mainz, Cologne, and Coblenz, and returned to Heidelberg, where he remained studying until October 4. Then he started for Italy once more, by way of Frankfort, Carlsruhe, Strassburg, Basle, Zürich, Rapperschwyl, St. Gall, Ragatz, Coire, and the Splügen Pass. In Italy he went to Chiavenna, Colico, Bergamo, Brescia, and Venice, where he stayed three days,— to Padua, Ferrara, Bologna, and Florence. The last entry in his journal is that of October 22, and ends abruptly, in the midst of a description of Florence by moonlight.

IV.

During the winter of 1858–1859, after his return from Europe, Potter remained in Cambridge as a candidate for the ministry. He preached at New Bedford several times in July, 1859, and finally received an invitation from the wealthy Unitarian society there to become its minister. His ordination took place on December 28, 1859, the ordination sermon being preached by Rev. Dr. William H. Furness; and his first sermon as pastor, printed in the volume which he published in 1885 with the title, "Twenty-five Sermons of Twenty-five Years," was delivered on January 1, 1860.

In the spring of that year, he began keeping house with his sister, Mrs. Ruth Almy, and her husband. In July, 1861, he preached at Washington on the day of the first battle of Bull Run; and he visited the camps in the vicinity during the terrible confusion that ensued. On July 23, 1863, he was drafted; and on the following Sunday, July 26, he delivered a sermon on "The Voice of the Draft," declaring his resolution not to disobey the call of his country in her hour of need. He tendered his resignation as minister of the Unitarian society, which, however, refused to accept it, granting him leave of absence for a year and giving him five hundred dollars. In the latter part of August, he went to Washington at the special request of Secretary Stanton, who had heard of his patriotic course, and who had written the following letter to Hon. John H. Clifford of New Bedford:

WAR DEPARTMENT
WASHINGTON CITY, Aug. 9, 1863.

My dear Sir:
I am infinitely obliged to you for the sermon delivered by Mr. Potter. Such outpouring of a noble spirit cannot fail to do good. I have directed its

publication in the Army and Navy Gazette as the best exposition of the Enrolling Law that has appeared. I think he is right in the belief that the time has come for him to have a nearer view of the great movement of which the war is a development. For this reason I wish to see him. It cannot be otherwise than that he is *drafted* for no ordinary service — a service that needs not, nor can be excused by a surgeon's certificate. Please tell him I wish to see him, and give him my thanks for what he has already done. . . .

Yours truly,
EDWIN M. STANTON.

The result of his interview with the great war minister was that, after preaching his farewell sermon on September 6, Potter was assigned the duty of "visiting and inspecting all the United States hospitals in and near Washington and Alexandria." This duty he faithfully discharged, making elaborate notes of the condition and needs of all the hospitals under his care.

Returning to New Bedford in November, on a furlough, he preached again to his society, and, on November 26, was married to Elizabeth Claghorn Babcock, daughter of Spooner and Lydia Delano Babcock of New Bedford. They proceeded at once to Washington, and in January, 1864, began to keep house in a little one-story hut in the Convalescent Camp, Alexandria, where he had been appointed chaplain. In May, he resigned his position as chaplain, and returned home with his wife. Leaving her there, he went back to the front, and served on the Sanitary Commission. He remained on duty in hospital during the campaigns near Fredericksburg, and was often under fire. In August, 1864, he returned home, his leave of absence having expired, and resumed his duties as minister of the Unitarian Society.

From 1866 to the end of his life, Potter was profoundly interested in the Free Religious Association, and his work in its behalf constitutes, in fact, his chief claim to public remembrance and gratitude beyond the limits of his society and the city of his adoption. He was Secretary of the Association from its birth in 1867 until 1882, and President of it from 1882 to 1893; he was familiar with its inside and outside history as no man could possibly be who had not given to it, as he had done, the faithful continuous service of twenty-six years; and it is a cause of deep regret that he never took up, as I repeatedly urged him to do, the task of compiling an accurate and full history of the Association from the original records, interpreted and enriched by his own personal knowledge. Such a history would have been of priceless value hereafter; and now it can never be written. He shrank from the task, yet was attracted by it, too; and it is more than probable that he would have undertaken it, if his life had been spared ten years longer. What further I may have to say on this subject of the Free Religious Association and of Potter's connection with it must come later.

In the winter of 1872-1873, his eyes gave out, and

his general health became impaired; this obliged him to spend the months of March and April in the milder climate of Florida, where he recovered his strength.

In the spring of 1875, he spent a few weeks in Washington on account of his wife's health — a sad forewarning of the greatest sorrow of his life; and again, in the winters of 1875-1876 and 1876-1877, the same reason took them both South once more, first to Columbia, South Carolina, and afterwards to Kittrell, North Carolina. In June, 1877, still for the same melancholy reason, the whole family removed to Grantville, Massachusetts, now Wellesley Hills, which obliged Potter to travel to New Bedford every week in order to discharge the preacher's duty. His gentle and lovely wife died on December 7, 1879, leaving her husband alone in the care of their two young children. He returned with them from Grantville to New Bedford in May, 1880, but not to the old home. Over this sacred grief let the veil be reverently drawn. Enough to say that no father ever fulfilled his duty more conscientiously or more tenderly or more wisely than did this bereaved and great-souled man.

When "The Index" was founded in Toledo, Ohio, and its first issue appeared on January 1, 1870, Potter assumed charge of a special page devoted to the Free Religious Association, and edited it independently, as Secretary, during the first year of that weekly journal. At the end of the year, this special page was given up, but the leading officers of the Association, together with other invited writers, became henceforth "editorial contributors." This arrangement continued till July 1, 1880, when the original editor of "The Index" resigned; and the Index Association, of which Potter was the President, gave to the Free Religious Association the entire property and goodwill of "The Index," valued at over five thousand dollars, on condition of continuing to publish the journal in the cause of "Free Religion." Proprietorship of "The Index" was now vested in trustees selected by the Free Religious Association, and Potter became editor, with an assistant, of "The Free Religious Index"—a name subsequently changed back to its original form. This function he continued to discharge, going to Boston weekly to supervise the "making-up" of the paper, till the end of the year 1886. At that time "The Index" was given up altogether; and the Free Religious Association, ceasing to have a weekly exponent of its ideas, lost greatly in influence and power. During the entire seventeen years of its existence, "The Index" enjoyed the unwearied support and coöperation of Potter's mind and heart; and in its columns are still to be found some of the ripest and richest products of his brain.

The twenty-fifth anniversary of his settlement as minister of the Unitarian Society was celebrated at New Bedford on December 28, 1884. His own anniversary sermon, together with the speeches of Thomas M. Stetson, Esq., and the Hon. William W. Crapo, may be found in the volume already mentioned, "Twenty-five Sermons of Twenty-five Years," which was published in compliance with the request of "many friends" who desired a permanent memorial of their beloved pastor and preacher.

In the spring of 1887, Potter's health was again much broken by sleeplessness and impaired nervous energy, but was restored for the time by a month's trip to the South. In 1889, from January to June, he was compelled to take another and longer rest in Florida and South Carolina. So much discouraged did he feel at last, in consequence of these repeated failures of health, that he tendered his resignation in April of this year; but his society, which was devotedly attached to him, refused to accept it, and insisted on lightening his labors by giving him a colleague. A young graduate of the Harvard Divinity School in whom he had become deeply interested, Mr. Paul Revere Frothingham, was invited to become his associate pastor, and, in accordance with Potter's own earnest wishes, was ordained as such on October 9, 1889.

But the long and faithful service was drawing to a close. In January, 1890, Potter was once more obliged to seek rest and recovery at the South; and, feeling that his life-work in New Bedford had been fully accomplished, he sent in his final resignation on October 2, 1892. To all entreaties to withdraw it, he remained inflexible, and his decision was communicated to the society in the following letter: —

NEW BEDFORD, Sept. 27, 1892.

To the Members of the First Congregational Society in New Bedford:

MY DEAR FRIENDS,— The time has come when I am constrained by a sense of duty to announce to you my desire and purpose to withdraw from the pastoral office which, by the kindness of this Society, I have held nearly thirty-three years.

I am moved to this action by no sudden impulse, nor is there need to assure you that it arises from no break in the harmony of our parochial relations.

For a considerable time I have contemplated such a step,— not with the view of retiring from the ministry, but that I may be free, after possibly a brief interval of rest, for a somewhat different kind of professional labor; or, at least, for carrying elsewhere the religious message which these years have made so familiar to you. During the period of active work which remains to me, and which I trust is not to be brief, I am convinced that I can use my resources to better advantage in a different field.

It is to be, I am aware, no easy nor pleasant incident thus to sever the various ties which bind us together — ties professional and personal, which, for many of you as for me, have been forming through the lapse of a generation. In bonds of sorrow and of joy, as well as by the interests of united religious endeavor, our lives have been knit into each other.

Nowhere else can I expect again to establish the home-feeling which has grown up for me among you, and in this place so near the spot of my birth and the homes of my ancestors and kindred, and I shall hail it as a kind fortune if I shall be permitted, after my working days are finished, to return hither to spend in this community the remnant of my life. But that time is not yet; and meanwhile the voice of duty rather than sentiment is to be heeded. Believing that in the years immediately to come I can labor more advantageously elsewhere, I ask that you will grant me a friendly release from our compact.

By the terms of my settlement, notice of a desire on either side to terminate the relation was to be given six months previous to the act of dissolution.

The Society, however, would confer on me a special favor, if it should so far waive this condition as to allow my resignation to take effect on the 28th of next December, which will be the anniversary of my ordination and will bring my ministry to the full period of thirty-three years.

I feel the more free to request this concession, inasmuch as the junior pastor, who in his three years of service has proved himself amply and acceptably equipped for all pastoral duties, will then have returned from his absence in Europe, and will be on the spot to take up the work of the parish, with no break in its interests. I am happy in the thought that I can thus leave the Society well organized in its various departments, and advancing under earnest and vigorous leadership to improve new opportunities.

In the future as in the past, the harmony, progress, and welfare of this Society will ever be dear to my heart. By its generous liberality and aid, I have been enabled to do what must now stand as the main work of my life. Both parochially and individually, beloved friends, my best wishes will remain with you and for you; and all your successes in the things that make for the highest interests of human existence will find grateful place among my own purest satisfactions.

With sincere and affectionate regard,
Your friend and pastor,
WM. J. POTTER.

Reluctantly acquiescing at last in Potter's own view of the matter, the Society accepted his resignation with universal sorrow on October 2, in the following resolutions:—

"*Resolved*, That the Senior Pastor shall on the 28th of December next be liberated from all duties to us in New Bedford, to the end that he may be enabled to preach or publish elsewhere the views so faithfully and well preached in our pulpit. He has been a moral power and intellectual centre in our city.

"His preaching has profoundly satisfied the loftiest spiritual and religious needs of ourselves and the many visitors to our services.

"While our love for him and our estimate of his value to us would never permit us to voluntarily allow his departure, yet, as it is solemnly required by him, we can still rejoice that others in other churches and in distant communions may share in the high expositions hitherto confined so much to us.

"Though we are but pupils of his, yet the views

upheld here are widely deemed to represent the status of this church, and it is fitting that in some sense we have our missionary. We extend to him our earnest wishes that his efforts may be blessed with success, and, to assist him therein, we request that he will accept from us the sum of $2,000 annually for five years to assist him in his proposed work.

"We shall be glad to hear his reports of the progress of the Liberal Faith, wherever he may be. We sincerely hope that the kindness of the future may enable us to hear his voice often, and in accordance with his request now accept his tendered resignation, to take effect as above."

The story of this beautiful and unique termination of so long a pastorate will be brought to a full and fit close by the following responsive letter: —

NEW BEDFORD, Dec. 10, 1892.

To the First Congregational Society in New Bedford:

DEAR FRIENDS,— Most grateful acknowledgment is due to you for the very kind terms in which you have accepted my resignation of the pastoral office, and for your generous proposal to share the responsibility for the religious work which I have in mind to do elsewhere.

It is especially gratifying to me thus to have your moral support in the work, while the material aid you ask me to accept will relieve me from certain anxieties and make me much freer in the work than I could be without it.

I am pleased, therefore, to stand in this relation to

you, as your missionary preacher in other parts of our land.

Since, however, unforeseen circumstances may arise which may make it desirable to modify or terminate the relation before the five years named in your vote shall expire, I assent, with the understanding that this arrangement shall not be binding beyond the time when either party to it may desire its dissolution.

Let me also take this opportunity to return my deeply felt thanks for the numerous individual expressions which have come to me of your friendly regard and affection. Though I am to hold toward you but little longer the pastoral relation, it will be to me a constant happiness to keep your religious sympathy, and to deserve, if I may, your continued friendship and good will.

Most sincerely yours,

WM. J. POTTER.

On Christmas Day, 1892, Potter preached his farewell sermon on "Thirty-three Years: their End a Beginning." Henceforth he was a free missionary of free religion. Leaving Boston about a fortnight later, he preached in Chicago on January 15, 1893, and soon afterwards proceeded to California, where he spent about five months, preaching (mostly in Unitarian pulpits) in Pasadena, San Diego, Los Angeles, Fresno, and San Francisco. In June he went to Colorado, where he spent the summer in resting from the fatigues of the winter and spring. Towards the last of August, he returned to Chicago, to attend the World's Parliament of Religions at the Columbian Exposition, and to participate in the twenty-sixth annual meeting of the Free Religious Association, held in connection with the Parliament on September 20. The Parliament itself was the concrete historical realization of a dream of his own, declared in his own words twenty-one years before at the annual meeting of the Free Religious Association in 1872,— words which constitute one of the most remarkable prophecies ever uttered.

"Some of us here," wrote Potter, in the report of the executive committee on that occasion, "may live to see the day when there shall be a World's Convention, in London, or perhaps in Boston, or San Francisco, of representatives from all the great religions of the globe,— coming together in a spirit of mutual respect, confidence, and amity, for common conference on what may be for the best good of all; not to make a common creed by patching articles together from their respective faiths in which they might find themselves in agreement, but, emancipated from bondage to creed and sect, to join hands in a common effort to help mankind to higher truth and nobler living. It may be that the work of this Association will culminate in such a World's Convention — a peace convention of the religions. For that grasp of hands across the dividing line of opinion, with mutual respect for the natural rights of opinion, in a common effort to get truth and to do good, is the Free Religious Association."

Such a vision as this, which at the time was regarded as the outburst of an exaggerated and extravagant enthusiasm, was in truth a flash of religious genius. Seldom, if ever, has a prognostication of the future been so solidly grounded in the nature of things, or a piercing glance into the secret of a far-off evolution been so amply warranted and verified by the subsequent fact. Was there not a rare poetic beauty and fitness in the conjunction of circumstances that permitted the prophet to behold the fulfilment of his own prophecy,— nay, more, to be a part of it, and to drink the delight of helping to usher in the new epoch of Universal Religion which he had so glowingly foretold and labored for so long? There is cause for gratitude to all who loved him that he should have been allowed to taste this supreme satisfaction before he died.

For the end was near. He left Chicago for New Bedford, September 24, and began in Horticultural Hall, Boston, October 22, that noble course of Sunday lectures which was the summing up of all he had won of wisdom in his beautiful life and the grand consummation of his life-work. This course he completed in Boston on December 10, occupying a room meanwhile at "The Otis," 41 Mount Vernon Street — a room that it pleased him at the time to know was situated directly over the room in which his old friend the writer was born. He repeated these lectures one by one in Worcester between November 12 and December 17, when, after preaching in the forenoon for the last time to his beloved society in New Bedford, he went in the afternoon from New Bedford to Worcester, and delivered there once more the closing lecture of his Horticultural Hall course in the evening. That splendid discourse was his swan-song, his last word in public, the fit and beautiful ending of his faithful ministry.

On Thursday, December 21, he had the crowning happiness of performing the marriage service for his only son. His cup was full. His work was done. Late on that evening, while passing through the streets of Boston alone, the releasing summons came suddenly and without warning. Apparently he grew dizzy, and sat down to rest himself on the doorstep of No. 6 Province Court. Here he was found unconscious by passersby. Notice was given to the police, who carefully removed him to the station, where, without recovering his consciousness, he died about midnight. Identified by some papers in his pocket, he was at last delivered to his friends, borne to New Bedford, and buried, on December 26, from the noble old stone church which he had always loved and to which he had devoted the best years of his life. A great audience, comprising all the best elements of the community and filling the large auditorium, assembled in awed silence to express the universal sorrow for his death and the universal reverence for his rare personal worth — the universal appreciation of the power of his thought as a preacher, the nobility of his character as a man, the beneficence of his influence as a citizen, and the incalculable good which had come to the city of his adoption through the radiance of his life and the strength, beauty, and saintliness of his soul. Such feelings and thoughts were in the minds of all, and were uttered by his two old friends who had been summoned to speak the last words of love, grief, and hope over his lifeless form. This was laid in the earth beside that of the gentle and devoted wife who had left him fourteen years before, and whose premature departure had been the one great sorrow of his life. Thus William James Potter was gathered to his fathers, honored and loved by all.

V.

There is little in this record of an outwardly uneventful life to dazzle the imagination, challenge the applause, or even attract the eyes of the general public. But it is such lives that make the world worth living in. Not so much by what he did, or even by what he said, as by what he was, Potter has left an indelible impress upon the community that knew him best. He was not a great master or manager of affairs, but commanded universal respect for the soundness of his judgment and the weight of his influence. He was not a great thinker or originator of ideas, but knew how to make the best ideas of his age tell for the purification of character and of society. There was a singular moderation in his mental action which, while it hindered him from becoming a discoverer or beating out new paths of thought, qualified him admirably for the most important function of a free preacher in a free community — *persuasion*. Bold and sincere in a rare degree, he knew how to carry his people with him and keep their sympathies, yet without stooping to conciliate their prejudices or to withhold any part of the message he felt bound to deliver. Preëminently a reformer and innovator in religion, the calmness of his temperament, no less than the tenderness of his spirit, preserved him from arousing opposition by pressing the logic of reform beyond the willingness or ability of his hearers to follow it. Probably he owed this balance of courage and caution, this tempering of the demands of logic by the claims of sympathy, to his Quaker ancestry and early environment. But, whatever its origin, his temperamental moderation both in action and in thought saved him from that grim remorselessness in pursuing a principle to its last results which makes at once the strength of the speculative pioneer and the weakness of the practical reformer. He always stopped a little short of the extreme logic of the case. There was nothing in this that savored of concession or compromise; it was a characteristic rooted deeply in the essential quality of Potter's mind, and lay at the bottom of his success as a preacher; it made him dear to those whom he so gently led to higher levels of religious thought, because, although they felt that he did not go too far or get out of their reach, they could also feel that he was uncompromisingly true both to himself and to them. The preacher's success is founded upon the people's belief in his sincerity, but no less upon their sympathy with the substance of what he preaches; and the very slowness with which Potter's intellect, logical as it was, moved to the remoter and subtler implications of his own thought, was a limitation which proved to be a positive power in his preaching and gave him a stronger hold upon his people's hearts. No audience on earth will travel very far on the track of an idea or a principle; for nothing is feebler in the average man, at the present stage of human development, than the sense of rational continuity or logical necessity. Whoever taxes this capacity too severely from the pulpit will find few to follow him; he will defeat his own object. Potter made no such failure. The strength of his preaching was its large general intelligence, its sobriety of speech, its elevation of tone, its profound religiousness of spirit. His eloquence was that of a whole man appealing to the whole humanity of his hearers, and making them conscious of a wider horizon, a purer atmosphere, a less beclouded sky; his strongest appeal of all was the simple fact of his own presence and his own spirit, as one with the Eternal whom he interpreted. Strong, self-contained, and self-consecrated to the best, he delivered his message in all simplicity and self-forgetfulness; and the loyal adhesion of the New Bedford society to their minister for a whole generation, in these days of short pastorates, was the highest tribute of appreciation and gratitude which they could possibly have paid to this incorruptible servant of whatever truth he saw.

VI.

But Potter was more than a preacher — he was a citizen. He took the utmost interest in the welfare of the city and of the general community, and extended his influence for good far beyond the narrow limits of his parish. Bold and free of speech as he was, the benignity of his nature and his complete freedom from the spirit of antagonism — he was a true man of peace, like his ancestors — rendered him a favorite with the other ministers of the place, and it was said at the time that every minister in New Bedford attended his funeral. Among the topics of his sermons came often those most closely connected with local affairs, the business interests of the city, political issues, not only during the war, but to the end of his life. He was alive to everything that concerned the higher interests of the people, and took part in all promising reforms, if not with very active participation, at least with words of open and hearty sympathy. Temperance, woman suffrage, civil service reform, the rights and wrongs of the freedmen and the Indians and the Chinese and the oppressed of every name, the cause of education and the young — all these things and more of the same kind enlisted his earnest efforts for the betterment of the world. Particularly deserving of mention in this connection is the active part he took in the establishment of the Swain Free School, one of the most important institutions of New Bedford. I owe to the kindness of Mr. Andrew Ingraham, the accomplished and successful principal of this School, the following extracts on this subject from Ellis's "History of New Bedford and Vicinity:" —

"In 1880, Charles W. Clifford, William J. Potter, Charles H. Peirce, and Edmund Grinnell were chosen members of the Board of Trustees."

"What should the Trustees do? Fortunately the testator himself, by the very terms of the will, and more particularly by the codicil of April 26, 1858, had shown his foresight of changed conditions. Indeed, the courts of Massachusetts have favored that interpretation of the language of public bequests which recognizes that testators have some knowledge of human affairs. Twenty years had passed since the death of Mr. Swain. The city schools had reached a high degree of efficiency, and there were flourishing private schools. The field seemed to be already occupied. What was to be done?

"The solution of this problem was due to the sagacity of the Rev. William J. Potter. He conceived the idea of university extension before that phrase was heard among us, or rather of something that contained the essential element of university extension — of something that competent judges pronounced better than university extension — of something, however, that may be worked in harmony with university extension: of a permanent local institution for higher education, not a fitting school, necessarily, to prepare the young to pass a definite examination, not a training-school, necessarily, where constant practice for many hours a day and for many days in a year must be enforced to insure quickness and accuracy in doing something useful. These things might be secured incidentally, but the main purpose should be to furnish opportunities of culture to those who either had or wished to have the sentiment and the idea of culture.

"With ages ranging from fifteen to sixty; with no other occupation than school work or with the cares of household and business; attending constantly or unable to attend except at rare intervals; studying for a livelihood or for enlarged experience; both men and women and girls and boys have appreciated the efforts that have been put forth to meet their wants, and have helped to make the school a monument to its founder."

VII.

With all this varied and successful activity as a preacher and a citizen, however, Potter exerted the deepest, widest, and most lasting influence of his life through the Free Religious Association. One of its three original founders in 1867, from its foundation to his own death, a period of twenty-six years, he was pre-eminently the directing mind of this Association, serving it for fifteen years as Secretary and for eleven years as President; and his connection with it has made his name historic. For no history of the development of religious thought and life in America, from the close of the Civil War, in 1865, to the Columbian Exposition and the World's Parliament of Religions, in 1893, can possibly be written, unless the intellectual movement from CHRISTIANITY to FREE AND UNIVERSAL RELIGION, represented by the Free Religious Association, shall be made its fundamental theme. This intellectual movement, it is true, has been very much larger than any visible activities of the Association; but the Association remained during that period its chief social expression, while "The Index," so closely connected with the Association, remained for the greater part of that period, from 1870 until 1887, its chief literary expression. The movement itself, in general, was the intellectual advance from Transcendentalism or Mysticism to Scientific Method in religious philosophy, and from Christianity to Universal Religion in ethics and social organization. These two great transitions, which in truth are co-extensive with the religious movement of the whole civilized world, are still very far from being completed; we are still in the midst of them; and the Free Religious Association itself, as their most advanced representative or exponent, has lapsed since Potter's death, and mainly because of the loss of his sagacious leadership, into a state of arrested development.

For, after a year's experience on the Pacific coast as the free missionary of free religion, and after the powerful stimulus to thought imparted by presence and participation in the great religious Parliament at Chicago, Potter returned to the East with a deep and clear conviction of the necessity of what he called a "new departure" in the work of religious reform. At first he was inclined to believe that this "new departure" must be made independently of the Free Religious Association, which perhaps had already fulfilled its mission and might now gracefully give way to a new society, founded on perception of the practical as well as theoretical impossibility of reconciling the principles of Universal Religion with the mutually exclusive claims of the various historical religions, and devoted to the enterprise of organizing local congregations, in "avowed independence" of all historical religions, on the basis of Universal Religion alone. This was his own unprompted proposal. To the suggestion, however, that the constitution of the Free Religious Association, which had originally been drafted in accordance with the spirit of Universal Religion, and from which even the mention of Christianity had been intentionally excluded, might easily be developed into a form which should realize the "new departure" through the Free Religious Association itself, Potter lent a ready and sympathetic ear. After careful deliberation, he concluded that the wisest plan was to submit a proposition of constitutional amendments to the Free Religious Association at the Annual meeting of 1894, and allow the fate of this measure to decide the question whether the imperatively needed "new departure" should be effected through this Association, or through a new one specially framed for the purpose. Owing to the temperamental moderation and caution already alluded to, Potter had not arrived at the conclusion that this "new departure" was the clear need and duty of the hour, until his own experience, as a missionary of free religion, and as both a spectator and a participant in the World's Parliament of Religions, had convinced him that it was a practical necessity of the actually existing situation; he waited until the logic of ideas was confirmed by the logic of events. But, this once made plain to him, he hesitated no longer. When I asked him directly whether, if the Free Religious Association should decline to take up the work of organizing local societies on the basis of avowed independence of Christianity and avowed acceptance of Universal Religion alone, he was ready to favor practically the formation of a new Association for that express purpose, his reply was an emphatic *yes;* and he added that, in this case, Chicago would probably be a better place than Boston for starting the new movement. It was this answer which induced me to attend the conference of friends of the Free Religious Association in Boston, December 11, and to lay before them a draft of amendments, previously approved without hesitation or reservation by Potter himself, which would adapt the constitution of the Association to the positive and energetic prosecution of the "new departure." But, scarcely three weeks from that day, that noble heart had ceased to beat. Deprived of its long revered leader, the Free Religious Association adopted the amendments, indeed, but in a mutilated form which, by omitting the cardinal point of "avowed independence," deprived them of all significance as a "new departure." The death of its leader was the death of its own leadership, too, and the world waits for its successor.

Further details are unnecessary here. But justice and fidelity to Potter's memory require that so much as this be recorded in this place. When, half a century hence, not only America, but the whole world as well, shall be thickly dotted with temples to Universal Religion, devoted to the pursuit of religious truth in the freedom of the scientific method, and emancipated from all dependence upon Brahmanism, Buddhism, Judaism, Christianity, Mohammedanism, or any other particular historical religion, let it not be forgotten that William J. Potter was one of the few prophetic minds of the nineteenth century who welcomed the dawn of that wider and wiser civilization, and spent his life in the effort to hasten its coming. Let it be not forgotten that he who did more than any other one man, nay, than all other men together, for the Free Religious Association, and who would fain have led this little company as explorers and pioneers and first possessors into the "promised land," died with the clear Pisgah-vision of its beauty in his soul and before his eyes. Doubt of this statement must disappear before these words in his leading address at Chicago, September 20, 1893: "Following the logical lines of a growing unity in thought and purpose among the most enlightened and spiritual minds of all faiths, the Free Religious Association has been prognosticating the actual ultimate union of all the great faiths of the world in one religion; and this not by the conversion of all the others to any one of the faiths, but by the conversion and education of them all to the perception of a higher realm of truth. A quarter of a century ago, when the Free Religious Association was organized on a basis which, as to rights of membership, obliterated the line separating Christianity from other faiths, such a prophecy as this was sometimes ventured, but was apt to be regarded as the wild dream of a mere visionary. But to-day our most glowing visions pale before advancing reality. I make bold to say that we who are now living will behold — nay, may already behold — the dawn of the day of a new religion, which is to be really universal in its principles and as broad as humanity in its boundaries; which is not, however, to be Christianity, nor Judaism, nor Buddhism, nor Neo-Brahmanism, but a new faith into which the specific religions are in form to die that they may continue to live in spiritual substance. The meaning of the Free Religious Association, to me, culminates in this thought; and, in the remaining time during which I shall ask your attention, would that I had the power to impress the thought on your minds with the force with which it sometimes comes to my own!"

The last great effort of Potter's life was dedicated to the practical realization of this thought in the Free Religious Association itself. He died before the effort had succeeded; and without him the effort failed. Through this Association he would fain have laid, in concrete reality, the corner-stone of the church of the future, the free church of the Ideal; but the Association lacked insight or courage enough to take that next step forward in its own development which would have consummated the hope and aim of its dead leader, or to rise to his spiritual height. This testimony must his old companion for twenty-six years, his friend in private and his comrade in public, bear to the purity of his spiritual perception, the splendor of his moral courage, and the crowning act of loyalty in his lifelong self-consecration to the truth. The future will recognize this forward-facing movement of his latest leadership as the most enduring monument to his memory; for it indissolubly associates his name with the advent of Universal Religion as the supreme renovating force of human history, the supreme hope of the world in the long centuries to come.

VIII.

Preacher, citizen, religious leader — Potter was all of these, not, perhaps, in the superlative sense, yet still in a sense so full and noble as to insure a grateful remembrance of his work for many generations. But the faithful worker is always greater than his work, and Potter was most of all a *man*. Some miscellaneous extracts from the few early journals alluded to, insertion of which in the order of time would have had the effect of giving to those early years a disproportionate prominence, as compared with the later years of which I have no records at command, will throw a stronger light on some of the most striking traits of his character than could be thrown by any abstract analysis or description.

North Dartmouth, Nov. 23, 1847: "The idea entered my head to-day of going to Bridgewater to Normal School. Think I shall ask father again, though I do not want him to pay my board. I know that he wants me to be a farmer, and that I shall have to oppose his wishes to be a teacher. But I feel as though farming is not intended for me, and that I shall do more good in some other sphere. The question has often occurred to me, whether we should be directed entirely as to our employment by the choice of our parents. It seems to me that there is in each of us something which seems to point out our allotment — the sphere in which it is designed for us to labor. I am aware that this may at times, like the magnetic needle, be attracted out of its natural direction. But this is far from being necessarily the case, and, when it does happen, is the result of mismanagement. I would not without reason oppose my father's wishes. I exceedingly dislike to do so, even when there is reason for it. Most gladly would I remain here, did I consider it for my benefit, and, perhaps it will not be too much to add, the benefit of my fellow-men. Here are my sunniest moments; *home* is, and will ever be, the centre of my enjoyment. It radiates every circle in which I tread, howsoever far removed, and thus will it ever be. Farming would be delightful, could I be satisfied with it; but I should not feel that I were doing all that I had the capability of. I do not leave it from any dishonorable motive. I respect it as an employment. Earth has not a more honorable one."

Nov. 25, 1847: "Inquired of father to-day in relation to going to Bridgewater. He spoke very discouragingly, and almost induced me to resolve to say no more about leaving the farm, but to content myself to remain upon it through life. He overcame my feelings by alluding to the probability that he would not dwell on earth much longer, and that then there would be no one to take his place. In the bitter thought of the moment, I believed that I had been doing wrong, and that it would be right for me to sacrifice all my plans of future life and live at home as contented as possible. But I am myself again; and reason, and, I think I may say, conscience, tell me to still press forward; and press forward I must."

Nov. 29, 1847: "Well, it is decided that I shall go to Bridgewater. A committee-man of Westport came for me to take a school. I asked father which I should do — take the school or go to the Normal. He told me to take my choice; which, of course, I did. He seems quite reconciled to my going — more so than at either of the last two terms that I have spent at Providence. I am glad that it is so; it has always been a source of regret to me to be at school without his entire and free consent."

Who that knew Potter intimately in his later life can fail to recognize, in this simple and serious story of his own action by the boy of eighteen, almost all the traits that characterized the mature man — the "sweet reasonableness," the fairness and soundness of judgment, the ready response to any appeal made to his sympathy or natural affections, the tenderness of his heart, the elevation of his motives, the modesty and conscientiousness of his disposition, and withal the quiet and amiable but indomitable pertinacity with which, notwithstanding any and all opposing considerations, he always adhered in the end to any conclusion in thought or any decision in life at which he had once independently and deliberately arrived? Never was there a better illustration of the truth of Wordsworth's famous line: "The child is father of the man." In Potter's vocabulary there was no such word as *surrender*.

Bridgewater, Feb. 13, 1848: "I observed yesterday a father drawing his little son on a sled. The little boy said, 'Why don't you go into the road? You said you would.' What caused that boy to ask this question but an instinctive consciousness of moral principle — an idea that his father was bound to do as he had promised? Had that boy's heart been depraved, evil, and corrupt, had he known by nature the sins of lying and deceiving, would he have thought it strange that his father should not do as he said he would?"

Yarmouth, July 9, 1848: "Have given up the idea of going to Roundout, so that I have quite a different story to write from that of last night. After I concluded to go, I could not feel quite easy about it. To go off without the consent of my father was something I had never done, and, though I did not *think* he would have any objection, yet I did not *know* it. At any rate, he could not tell me I might go. This was a thought which troubled me at Nantucket, and probably prevented my staying more than anything else. In meeting, to-day, I looked over the reasons on both sides of the question, the motives which were operating to induce me to go, and the obstacles which seemed to be in the way, and I came to the conclusion that it is my duty to go home. I feel under some obligations to work a little this vacation. It was very kind in father to let me have the time and money to make this visit, and I think I ought to make some return and not take more liberty. The thought of the pleasure which I should derive from the journey would sometimes intrude itself, and somewhat shake my convictions of duty. But conscience finally approved my judgment, and I settled the matter by saying to friend A. after the meeting, 'I shall not go to Roundout.'"

Kingston, Dec. 10, 1848: "He [Potter's successful predecessor in the Kingston school] was easy, social, familiar, fond of activity, and, I should judge, rather averse to retirement. My character, if I can rightly judge it, is compounded of some qualities very opposite. I am stiff, unsocial, distant, so reserved as to be almost uncivil, apparently preferring solitude and self to all else. To all of these charges my first appearance will bear full evidence. But to the last of them, in justice to myself, I shall plead 'not guilty,' I sometimes love solitude; it is a part of my nature to love it, and I have taken little pains to wean myself from it. But I do not love it *always*. I am sometimes as *lonesome* as other folks, and suffer as much from this cause as any one need to. I cannot at one step make strangers my acquaintances, and, until I am perfectly acquainted, I cannot feel at home. All my intimate, real acquaintances are few and slowly formed. I now greatly, severely miss a few bosom friends to whom I can unburden my pent-up thoughts. But I must wait till they are found. Perhaps the materials for them are here somewhere in store for me; and yet I may leave Kingston and not have a single real acquaintance! This may appear improbable, if not insane, to others, but to me it is far otherwise. I know myself as I think no other does, except Him who knows us all. What I mean by a real acquaintance is one with whom I can associate for hours, days, or any length of time, and feel perfectly at home, exhibit unrestrained freedom, and feel that it is no effort to converse. Now, when I look back upon my life and think of the people with whom I have mingled, and find so few among them whom I can call *real* acquaintances,— when I reflect that during my whole course at Bridgewater I formed scarcely more than half a dozen such, and that my room-mates, one for fourteen weeks and another for twenty-two, are not of this number, the thought that I may leave Kingston without a single acquaintance is to me far from visionary. It is an idea whose *reality* I dread. Not that I shall have no friends here; I have some already whose friendship I prize. Neither would I say that all my Bridgewater friends can be reckoned under the figure o, for it would be unjust both to them and me. No, many, many are the choice spirits whom I can number as my friends, and to meet whom would give me extreme joy. But they are not all such intimate acquaintances that I feel perfect freedom in their presence. Friendship may exist without a perfect acquaintance. Close attachments may be formed between those whose everyday thoughts and feelings are unknown to each other. It is not necessary that our simplest, undressed, and most common thoughts should be known to another, in order to gain his esteem, attachment, and affection. These are known only to ourselves, our God, and *real* acquaintances. We sometimes want to let these thoughts escape. They become burdensome, and it is then that we feel the need of an *intimate*, *real* acquaintance — such a one as I am aching for now, before whom I may once more appear just as I appear to myself."

Kingston, Dec. 18, 1848: "Another beautiful

day. School has been large and pleasant. Had forty this afternoon. I have been in good spirits, and the scholars appeared so, too. In fact, I have felt quite happy all day. This evening I have made two visits: one at Deacon ———'s, a fine old man of sixty-eight, who has a very comfortable home, quite a property, a social wife, and a handsome niece living with him; the other at Mr. ———'s, who has also a comfortable home, with a fine wife and three children. They are all boys, and all come to school. They came part way home with me, and commenced talking about the stars. I pointed out some of the finest constellations and brightest stars, giving some of their names. They appeared interested and desirous of knowing more, were very respectful, and seemed happy to have my company. I was no less so to have theirs. It really did me good. I wish I could be with a few of my scholars at a time every evening. I do not like to see them shy of me. I want to be free, candid, and familiar with them; I want to make them feel that I am not merely their 'master,' but their real teacher and friend. This day has been one of hope; may it not be succeeded by a morrow of disappointment! Wilt thou bless it, O Father, from whom all our blessings flow! May I receive fresh encouragement and renewed strength to press forward in the responsible work I have undertaken, doing nothing to the injury of my little flock, but with thy assistance bringing them nearer and nearer to thee!"

Kingston, Jan. 3, 1849: "I have to-day attempted a little matter of discipline which may be worth recording. I have noticed for several days small balls of paper in considerable numbers upon the floor, and had discovered two of the rogues who helped to get them there, but had not informed them of it, as I was satisfied there must be others. After all the books were laid aside this forenoon, I mentioned the circumstance, and also that I knew two of the offenders, but did not give their names. I spoke some time of the wrongfulness of the act; that the fact that they had tried to conceal it was strong evidence that those scholars who had performed it knew it was wrong and that they might justly deserve punishment; but that I was in hopes the thing might be stopped without it. Here one of the boys voluntarily confessed himself guilty, and gave to me the instrument he had used to blow the paper about the room. I then asked all who would be willing to acknowledge the fault, had they committed it, to rise. All rose. I then asked all who had done so to rise. Eight of the boys rose, several of whom, without my asking, resolved that they should not do so again. I then asked how many were willing to join in the resolution, and found that all were. Then I told them I should inquire at the close of the week how many had kept their resolution. It has been kept well this afternoon, as far as I have observed."

Kingston, Feb. 4, 1849: "A week ago to-day I went over to Duxbury to see Mr. Kendall, and had the good fortune to meet some other Normal friends. I had a very fine visit, well worth the walk over and back again. I have come back, though, with my desires for going to College rekindled. Mr. Kendall will enter at next Commencement — wish I were ready to go with him, but how I am to go is not yet revealed to me. Sometimes I feel as though I would say, I will go, and will press forward in spite of all opposition until my *will* is affected."

Sandwich, May 20, 1849: "The characteristic unfixedness of my vocation has at length brought me here, just into the limits of Cape Cod. I engaged a school here, before I went home after my winter's siege in Kingston. . . . My winter's labors, trials, and failures had somewhat diminished my zeal; they had given me a truer and more practical sense of the duties, responsibilities, and difficulties of the profession I had chosen, and had taught me the useful, though humiliating fact, that I possessed not the ability to do what I had once looked upon as an easy task, or rather no task at all. But, though I had gained a more perfect knowledge of my inability for the work of teaching, though my ambition was somewhat humbled, my hopes crushed, my prospects clouded, yet duty pointed out no other course of life; inclination fastened upon no easier nor more lucrative employment. To become a teacher had long been the object of my desires, for which I had in some measure prepared myself, and to attain which I had met some crosses, encountered some opposition at the risk of being thought wanting in filial duty, made some sacrifices. Thank Heaven that my purpose was too fixed, my plan of life too far matured, to be overthrown by fickle fortune or undermined by dark discouragement. Most rejoiced was I, when I reached home, to find that I should no longer have to oppose a father's wishes by continuing in the course I had commenced. His views seemed more nearly to accord with my own than they had ever done before. He was perfectly willing, and I think considered it best, that I should pursue teaching; indeed, I did not complete my engagement here, until he freely expressed his consent. I can now labor more easily, more freely; a burden seems lifted from my shoulders. But I fear I have soon again to oppose his wishes, or give up *hopes* which have long lived in my bosom with little prospect of becoming realities, until recently, when they have assumed the more definite form of *plans*, only awaiting *time* to become *actions*. I have finally formed the determination to go to college, and have even set the day. If all things go favorably till then, I think of entering one year from next Commencement. Am going to spend all my spare time this summer in preparing. I am induced to take this step, not because I think college celebrity is necessary to success, but because I think college study will make me more useful. Men to become self-taught must possess a peculiar turn of mind, and it will not do for all or for many to trust to themselves. I am aware I shall go among numerous temptations, but I believe I shall be preserved. We live in a world of temptation which we cannot shun, but must meet. No one can live through the college course without being strengthened in virtue or tainted with vice. The former is certainly desirable, and by caution, watchfulness, and prayer can be attained."

North Dartmouth, June 26, 1849: " Rose at half

past four. Dressed and went into the garden, and worked, with the exception of twenty minutes for breakfast, till half past eight. Came in, bathed, changed clothes, and commenced studying at nine — continued till twelve — read six pages of Cæsar. Was intending to study Greek this afternoon, but father wanted me to make hay, which I have done; and, to testify to it, I have six fine blisters upon my hands — my shoulders feel lame and my legs very stiff. This evening I have read three and a half more pages of Cæsar, which finishes the fourth book. I commenced it last night; there are seventeen and a half pages in it. The clock strikes ten, and I must go to bed. Rise to-morrow morning at four."

North Dartmouth, June 27, 1849: "Have been to monthly meeting. There were several strange ministers present, two from England. One of them delivered a long discourse on the commencement and experience of the true Christian. I presume it was good Quaker doctrine, but it savored too much of 'human depravity' and of 'self-abhorrence' to suit my taste. I cannot understand why we should so utterly and completely abhor ourselves. God has made us, and should we abhor any of his works? We *should* abhor and endeavor to cast out the sin that is within us; but that we are *all sin* I cannot believe. A great deal of Quaker theology grows more and more mysterious to me, the more I think about it. I have always considered myself a Quaker on all the great points of their doctrine, but it is merely because I have been accustomed to take them as truth without any thought at all. I am inclined to believe that this is the case with a great many birthright members, and that the Society suffers greatly from such members. They are Quakers simply because they were brought up in the Society, having no actual convincement of the truth of its doctrines. My mind at present is totally unsettled in regard to what orthodoxy and even more liberal sects would deem the essentials of a Christian. I never expect and never care, while I have my present views, to find a church whose creed I would adopt. I am perfectly sick of everything in the shape of a religious creed. What a vast variety there is! And all interpretations of the Bible! One would suppose that, if the Bible was revealed from God, it would be sufficiently plain to every understanding."

North Dartmouth, June 29, 1849: "'When I would do good, evil is present with me.' I sometimes almost despair of there being any one to help me, even an Almighty. What evidence have I of his existence? Do I even feel an inward consciousness that he exists, as I do of myself? Have I a real, living, moving faith in the superintending providence of a God, or do I only believe in him from tradition? O Almighty One, if there be such a being, what art thou? How can we know thee — how feel thee? Is there such a thing as man's actually holding communion with thee? If so, what is it? How can it be done? Can my spirit ever attain to this honor? How can spirits mingle together? How *know* they mingle together, and the time? How do they become acquainted? How enjoy each other's society? O, will my poor, sinning, trembling soul ever know these things? Shall I ever have faith — shall I ever cease to doubt? I know that all Nature speaks a God; but I want to *know*, I want to *feel*, I want to *speak* to that God myself. I feel sometimes impatient for my spirit to leave this body, that I may know what is behind the curtain that is spread between time and eternity. But am I prepared for this? If Death should come to-night, this moment, should I be willing to meet it? O no, I should plead for a little longer; I should try, I fear, to cheat Death by fair promises of what I would do, if he would suffer me to remain. What omissions of duty, what commissions of evil, would crowd themselves upon me! And when will they be less — ah, when? I pray that it may be soon."

North Dartmouth, July 1, 1849: "My mind has become somewhat calmed, though it is still full of doubts in respect to almost all the great doctrines of our various religious sects, and particularly those of Quakers. I long ago resolved to submit everything, whether of a religious nature or otherwise, to the test of reason, being satisfied that Christianity is a rational religion, and capable of withstanding the search and the criticism of the keenest intellect. I knew that I considered many things as true solely because I had been brought up among them, where their truth was never questioned; and I know I hold many such things about me now, but they are becoming less and less. Every day I find myself resting upon another's convictions, pinning my faith upon another's sleeve; and every day I try to tear myself away, even though strongly attached thereto, and I find nowhere else to rest. Sometimes I feel as though the very foundations of my soul were breaking up, and that I should never find a settling place. But it matters not whether I ever come to any conclusion upon these subtile points of theology, if I can only settle upon true Christianity. But, should I tell all my thoughts, I should hardly be considered a friend of this by very many professing Christians. The great points that are a burden to me now are the character of Christ, the atonement, the nature of salvation, immediate revelation, the authority and inspiration of the scriptures, the ministry and worship. Among this vast multitude comprising what are considered the most essential truths of the Gospel, I do not feel that it is essentially necessary, however desirable it may be, to decide upon either. The language arises spontaneously over all my inward strivings: 'If thou doest well, shalt thou not be accepted?' Teach me, O God, of thine own wisdom!"

The last three extracts, portraying as remarkable and as pathetic a struggle as ever took place in a human soul between the imprisoning forces of an inherited thought-system and the irresistible vital energies of nascent reason, could not have been omitted without leaving in utter obscurity the origin of much that was noblest in Potter's character and career. But I have hesitated not a little whether it would be wise to publish without at least one omission the record of his thoughts on the day of his majority. Ought so frank a reference to his personal appearance as is contained in the following entry to be submitted to alien eyes? In answering this question, I have allowed myself to be governed by the effect of that passage on my own mind. It is so characteristic, so full of a pitiless sincerity and uncompromising truthfulness and rarest freedom from all the delusions of personal self-conceit, that it seems to me to have sprung unconsciously out of the innermost nobilities of his nature, and to tell as nothing else could how strong a passion for truth burned in his heart's core. Even if this early photograph of the boy had remained a correct likeness of the man, it would still be invaluable in its ethical aspect. But whoever saw Potter in public when his fine face was lighted up with the glow of great ideas and lofty ideals,— whoever met him in private and had insight enough to see the inward majesty of the soul mirrored in the whole outward aspect of the body,— must recognize, in this striking contrast between the boy and the man, a wonderful instance of the way in which Nature makes the psychical dominate the physical and write out the story of the victorious spirit in the gradual transfiguration of features and form. Let the ruthless description stand, if only as a foil to the serene and noble presence which we all loved to see, but shall see no more!

Taunton, Feb. 1, 1850: "My twenty-first birthday. I am now *legally* a *man*, a *free*-man. The day has come which years ago, in my early youth, I was accustomed to anticipate with so much impatience and hope. Are my anticipations realized? No.

The years between looked long and weary. I expected to find myself at twenty-one a new being, possessing hardly a quality by which I could recognize my then insignificant existence. I thought to feel, to act, and to know myself differently. I believed I should scarcely identify the boy in the man; that I should outgrow myself, and by some mysterious process be converted into another being of different perceptions and functions. But *do* I feel, act, and know myself any differently from what I did ten years ago? Can I not identify the spindle-bodied, long-legged, large-nosed, freckle-faced, red-haired boy of eleven, in the somewhat taller but similarly featured form that I now wear? And do I not inwardly perceive myself the same as then? I certainly do. The man is but the boy larger grown. But have I not changed? I as certainly have. But the change has been rather a change in size than in nature — a development of what I then possessed rather than an exchange for something else — a slow and steady growth from the green and tender sapling to the height and magnitude of a tree. Thus grows the character — so slow the progress, so gradual the transition from one stage to another, so perfectly adapted the past that is to the past that has been, and the past that will be to the past that is, that we never lose the consciousness of its sameness. But, could I have been transported at once from myself in 1840 to myself in 1850, I opine I should not find it so easy to know myself; and, could several characters be similarly transported across ten years of life, and then shaken up together and drawn out by those who were their owners, I imagine there would be some curious mismatching. What a scramble there would be after a character! And what kind of a character would be most in demand? Sinful and grovelling as many are, and prone as we all are to evil, yet, so strong is the natural love of the heart for the virtues and the holy, that I am inclined strongly to the belief that each would choose and claim a virtuous character. Men do not plunge headlong into sin, any more than they rise at once to a sublime height of virtue. But no one sinks so low that he cannot distinguish and honor high-minded, consistent virtue, and that he would not gladly exchange his evil for good, could he do so by a simple act of the will. But the struggle is long and hard from vice to virtue; his heart fails within, and the world without affords little sympathy or encouragement.—Twenty-one years of my life have gone; more than a quarter, should I live to a 'good old age,' and a much greater part, probably, of what my life will probably be. I do not count upon a long sojourn here, nor do I wish it. I scarcely anticipate another twenty-one years. But how different the twenty-one years to come from the twenty-one years that have passed! These have been spent mostly in the quiet of home; now I am to come out into the broad world. The past is the foundation on which the future is to be built. It is yet to be seen how it will stand the stormy elements of human society; whether the structure of active life raised thereon will wave hither and thither at every shift of public opinion, and tremble at the blow of the critic's pen, and fall before the rush of opposition, or whether it will stand firm and unshaken, ever pointing upwards to God as the centre of trust and faith, and as if upheld by the strength of his eternal arm. Principles that I have formed are now to be tested, theories to be practised, opinions to be expressed, and an influence to be thrown out into the mixed, fermenting mass of human materials around me. Am I ready for this? Am I ready for life? To go out into the world, to combat its ills, to withstand its snares, to endure its scorn and meet its opposition? *Some* dread to *die; I* rather dread to *live*. Life is a fearful, awful thing, great in responsibilities, filled with duties. But it must be met. Its responsibilities must be borne; its duties must be performed; and *he only* who is ready for these, ready to live, is ready *to die*."

Taunton, July 17, 1850: "Those dreaded days have come and gone, and with them all anxious thoughts and dreary forebodings. To me the result is more than satisfactory. I can scarcely realize it. I am in college and free from all conditions — a thing I dared not dream of. I expected certainly to have two or three deficiencies to make up, and had made up my mind to consider myself lucky even with these. But when, last evening, I took in my hand the proffered paper, hardly daring to look at it, dreading the fate it was to reveal, and saw the announcement actually written out in words that I was a real member of the freshman class in Harvard College, clear of conditions, my mind would scarcely give credit to my senses. But so it was; yet I could not believe it, until I was assured by Mr. Wheelwright, and others who had passed through the ordeal, that there was no delusion. My joy was irrepressible. It burst through every pore of my skin, lightened every motion of my limbs, could be heard in every sound of my voice. My mind seemed at once relieved of a heavy burden, a burden which for the last six weeks had pressed upon it so unremittingly that my only thought, speech, and act had been in reference to this one thing—*college*. My spirits at once resumed their wonted elasticity, and with a light heart I leaped upon an omnibus, in company with Mr. W. (who seemed equally joyous at the success of his three candidates), bound for Boston and thence for Roxbury, where I spent the night. An occurrence happened in Boston rather calculated to check the exuberance of my emotions. A gentleman who left the omnibus before myself took my valise instead of his own, which he left for me and bid fair to be as much use to me as mine to him. What made the matter worse for myself, in the ecstasy of feeling with which I left Cambridge, I entirely forgot to take my pocketbook from my valise, which contained all my money, except a little change in my pocket. My sudden depression of spirits was but momentary, however, as Mr. Wheelwright assured me that he knew the man who had taken it, that he was a good honest clergyman, and would probably be in Cambridge at the Commencement to-day, when, if I would go back again, I might make the exchange. Feeling perfectly satisfied that I should get the valise again, I comforted myself for the night, being without a change of clothing and the indispensables of making a toilet, with the thought of the good minister's ideas when he should find that he had purloined a valise, and was without nightshirt or razor and perhaps *minus* some of his sermons. This morning I went over to Cambridge, and there learned by inquiry that my valise was left at the omnibus office in Boston. I accordingly went back to Boston, made the exchange, and this afternoon, tired, heated through and through with the burning sun, which I had hardly been in contact with for several weeks, dusty, dirty, sweaty, and sleepy, I found my way back to Taunton again. 'Action and reaction are equal and in opposite directions' is no less a truth of mental than of physical philosophy; hence I am now beginning to experience a vacancy of life and activity corresponding to my fulness and buoyancy of spirits last night. Sleep, perhaps, will restore me, and to sleep I go."

North Dartmouth, June 20, 1851 : "Spent last week at Newport — went on with father to the Yearly Meeting, which I had given up all thoughts of ever attending again. This probably is the last time. I find little in the Quaker Society that commends itself to my understanding or my heart. I am no Quaker in doctrine or in spirit. They are too Calvinistic in the former, too sectarian in the latter. I do not like this keeping apart from other societies and the world. We want more of brotherhood among mankind — more of the family union; this the Quakers do not cherish."

Between July 18, 1851, and August 6, 1857, when

he "left home for Europe," Potter seems to have kept no journal; at least, none has been found. On August 9, he sailed from New York for Europe, where he travelled and studied over a year. The following passage from his journal on the outward voyage is of more than usual significance, as marking a phase of his theological thought which was never wholly abandoned in subsequent years, and yet was never logically developed in either its theoretical or its practical aspect — a development which, in a mind so conscientious as his, would have led to an early retirement from the ministry. The conception here outlined remained undeveloped even in his own mind; yet I think it was a source of some vagueness and confusion in his preaching, so far as its philosophical side alone was concerned, and would have impaired even its practical value, if his deep religiousness of nature had not come to the rescue and saved him from a too rigorously logical evolution and application of his own conception : —

At sea, Aug. 14, 1857: "The lesson that I learned from the ocean was, in fact, the confirmation of my theology, or perhaps more properly its reflection: namely, that the Infinite becomes manifest to itself only in the finite, — that the Infinite, Absolute, Eternal, lies as a vast boundless sea, without soundings and without horizon, in perfect, unconscious rest, a great storehouse of powers in perfect harmony and repose; so soon as motion, form, thought appear, so soon as these powers come into activity, there begins the finite. Our ship, too, as she took up the winds, and rode triumphantly over the waves, was a symbol to me of man's relation to God. The ship, by being built in conformity to the ascertained laws of fluids and of mechanics, was able to use the great powers that lay in the sea and the winds. So man, learning the laws of his being and conforming his character and conduct thereto, brings into action the very power and strength of God."

Berlin, Oct. 15, 1857: "To-night I am in new quarters — find my room much more cheerful than the old one — feel more at home and better able to work. I had quite an amusing adventure with my *Wirth* as I left him. I thought his bill too high, and struck off from it one thaler and ten sgr., giving him my reasons. Of course, they were not sufficient for him, and he insisted upon the whole. I then told him to receipt the bill for so much, and, if he wanted more, to go to the *Universitätsgericht* — which I had been told was a sure way to bring an exorbitant *Wirth* to terms. He still refused. I then told him to make out an honest bill, and call upon me at my new room when he was ready to settle it honestly; whereupon I took my carpet-bag and shawl to go out. My trunks were already on a *droschke* at the door. He stepped quickly before me and fastened the door, calling at the same time to his wife to summon a policeman. My *Wirth* and *Wirthin* pleaded their cause before him in their fluent German. I, luckily perhaps, knew but few words for stating mine, — told him the proposals I had made, which I again repeated, again offering to pay what I thought just and accept the bill receipted for that amount. My *Wirth* still not acceding to this, the policeman told me to leave the things I had in the room for security and go without paying. But, not knowing precisely what security I was to have for the things, which were, moreover, articles of indispensable daily use, I demurred to the decision. The policeman went off, and matters stood as before, I a prisoner. The only way the *Wirth* could keep me in the room was to stay there himself, and so it seemed that the case would have to be decided by the sitting-out process, which we commenced in good earnest. My *Wirth* soon began to show signs of yielding. He offered to strike off one item of ten sgr. (25 cents); which I informed him was very good, but not enough. Again another long sitting. My *Wirth*, perhaps, begins to calculate how many shoes he is likely to lose the mending of by this process; and by and by he offers to strike off another item of one-half a thaler. Prudence would perhaps have suggested that I should not push my cause any farther, as he had now come more than half way to meet me. But, as I regarded myself the representative of justice, I was determined to stand or fall with it, and so again informed him that his offer was very good, but still not enough. Again we resort to the argument of sitting, and this time he is convinced of the propriety of my proposal, accepts what I had offered to pay him, receipts the bill for so much, opens the door, and I go out in triumph with my property, fully confident that I shall hear nothing more of my *Wirth* or the balance of his bill. I feel that I almost deserve a triumphal procession from the hands of all foreigners for this victory over a Berlin cheat, in which I trust I may be pardoned if I take an honest pride."

Berlin, Oct. 31, 1857: "I was summoned to-day before the *Universitätsgericht* to answer an action entered by my old *Wirth* to recover the balance of his bill; and so the comedy is likely to have several more acts, and perhaps (for me) prove a tragedy, after all. To-day there wasn't much progress in the action of the drama. The court couldn't understand English and the defendant couldn't understand German — case deferred till Dr. Lolly, the English professor, could be present to interpret. As I went out through the anteroom, I paid five sgr. to the attendant as the summons-fee — noticed that my *Wirth* went out without any such demand upon him."

Berlin, Nov. 4, 1857: "Third Act to the Drama of My *Wirth's* Bill. Again summoned before the *Universitätsgericht*, Dr. Lolly present. I grounded my defence on the fact that several German students, to whom I had shown the bill, had all declared the charges too high — that I was charged more for the same things than a German student under the same *Wirth*. In reply, the court said that it was a custom in regard to certain services, unless there was a special bargain made at the outset, to charge double the usual price; that is, a custom of cheating a stranger until he shall discover the cheat. But *custom* is *common law*, and so, of course, my defence in this respect was completely demolished. I had made another point against a special item for doing errands, nothing of consequence having been done for me. Here the court again met me with a custom from the university at Halle, where, the court said, it was the usage among the amiable race of *Wirths* to make an extra charge for everything, even for the use and the making of the bed. I congratulated myself that I had not gone to Halle, but did not precisely see how this useful piece of information met my objection to paying for service which had not been done for me in Berlin. However, the court decided against me, and I was reduced now to make a point out of an item which I had before allowed to pass unquestioned. I was with my *Wirth* but twenty-seven days, and, of course, had eaten but twenty-seven breakfasts; he had charged, however, for a full month, thirty. Being reduced to extremities, I now brought up this fact, which, to my surprise, seemed to the court well made; but, either from the fact that the court had forgotten its arithmetic or because it was of opinion that the objection was only two-thirds just, it deducted two breakfasts instead of three (six sgr.), and gave its decision that I should pay the rest of the bill. I was not disposed further to martyr myself for the sake of justice by appealing to another court, having had quite enough experience of courts, and so laid down the cash, which my *Wirth* took with a malicious smile of victory. There was then a little afterpiece of half a thaler to pay for costs of the suit, and five sgr. more for the second summons. I again observed that my *Wirth* went out without paying anything. And so the second part of this drama ended not quite so triumphantly as the first; I am now a conquered, crest-fallen hero, my pride and my plumes trailing in the dust."

Berlin, Dec. 10, 1857: "My Berlin life is becoming so regular that I find little new to be noted from day to day. The lectures, reading German and talking whenever I can find opportunity, concerts, the picture gallery, and walks in and about the city, use up my time. As in America, so here I find myself generally alone. My progress in German is almost imperceptible. To master the language must be the labor of a life-time. I hope, however, to be able to enjoy Goethe and Schiller in their own tongue. I am now reading *Iphigenie von Tauris* with great delight."

Berlin, Dec. 15, 1857: "The greatest day I have yet had in Berlin. Saw Humboldt at the American minister's, and had an opportunity of hearing him converse for a couple of hours. The Americans in the city were all invited there to meet him. As he entered the room and we all rose to receive him, he seemed a little embarrassed, but, as soon as he commenced to talk, became perfectly at ease. In his manners he is extremely simple and childlike. Though in his eighty-ninth year, and this winter weakened by sickness, he would not sit so long as the ladies were standing. In stature he is much below the medium size, or, at least, seems so now that he is bent somewhat with years; but his head is enormous, very high and large in front, and quite thickly covered with gray hair — his face rather small and flushed, eyes small, but very bright and piercing. In conversation he is wonderfully fluent, and very rapid in his transitions from one topic to another. He shows his immense learning, but without the slightest appearance of show. There is little need that any one should talk except to answer his questions, of which he puts very many. He is still lively, brilliant, and fond of humor — told a story capitally of a man who some twenty years ago took a plaster cast of him. The man, he said, remarked that he was always most fortunate with the casts of men who died soon after he took them. With a cast of Schiller (Schleiermacher?) he was very fortunate, since he happily died a short time after it was taken, so that there was a large demand for it, and he sold a great number. 'The man, I think,' says Humboldt, 'must have been very unhappy with mine and very angry with me, since that was twenty years ago and I live yet.' Stuart, he said, painted a portrait of him while in America, for Jefferson, which was very good. He speaks English fluently, yet makes mistakes — forgets languages, he says, as he grows older and ceases to use them. He frequently exclaimed in the course of his conversation against his 'horrid English'— remarked that the similarity of the German and English makes it more difficult for a native of one country to speak well the language of the other, since he is continually making literal translations and so failing in idioms. Some one asked him if he saw Jefferson while in America. He replied very quickly, 'I saw *but* Jefferson, and that is the reason why I am so ignorant of the United States. I was in the United States but three months, half of which

I spent with Jefferson at Washington.' He was in the United States in 1802 or 1803. His memory is most extraordinary, yet becoming somewhat impaired with regard to recent everyday affairs. He knows our early history most accurately — better, I think, than did any of his American audience — gives dates as if he were reading from a book. He had read Professor Lieber's Geology of South Carolina — thought it excellent, and wished that Lieber might be sent as a geologist to California, of which all the geological accounts he had seen were very confused and gave him no idea of the formation of the land there. He spoke several times, and with earnestness, of the bad influence of excessive immigration upon our country — thought the evil was not sufficiently apprehended by our people, that the foreign element would before long give us much trouble, and, he feared, prove disastrous to the government. He is at present at work upon the fifth volume of the Kosmos, getting it ready for the press, in which he seems to be insensible to fatigues and the infirmities of age. His step was a little uncertain, as he went down the stairs to take his carriage, and his servant supported him. And I thought, as I saw him move away, that, had I waited to visit Europe twelve months later, it would have been too late to see this greatest marvel of learning that this age, or perhaps any age, has known."

Heidelberg, Sept. 7, 1858: "I got a new view and a most magnificent sunset this evening from the Geissberg. The whole Rhine valley seemed to be covered with an atmosphere of molten gold. And, as I was returning to my room by the road that winds around the side of the hill, I came upon another view of the town and Neckar valley, as charming as any I have found. The castle is also seen to good advantage. One is much lower down, indeed, than the summit of the Geissberg, but, by the help of a platform which has been built out upon a projecting cliff, stands almost directly over the town, and looks down into the streets and squares and yards of the houses. As I stood there, the bells were ringing out their evening summons to rest, while the busy crowds were hurrying through the streets on the last errands of the day. The night crept slowly down the valley of the Neckar, drawing his curtain around one object after another, till at last he wrapped the old castle up in his thickest vestures of black and spread out a milder darkness over the whole expanse of the great Rhine plain. Only in the town was his course resisted, where the lamplighters with their ladders were running through the streets, and each marking his path by the train of fires he left behind him."

Heidelberg, Oct. 3, 1858: "To-morrow I leave Heidelberg for Italy, and so to-day I have been visiting for the last time and taking leave of all my favorite haunts. I have no friends to part with — nothing but nature and the castle. I stood long to-night, just after sunset, upon the great terrace, and gazed upon the noble ruin, till the shadows of night enveloped it. More lovingly than ever did the ivy seem to cling around the old weather-beaten stones, as if to hold them up against the assaults of time and the elements. The trees within the walls, looking through the windows and reaching out their arms, I imagined, were inviting in the birds to give them shelter for the night. And with what strength the great octagonal tower stood there against the western sky! And the hill-side below the ruin, with its fine wood of locusts, seemed to decline more gracefully than ever into the green lawn beneath, and then to slope away into the Neckar valley and the shadows of evening. I had previously taken my last look at the old knightly statues in their niches of stone and ivy, and at the beautiful front of Otto Heinrich's Building, which, according to the books, was constructed from a design by Michel Angelo. If so, one may still venture to admire it. It is a curious circumstance that on this wall are combined the statues of Christian saints, of Roman celebrities, and of heathen divinities; and at the very top, projecting entire above the whole ruin, and in such an exposed position that it seems a marvel they have not been thrown down in any of the convulsions which the castle has suffered, are the statues of the two pagan gods, Jupiter and Pluto. They stand there, overlooking the whole ruin and town, as if to teach modern visitors humiliation at the thought of the *Christian* scenes of war and outrage which these old heathen deities have witnessed from their high stations, and also to proclaim that heathenism had its side of truth which neither time can injure nor opposing systems shake to pieces. I lingered long in the enchanted grounds after the crowd of Sunday visitors had departed, and then went up on the hill-side back of the castle, where on music-days I have often sat under the great chestnuts in order to get away from the noise of tongues and beer-glasses. I have fancied, too, that the music, as it came winding up among the trunks of the old trees, was all the sweeter for the fragrance of the fresh air and the foliage which it caught in the ascent. It was here that I took my final leave of the castle, to return to my room to the very unsentimental business of packing."

Verona, Oct. 9, 1858: "I was struck, too, with the fact that many of the monuments [in the cemetery at Brescia] had been defaced with writing and images in pencil, while the more costly were protected from such desecration by a covering of iron net-work. Could any American boy scribble upon a tombstone? Perhaps there is something superstitious in that feeling of awe with which we at home are accustomed to walk among graves; and yet, let us have this superstition a thousand times rather than the Italian, or perhaps more truly Catholic, indifference to the dead. I saw the same hollow heartlessness more strikingly exhibited at a funeral ceremony in one of the churches. Some priests were performing the usual burial ceremony over a coffin in the centre of the church. I approached, feeling almost as if I were an intruder. It was the coffin of a child. But there was no mother there to shed her last tear over its remains, nor a single mourner around it. There was no one but the priests to perform their hollow service, and a few ragged children, who had followed the coffin in from curiosity, or, as I afterwards saw, for its spoils. The ceremony over, the priests departed. The sexton, with little regard to its contents, gave the coffin into the hands of four of the children, and it was carried out into a side room. Here, with as much handling as if it had been a bale of goods, it was stripped of its black drapery and of various ornaments of lace, gilding, and artificial flowers. These were eagerly divided and carried off by the children, while the coffin, tossed aside upon some others that stood there, was left a shapeless rough box."

Padua, Oct. 13, 1858: "We here picked up a cicerone, and in a few hours saw all that is worth seeing of this once famous town. There is not much that I shall remember except a picture by Guido Reni of 'John in the Wilderness,' which impressed me very much. I have seen nothing of Guido's before that I liked. But this is just such a painting as I would like to have in my room, ever before me. The attitude is a wonderful combination of ease with energy. There is a youthful simplicity in the whole figure, which one sees well will grow into manly honor and dignity; and the countenance and eyes are all a-glow with a true boy's enthusiasm, which is to ripen naturally with age into prophetic inspiration. It was but a few moments that I looked upon this picture; but I shall see it all my life-time."

The life-story has been told — an uneventful story, and most inadequately told. Yet it is the best that can be gathered out of the obscurity that always hangs over the deep things of the human spirit. Such a life as that of William James Potter yields no material for the romancer or the dramatist, and leaves its abiding record chiefly in the lives of others, lifted up to higher planes of thought and feeling and silently influenced to aim more steadily at the "beauty of holiness." Strength and vigor of moral character, loveliness of spirit, saintliness of life,— undemonstrative yet tireless enthusiasm in the cause of soul-freedom and soul-fidelity, undaunted pursuit of pure truth in the face of myriad influences in society that tend to tarnish its purity and subordinate it to meaner ends, unbounded faith in the immanent and ever-active presence of the Divine in the human,— in a word, lifelong self-consecration to truth, righteousness, and love: these were the impressions of the man that were left on all who came within reach of his shy yet potent influence. To the few who were admitted into the sacred places of his companionship, veneration and affection contended for the mastery. Yet nothing could be less mystical or unreal than his participation in the commonest affairs of life. Greater than his purely speculative capacity was his rare soundness of judgment in all practical matters, in which he made fewer mistakes than almost any one that could be named. It was this quality that made his opinion weigh so much in his own city, even among hard-headed business men; they saw that he was wise in the things of the world, and this gave them an instinctive confidence that he was wise in things of a higher order. In times of trouble, when ordinary ambitions lose their hold even on the worldliest minds, a soothing and uplifting influence emanated from his words and manner, nay, even from his mere presence and aspect, which attached to him those who could by no means fathom the depths of his spirit. Little as he performed the ordinary offices of the conventional "pastor," he yet ministered to his people in a way that held them to him with "hooks of steel," and rendered him their helper, comforter, and friend. How sweet and gracious and consoling were his sympathies with their sorrows, they knew, if strangers knew not; and the reluctance with which the long pastorate was at last ended tells its own story in these days of swift and frequent change. Perhaps the secret of his power over their hearts is let out, in part, in a letter of his which may fitly close this sketch of his life, and show the beauty of its sunset.

41 Mt. Vernon Street,
Boston, December 9, 1893.

My dear Friend,— Shortly after you left me to-day, your letter was handed in. Though constrained to silence, we understand each other. Our hearts are linked together, in this experience of a common pain, by the chain of a wordless sympathy. Yet I believe I can assure you that it is a part of "the All-Love" in the nature of things to soften gradually and tenderly the first sharp pangs of such pain, and that, too, without benumbing our sensibilities to the irreparable loss we have sustained. With the glorious memory of my wife shining through the fourteen years since she left me, I find in the ties of work and affection that remain so much of satisfaction and joy, that I cannot now quite respond to your expression that "the happiest day that awaits either of us on this earth will be the day when we leave it forever." Yet I can perfectly understand how you, in these desolate days of a bereavement so fresh and poignant, should feel so. But, dear friend, may you live to understand also my present feeling, that life, with all the bereavements behind it, may still have a joy and beauty which we shall not be eager to leave . . . .

Yours most sincerely,

WM. J. POTTER.

IN THE GRAY STONE CHURCH.

DECEMBER 26, 1893.

Forth went from his dear homestead's doors
    The Reaper-Youth at morn,
To toil as toiled his ancestors,
    And reap his field of corn.
All day he labored in the sun
    And bore the heats of noon,
Nor once forgot the task begun,
    Nor laid his sickle down.

Back to this dearer home returns
    The Reaper-Man at night,
And love, exulting while it mourns,
    Bends reverent at the sight.
He comes, alas, to reap no more,
    But with a wealth of sheaves,
Where once the field he labored o'er,
    He now his harvest leaves:

His harvest, not of yellow corn
    Such as his fathers prized,
But souls to nobler issues born,
    To holier lives baptized,—
Souls stirred to seek the lofty ends
    Of freedom, wisdom, love,
And make their own the truth that blends
    The Serpent and the Dove.

O prophet-preacher, wise and just,
    Pure, gentle, tender, free!
Marble is dust and bronze is rust;
    We build not these to thee.
Yet one memorial shall remain,
    Long as the seasons roll:
Thy monument of growing grain,
    Thy harvest of the soul!

                F. E. A.

LIST OF PUBLICATIONS.

[NOTE.— In the following list no attempt has been made to enumerate Mr. Potter's many articles in the *Index*, to which he was a constant contributor, and of which he was for six years (1880–86) the editor. He also edited for a number of years the annual reports of the Free Religious Association. Many of his sermons were printed entire in the New Bedford daily papers from his manuscript; but it has not been found expedient to include them here.]

DISCOURSE [TO THE MEMORY OF MRS. SARAH R. ARNOLD, preached Sunday, May 13th, 1860. New Bedford, 1860.] 8vo. pp. 18.

[The same.] 8vo. pp. 17.

THE INNER LIGHT AND CULTURE. An address delivered before the Alumni Association of Friends' New England Yearly Meeting School, at their third annual meeting at Newport, 1861. New Bedford, 1861. 8vo. pp. 16.

A PULPIT VIEW OF THE BUSINESS INTERESTS OF OUR CITY. [Discourses preached Jan. 18 and 25, 1863. New Bedford, 1863.] *Broadsides.*

THE VOICE OF THE DRAFT. [New Bedford, 1863.] *Broadside.*

This was reprinted in the *Army and Navy Official Gazette*, Aug. 11, 1863. (Vol. I., pp. 87-89.)

THE NATIONAL TRAGEDY. Four sermons delivered before the First Congregational Society, New Bedford, on the life and death of Abraham Lincoln. New Bedford, 1865. 8vo. pp. 67.

A TRIBUTE TO THE MEMORY OF JAMES ARNOLD. [New Bedford, 1868.] 8vo. pp. iv, 19.

REASON AND REVELATION. A discourse. New Bedford, 1868. 16mo. pp. 22.

THE DOCTRINE OF PRE-EXISTENCE AND THE FOURTH GOSPEL. Reprinted from the *Radical.* Boston, 1868. 8vo. pp. 13.

TEN YEARS' MINISTRY. A sermon preached to the First Congregational Society, New Bedford, Jan. 2, 1870. [New Bedford, 1870.] 8vo. pp. 13.

WHAT IS CHRISTIANITY, AND WHAT IS IT TO BE A CHRISTIAN? A discourse before the First Congregational Society, New Bedford, Dec. 28, 1873. [Reprinted from the *Index.*] Boston, 1874. 16mo. pp. 21.

A DISCOURSE ON CHARLES SUMNER, delivered at the First Congregational Church, New Bedford, March 22, 1874. [New Bedford, 1874.] 8vo. pp. 6.

LESSONS FROM THE ELECTIONS FOR THE VICTORS AND THE VANQUISHED. A discourse delivered before the First Congregational Church, New Bedford, Nov. 9th, 1874. New Bedford, 1874. 8vo. pp. 19.

SOME ASPECTS OF UNITARIANISM IN ITS PAST AND PRESENT HISTORY. Two discourses delivered before the First Congregational Society, New Bedford, Nov. 22d and 29th, 1874. New Bedford, 1874. 8vo. pp. 38.

CHRISTIANITY AND ITS DEFINITION. *In* "Freedom and Fellowship in Religion." A collection of essays and addresses edited by a committee of the Free Religious Association. Boston, 1875. pp. 178-221.

IN MEMORY OF MRS. CAROLINE MORGAN, who died April 20, 1883. [New Bedford, 1883.] 16mo. pp. 18.

Contains address at the funeral service and "The Higher Life,' a discourse preached April 29, 1883.

WILLIAM H. ALLEN. [New Bedford, 1883.] 16mo. pp. [20.]

Contains the address made and selections read at the funeral, and a portrait and brief life of Mr. Allen. Printed on one side of the leaf only.

TWENTY-FIVE SERMONS OF TWENTY-FIVE YEARS. Boston, 1885. 8vo. pp. [x] 417. *Portrait.*

THE FAITHS OF EVOLUTION. (Unity Short Tracts, No. 6.) [Chicago, 1885?] 16mo. pp. 8.

An extract from the sermon preached on his twenty-fifth anniversary.

A COMPLETED LIFE. A discourse preached in the Unitarian church, New Bedford, Mass., Oct. 24, 1886, as a tribute to the character of Joseph C. Delano. [New Bedford, 1886.] 8vo. pp. 20.

THE FIRST CONGREGATIONAL SOCIETY IN NEW BEDFORD, MASS. Its history as illustrative of ecclesiastical evolution. New Bedford, 1889. 8vo. pp. 151.

SERVICES at the ordination of Paul R. Frothingham as associate pastor of the First Congregational Society in New Bedford, Mass., Oct. 9, 1889. [New Bedford, 1890.] 8vo. pp. 31.

Contains sermon, "Liberty, but Religion also." By William J. Potter, senior pastor. pp. 7-30.

A Noble Motto for the Conduct of Life. A memorial discourse [on Dr. G. Felix Matthes], delivered in the First Congregational (Unitarian) Church, New Bedford, Oct. 20, 1889. New Bedford, 1890. 16mo. pp. 18.

The Late Lesson from our County Court House: A Pulpit Trial of the Egg Island Crime. A discourse given in the First Congregational (Unitarian) Church in New Bedford, Oct. 25, 1891. [New Bedford, 1891.] 8vo. pp. 8.

The Free Religious Association: Its Twenty-five Years and their Meaning. An address for the twenty-fifth anniversary of the Association, at Tremont Temple, Boston, May 27th, 1892. Preceded by a brief sketch of the annual convention. [Boston, 1892.] 8vo. pp. 31.

Closing Sermon of William J. Potter, Dec. 25th, 1892. Opening Sermon of Paul Revere Frothingham, Jan. 1st, 1893. First Congregational Society, New Bedford, Mass. [New Bedford, 1893.] 8vo. pp. 44.

Mr. Potter's sermon, "Thirty-three years: Their End a Beginning." pp. 9-26.

Sunshine of the Soul, William J. Potter, Dec. 17, 1893. In the Shadow, Paul Revere Frothingham, Dec. 24, 1893. [New Bedford, 1894.] 8vo. pp. 36.

Mr. Potter's sermon, the last he wrote, pp. 3-20.

ARTICLES IN THE RADICAL.

IDEAS AND INSPIRATIONS. October, 1866. Vol. II. pp. 65-75.

WHO IS OUR SAVIOUR? February, 1867. Vol. II. pp. 347-352.

THE RESURRECTION OF JESUS. May, 1867. Vol. II. pp. 558-571.

THE DOCTRINE OF PRE-EXISTENCE AND THE FOURTH GOSPEL. April, 1868. Vol. III. pp. 513-525.

THE DOCTRINE OF DIVINE INCARNATION. June, 1868. Vol. III. pp. 673-688.

CHRISTIANITY AND ITS DEFINITION. February, 1870. Vol. VII. pp. 81-108.

THE DOCTRINE OF IMMORTALITY IN THE LIGHT OF SCIENCE. June, 1871. Vol. VIII. pp. 314-336.

THE NEW PROTESTANTISM: ITS RELATION TO THE OLD. (Discourse before the Alumni of the Divinity School of Harvard University, June 27, 1871.) September, 1871. Vol. IX. pp. 105-128.

ARTICLE IN THE RADICAL REVIEW.

THE TWO TRADITIONS, ECCLESIASTICAL AND SCIENTIFIC. May, 1877. Vol. I. pp. 1-24.

RELIGIOUS SENTIMENT IN THE LIGHT OF SCIENCE.

PROBABLY there is no utterance of Hebrew piety which has come down to us that would be so generally accepted as the very quintessence, in expression, of the religious sentiment in one of its purest and most poetical forms as the Twenty-third Psalm, beginning, "The Lord is my shepherd." In the midst of perplexities, trials, sorrows, it breathes the innermost spirit of trust, confidence, serenity, hope, and peace. When we want words of comfort and calmness, we inevitably turn to it. Its sentences abide easily in the memory with a soothing charm. When read in the chamber of sickness, they have power to hush the moanings of pain. In the house of death they have power to subdue into reverent stillness, at least for the moment, the complainings of bereaved hearts. Over the grave they arch in a rainbow of promise. To many a man and oftener to woman, struggling to the verge of despair against life's actual hardships and bitterness, they have come with a strengthening of purpose, of courage, and of hope. It would be difficult, indeed, to find anywhere else, in so small a compass, throughout the whole range of religious literature, an utterance so completely covering all the hard exigencies of human life, and yet so charged with a confident belief in a ruling and overruling Providence for human personal good. We shall find the ethical side of religion more fully expressed elsewhere, as in the Beatitudes of the New Testament and in certain utterances of other religions,—as in Marcus Aurelius and Seneca and in Buddhism and the writings of Confucius and Mencius. We may find heroic appeals to religious action in some of the Hebrew prophets and in Brahmanism which are of a very high order of spiritual nobility, yet they strike a different key. But as a poetical expression of the religious sentiment *per se*, in all its fulness, ranging through the whole gamut of spiritual experience in the face of life's problems of good and evil, I think that the Twenty-third Psalm must stand as the classical masterpiece.

To the investigating rational understanding of the present age, however, clothed with scientific authority, there is no Holy of holies too sacred to enter. There is no veiled Shechinah from which modern reason dares not to lift the curtain; no traditional form of the religious sentiment, however venerable for its age or closely intertwined with the tendrils of the heart's holiest memories, which this same reason does not claim the right to approach and analyze. And this right must be freely granted. A human belief or a human institution, even on the theory that they were directly created by Almighty Power, cannot in themselves be regarded as more sacred than the plant or the mineral, which we unreservedly give up to science; for, on the same theory, the plant and the mineral were directly created by the Almighty Power. If the latter be a fit subject for scientific investigation, why not, then, the former? For one, I can have no sympathy with those persons who appear to be afraid lest modern rationalism is going to discover some disagreeable truth about the religious beliefs and usages they have been wont to hold. If it be truth, they should want to know it; for nothing can be more divine, more absolutely real, than that. It is on the presumption that these beliefs and usages have been supernaturally revealed as true that they have been adhered to. If not true, they are not what we have taken them for; and, if this be clearly shown by rational and judicial inquiry, we ought to be ready to discard them as errors, and not mourn for them as lost truths. And we should be thus ready, were it not that we often grow to love our own accustomed opinions more than we love the truth. When, therefore, this modern spirit of rational inquiry approaches the holiest shrines of our most cherished sentiments; when it asks, as it now does, for the reason of this or that usage in familiar forms of worship; when it studies, as it would other books, the most revered oracles of Scripture; when it takes even such an exquisite classic of religious literature as the Twenty-third Psalm, and, becoming more special and personal in its inquisitions, asks us here, for instance, who may be believers in the scientific doctrines of evolution and a natural divine immanence, and have parted company with the Hebrew conception of Jehovah, how we can harmonize with such modern beliefs our usage or any usage of the old Hebrew words, or how turn for truth or for comfort to the lines which picture the Eternal Power as the tender shepherd of mankind,— when inquiries like these press us, we ought not to evade nor blink them as if fearing some dire result, but be ready to give a reason for the faith or, if it be that, for the non-faith which may be in us. There is no result in religious things more dire than that intellectual tampering with truth which becomes insincerity in utterance and fraud in action.

Taking, then, such an utterance as the Twenty-third Psalm as one of the most noted high-water marks in the ancient expression of religious sentiment, what shall we say for it in the light of those rational views of religion which the new science of this century has been shaping? On the answer to this question will depend, perhaps, certain momentous issues,— as whether these new science-shaped views of religion will be merely critical, or positively and creatively religious. Will they remain on the plane of analytical religious philosophy merely, or will they be capable of nourishing the impulse to worship? I do not mean necessarily worship at fixed places and times, but that worship which is in spirit and truth and resolute noble purpose; and, what is more, will these new scientific views of religion give impulse to that consecrated and persistent action which will result in the continued moral progress and spiritualization of mankind? On these several and searching questions the discourses on the specific portions of the Psalm may throw some helpful light. But, primarily, the theme has such a large unfolding into the whole question of the relation of science to sentiment, and of sentiment as an essential factor of religion, that a prior consideration of these points will be helpful.

And, first of all, it must of course be borne in mind that we are here using the word "sentiment" in the sense given by the dictionaries as its first and most usual meaning; namely, as that function of the human mind which manifests itself in mental feeling, emotion, or inward sensitiveness to impressions from certain ideas or from outward things, as distinguished from the ideas themselves and from the faculty of mental perception and judgment. The term "sentiment," especially in the plural form, is sometimes used as a synonyme for "opinions," or mental views. But this is not a meaning with which we are now dealing.

A second point to be kept clearly in mind is that, when we are considering the present applicability of any past form of religious expression, whether it be an institution or usage, a work of art or a piece of literature, we must make a broad distinction between the expression of sentiment and the expression of beliefs or opinions.

On this distinction the whole question of adaptation to present use may depend for decision. For instance, the Hebrew-Christian Bible is a book of the most varied contents and texture. Large portions of it purport to be narratives of events, historical, biographical, cosmological. Other portions consist largely of dogmas, opinions, beliefs, and ecclesiastical regulations. These dogmas, opinions, beliefs, and regulations have to a large extent been passed by, outgrown. They belonged to their time, but have little use at the present time except for material toward a history of human beliefs and institutions. And, in every case, the question of their truth or error is to be submitted to the more enlightened reason of modern times. Of the narrative portions a large part has been proved to be unhistorical, legendary, mythical; and these parts can have no present use for ethical or spiritual profit, except that the legend is often morally suggestive. But, again, large portions of the Bible consist of religious poetry, prophetic preachings, ethical and spiritual precepts, the utterances of sage and seer. In these portions the religious or moral sentiment is spoken from and spoken to. And just in proportion to the height and purity of the poetic insight and the spiritual vision do these parts keep a permanent religious value and take their places as religious classics for the spiritual edification of mankind. Even in these utterances, beliefs of the time, no longer accepted by rational judgment, may mingle;

but they occur incidentally only, making a part of the setting of the gem, but not the gem itself: they are not the chief thing conveyed to our minds or touching our hearts. And herein we may find the proper rule for discrimination. Where the religious sentiment (including the ethical) so predominates over beliefs and opinions that it is not the latter which chiefly impress us, but the impress comes from the sentiment itself, and where that sentiment brings to us high solace or ennobling inspiration, there we have a Scriptural utterance, whether from the Hebrew-Christian Bible or any other religious literature, which carries its own proof of its continued spiritual value. Applying this rule to the Twenty-third Psalm, in my opinion it would abundantly meet the test. Beliefs may change, dogmas be discarded; but in the purest expressions of the religious sentiment there is a reality of truth which never becomes obsolete.

The correctness of this position with regard to the point under discussion is confirmed by noting that a similar relation exists between sentiment and doctrine, or belief, in other matters where sentiment is the chief ground of appeal. We may listen with edification and delight to a fine execution of the classical oratorios, though we may not accept the theology that inspired them and the words of which may still go with them. For music is an art which finds and addresses a sentiment which is underneath all words; and, when the art rises high enough, it may express that sentiment with such magical enchantment as to cause for the time being forgetfulness of the false words it uses. So Dante's great poems continue to find charmed readers, who discard the theological conceptions which his lofty muse used as the framework of her subtle art. And this is true of poetry in general. It is not necessary that the thought of a poem should be strictly modern to keep it alive, if only the thought be subordinated to sentiments or to certain fundamental principles of conduct which have common and perpetual vitality in human experience, and these sentiments and principles are touched by the wand of genuine poetic genius. Even the quaint plantation songs of the Southern negroes, with but a fig-leaf of thought and making use of the crudest imagery, have often power to draw our tears because of the pathos of sentiment with which they are charged. Yet, before leaving this point, it ought to be added that, when we have not only the richness of sentiment and the fine artistic genius, but, combined with them in any literary or musical composition, a range of ideas which are acceptable to our intellects, then there is additional gratification, since more of our mental faculties are addressed. Emerson and Browning have been poets who have particularly given to their admirers this third pleasure: they have been poets of to-day's thought. And not infrequently it is their thought which carries along a rough or halting verse. Still, it is not the thought which will decide the question of their permanence in the galaxy of the world's poets. Here their triumph will rest chiefly on the measure in which they have expressed imperishable sentiments by a masterful poetic genius.

But we are told to-day, and sometimes by persons who appear to represent a considerable part of the scientific thinking of the day, that sentiment itself is out of date and is to be relegated to the background of modern activities. So let me say a few words on this modern attempt to cast prejudice on sentiment in general. Sentiment is often derided as sentimentalism, the design being to cast back upon the parent-word the discredit that attaches to its verbal offspring. But the fact that a new word was coined to express that vicious extreme to which sentiment may run when unbalanced by other mental qualities proves rather the soundness of the original word and of that function of human nature for which it stands. We want to repress, of course, sentimentalism, and we want so to check and balance sentiment that it shall not fall into sentimentalism; but do we want to repress the faculty or function of sentiment itself? The faculty of reason does not always use sound logic, and sometimes falls into woful mistakes. Shall we therefore suppress it? Even conscience has gone astray, and committed terrible crimes. Shall we therefore discard it in the guidance of life? Nature has created in the human mind a variety of faculties, each fitted for a special function or service; and it seems probable that the great intent of nature concerning man, and of the Power behind nature, will be best fulfilled by a well-balanced development and use of all these faculties. Hitherto, the history of the world, from the very beginnings of history, proves that sentiment has played a most important part in the acts of nations and men. It has been the mainspring of some of the mightiest institutions and movements. Even we of this country are but a little more than thirty years away from one of the most magnificent demonstrations of sentiment on a continental scale that the world has ever seen,— the popular, Pentecostal uprising of the North against the slaveholders' rebellion, when the national flag was shot down. In the white heat of patriotic enthusiasm the iron barriers between churches and between political parties were melted away, and the North leaped as one man against that final outrage of the slave power. Sentiment needs the vigorous regulation, on the right hand and on the left, which is offered by reason and the lessons of experience; but it is itself the central impulse in a large domain of human action. It is the founder of the family and the home. It is the chief sustainer of moral law. It has been a founder and supporter of states as well as religions.

When, therefore, I hear of schemes for the suppression of sentiment in human life, I think that a task is undertaken a great deal larger than is dreamed of,— nothing less, in fact, than a revolution against human nature. I know what mighty power is possessed by moral agitators and reformers. They do sometimes revolutionize society and its institutions. But such reformers have a powerful sentiment in their philanthropy to spur them on. These new apostles to society, whose cry is, "Death to Sentiment," cut the very nerve of reform effort in the proclamation of their principle. They are not re-formers, but mal-formers. Their act, if they could accomplish it, would be a species of self-mutilation. Nature, therefore, may be trusted, by the pressure of all her vital and progressive forces, to resist it as a crime.

I doubt not that a scientific study of the great social problems — the problems of poverty, vice, and criminal degradation — will render most valuable aid toward their solution. I doubt not that in some respects a genuine social science is going to transform all our old methods, particularly in making the chief aim to be prevention of misery, instead of letting the misery come and then sending charity — necessarily then for very pity's sake — to misery's relief. But, if any think that these new scientific methods are to vacate the offices of the sentiment of benevolence in the solution of these grave problems, they most profoundly err. The plea of those critics to whom I have here referred is, Let not sentiment interfere to prop up the feeble-bodied and the feeble-minded against the operation of nature's stern law of struggle, with survival of the fittest. But by the natural law of evolution itself civilization and humanity have advanced far beyond this sheer animal stage of physical struggle for physical existence. The ethical and humane sympathies which do interfere with that old law of physical struggle and survival are among the most eminent signs of the high altitude to which human life has risen above savage and brute conditions of existence. On the human plane the survival of the fittest is thus made to mean the survival of the best. In fact, the new scientific methods of philanthropy will require larger and more constant services from personal sympathy and benevolent devotion than the old; and the best benefit of all methods of dealing with vice and misery must always come, not from the method itself, but from the personal sentiment of genuine neighborly love and helpfulness which the men and women who wield the method are able to put into it. As to that fastidious frowning on sentiment and on every kind of enthusiasm which appears in certain quarters of the fashionable world, it deserves scarcely any further criticism than that of silent contempt. With the suppression of sentiment, the faculty of thought in these persons seems also to have vanished, and nothing has power henceforth to disturb the decorous inanities of their days. Their characters are too feeble for perpetuation, and we need have no concern lest they shall revolutionize human nature. Nor need we more fear those bolder intellects who venture here and there to assert that the marriage institution should be taken from its ancient foundation in the sentiment of love, and that the state should select partners in marriage according to scientific principles of adaptation, and that the state, too, should take the children under its tutelage and not leave them to be spoiled by parental fondness. This theory is not wholly new to human history. Ancient Sparta tried it to a very considerable extent in both its branches. The theory produced a nation of soldiers. But they and Sparta went down with the rest of Greece, when that country of ancient genius vanished from history.

We see, therefore, that the great sentiments in general, which have moved human nature through all its past history, are likely to abide. They may be cultivated, improved, but not uprooted; for their roots are vital elements of human nature itself.

If this be true of sentiment in general, it is *a fortiori* true of the religious sentiment. Religion, as I am accustomed to define it, — seeking a definition which shall cover all its specific forms and possible phases, — represents man's threefold relation, through thought, feeling, and deed, to the Universal Power and Life. Feeling, or sentiment, is one of the three essential elements of religion, which must always appear when religion has its full symmetry of proportions and its full measure of legitimate power. Sometimes sentiment has held too exclusive sway, producing a religion of emotional ecstasy with the crudest thought and very slight ethical perception. Unbalanced by rational thought, disconnected from the moral sense and deed, the monstrosity of the dervishes' dance and the revival convulsion has been called religion. Nevertheless, without sentiment, religious thought may tend to dry dogmas, and moral deed be cold and colorless. The sentiment is that which imparts the life-giving, fructifying, mellowing atmosphere to religion. And it is difficult to see how this sentiment should not arise, though in very crude form perhaps, as soon as the first mental perception of relationship to some Power conceived to be supreme had dawned; and as difficult, nay, more difficult, to see why the sentiment should not continue as a necessary adjunct of all full-sided religious thought, under whatever degree of rational enlightenment and culture. Just look at the actual conditions a moment. Here we are, in organic, vital, present relationship with the Eternal Power from which all things have proceeded. That Power is the very breath of our life. Our consciousness, our affections, our aspirations, are phases of its existence. Our sense of duty and right is the behest of its august presence. Our dispositions to benevolence and generosity are the very channels which its love has made in our being at our welcoming gesture. Yet this Power, so nigh to us, so living in us — and this is what Science says — is that same Power which has existed from all eternity, creating the worlds and all that is in them, and which shapes the perfect crystal of the snowflake, clothes itself as beauty in the ripened leaf and in the first flower of spring and in myriads of forms, large and small, all around us on earth, and studs the heavens with gems of stars and planets. Can any human being actually think this thought about the Infinite and Eternal Power without some uprising of inward sentiment? without some emotion both of awe and of obligation? Even Science itself, for a moment, must hush its debates, cease its researches, and bow in reverence before the grandeur of its own conception.

Nor does legitimate Science make any opposition to sentiment either in religion or elsewhere. Sentiment forms a part of the phenomena which make the field of its researches. It is a more difficult field than that which is offered in physical nature; and Science does not claim that it can bring to the region of emotion the same tests which it would apply in the chemical laboratory or in botanic analysis. It only claims that the scientific method is to be used, and not the dogmatic; that is, the method of accurate research into and observation of facts, and then of their classification, and the discovery, if possible, of their law of relation. This method is now applied to the study of history, of language, and literatures; and there is no reason why it should not be applied to all the phenomena of religion. For science is simply systematized knowledge. But if, on account of the reconditeness of the field, Science is as yet unable to give a systematic explanation of all the phenomena of the religious sentiment, that failure does not invalidate the reality or the useful function of the sentiment. The blood circulated in the human frame precisely as now before Harvey discovered the law of its circulation. So religion and the religious sentiment existed for long ages before modern science appeared. Science has scattered or is scattering the crude explanations of their origin which have come down from uncivilized and uncritical times. By and by it may clearly show the natural motive and law of their development, and demonstrate their rational validity. Yet that validity will not depend on this discovery and declaration of Science. Science discovers a law of existence, but does not create it. The validity of religion is established in the constitution of human nature. It is Professor Tyndall who writes: "There are many things appertaining to man, over and above his understanding, whose respective rights are quite as strong as those of the understanding itself." "There are such things woven into the texture of man as the feeling of awe, reverence, wonder; the love of the beautiful, physical, and moral, in nature, poetry, and art. There is that deep-set feeling which has incorporated itself into the religions of the world. To yield this sentiment reasonable satisfaction is the problem of problems at the present hour." And, if I recall aright, it is Herbert Spencer who says, still more pointedly, in the line of the thought I have just been uttering, "The religious sentiment, like the desire for knowledge, is a phase in the energy of nature."

And when we have thus fixed the religious sentiment as correlated with the innermost essence of Nature's being, or, in other words, with that Reality and Power Eternal which is behind all phenomena, material or mental, as their source and sustenance, we need entertain no anxious fear lest this faculty of human nature, which has been so dominant in the past, is now to suffer extinction. Let us not believe that, under our rationalistic views of religion, the function of religious emotion must cease, that its place is vacated to be filled by some other faculty. The immediate objects of religious sentiment may change from age to age, but the sentiment does not thereby cease as a factor in human action.

I have spoken a few pages back of the religious sentiment as necessarily including moral sentiment when rightly cultivated, and without this combination there can be no genuine religion. And this necessity has been abundantly proclaimed and emphasized by all the great seers and prophets of religion in all faiths,—not always by theologians and priests, but by the world's galaxy of immortal spiritual teachers. But the fact that the strange deformity is not infrequently witnessed of a character in which religious sentiment is developed strongly and into great demonstrativeness of expression, and at the same time conscience in the same person is so weak as not to forbid most flagrant immoralities, — this abnormal fact has led not a few liberal thinkers to question whether religious sentiment has any real and permanent value in itself. Let me, therefore, call your attention somewhat more specially to this point.

Why, it is asked, make a distinction between the religious sentiment and the moral sentiment, since we admit, in accordance with the teachings of all the greatest religious prophets, that there can be no true religion without morality? Or, if psychologically there be a distinction, is there anything in the religious sentiment when it is developed by itself apart from morality that is worthy of preservation? What is religion apart from ethics but a mass of bigotry and superstition? Why not, then, reduce religion to what we admit is its best evidence and fruit, practical virtue, and, saying nothing of the religious sentiment, aim directly at that on which there is such general agreement?

Now there is a truth implied in these critical questions for which hospitable provision must be made in the institutions and practical efforts of religion. But, at the same time, the questions do not cover the whole of human nature, nor can the ethical aim alone permanently satisfy. I cannot believe that a correct philosophy either of human nature or of religious history will identify religion wholly with morality, and, much less, confound the religious sentiment with the moral sentiment. It is true that religion in its highest and purest form cannot exist without morality, true that the religious sentiment, when awakened to its best efficiency, must diffuse itself through the moral sentiment, and make the latter one of its most effective instrumentalities. Still, religion and morality are not the same. Religion, when genuine, includes and covers morality, but is more than morality. The ethical sentiment is one of the vital elements of the religious sentiment, but the religious sentiment has other elements of which the ethical sentiment knows nothing. The ethical sentiment may be defined as man's feeling of obligation to serve the right, and morality is the conduct that results from carrying this sense of obligation into practice. In other words, it is obedience to conscience, or to a rational view of what is best for individual and social well-being. But religion is something more than this. Even if we say that practically religion and morality come to the same result, — goodness, — it is goodness as seen from different outlooks, as reached by different paths, and as having a somewhat different quality. Matthew Arnold says, "Religion is morality suffused with emotion." This indicates the distinction partially, but does not wholly cover it unless a very large meaning be given to the word "morality," or the emotion be more specially defined as to its cause. No definition of religion, I think, will satisfy the philosophy of the subject which does not in some way denote the contact which the finite mind has with the vitalizing and sustaining Energy of the universe. It is not necessary that the definition should embrace the idea of a personal Deity, not necessary that it should attempt the impossible problem, which most theological systems do attempt, of defining the Infinite; but it must, in order to cover all the facts, in some way recognize the Infinite,— in other words, recognize that the human soul is conscious of a life that is not bounded by its material organism nor by any limits which itself can measure, but opens outward into the whole infinity and eternity of things, and is a natural, inherent part of the universal order. I should define the religious sentiment as man's feeling of his connection with the Infinite Life and Order, not in any supernatural way, but by the organic laws of his being; and religion, as the effort to bring his own life into harmony with what he conceives to be the demands of this higher and larger Life. And this rounded religious consciousness is not simple, but is a compound of several elements. Into it enter the idea of causality, the idea of truth, the idea of beauty, the idea of right and goodness. Without taking the ground that these ideas are innate, or forming any theory as to their origin, it is certain that through them the human mind finds itself confessing allegiance to a law of life that is not of its own creation and not bounded by the sphere of its own existence. These perceptions it learns to interpret as indicating the purpose and law of the Infinite Life, and yields itself to them in a joyful endeavor not only to attain harmony and good for one's self but to serve the universal welfare. This is to be rationally religious. It is to do by intelligent choice and free volition what the plants do by their structure, — to make a channel through which the ceaseless energy may work to its ends. But these perceptions thus peering out into the world's infinity of mystery and putting us into relations with things and forces that are illimitable, these perceptions that necessarily stretch back to the sources of all material and mental power and downward or upward to the primal cause of things, are naturally accompanied by emotions of awe, of wonder, of reverence, of adoration, of expectancy, of fear and hope, of solicitude and thanksgiving; and these various emotions, according to the understanding and culture of a people, will take shape in the various outward expressions of religion.

We may see now, I think, how it is that the religious sentiment, though needing the moral sentiment for its perfect development, may yet, since it includes so much more than the moral sentiment, be developed vigorously in some directions without it; and how, under narrow and ignorant views of the world and its powers and of man's relation to them, the religious sentiment should have often developed into crude and superstitious beliefs and revolting practices. These beliefs and practices vanish away through the influence of better knowledge and culture; but how the root of the religious sentiment itself, which is simply man's feeling of his relations to the Universal Life, is ever to pass away so long as man is not self-existent and self-derived, but is conscious that his life is related to the whole universe of things, I cannot conceive. The moral sentiment itself is endowed with a grander beauty and a higher majesty when it is thus felt to be one of the vital ligaments by which human life is connected back with the sources of all life, and is commissioned to work out a purpose that is not of self nor of time, but is eternal. The moral sentiment may, indeed, do its work, and do it fairly well, without this consciousness of its high descent and dignified destiny. The man may simply say, "This is duty, and must be done," without any thought as to what duty means in its universal relations, without ever inquiring into the nature of the pressure behind that little word "ought," which gives its authoritative power. When he acts thus, he is simply moral. But when to any person the consciousness comes, whether it shape itself into any formal belief or not, that, through this sense of "I ought," the eternal purpose of the universe presses to accomplish its high ends, and that he is agent of a power and purpose immeasurably grander than his own aims or his life even, then he becomes religious. Then he feels that the will of the universe is at his back. He becomes the subject of superb inspirations and courage and of high heroisms in action. He treads the earth as a master, holding a sovereign hand over its destinies, under the Eternal.

That this powerful sentiment is ever to abdicate its office I cannot believe. That it needs to be lifted to the full loftiness of its functions by enlightenment and culture, removing its abnormal excrescences, I concede and plead for. But human nature is not to be bereaved by its death. The power that built the wonderful cathedrals of the Middle Ages has not vanished nor abated aught of its marvellous and magical capacity, if to-day, instead of cathedrals of stone, it builds its visions of harmony, grandeur, and beauty, its wide hospitalities and generous sweep of human sympathies, into the characters of living men and women. The power which once set in motion the crusades might not be able to raise the smallest army for a like object to-day; but it is not exhausted so long as it summons men and women to nobler heroisms and purer causes. Guided by reason and the moral sense, pervaded and regulated by a wise culture, religious sentiment may be an element in human nature and life as vitally creative to-day as it has ever been in the past. When poetry shall die out of the human soul; when man shall cease to be moved by any of the sublime spectacles in nature; when his heart shall no more be entranced by exhibitions of heroic virtue; when truth shall no longer attract his admiring mind; when all visions of ideal excellence shall fade away from his eager eyes, and he shall no longer stand erect, with eyes lifted upward and forward toward the longed-for light of the better day to come; when the great mystery of Being, in which man lives and moves and has his being, shall have no power to stir a thought or a feeling within him,— in short, when he shall be no longer *man*, then, but not till then, will religious sentiment become a dead faculty in his nature. But so long as man remains a being capable of feeling the power of truth, goodness, beauty, and he is conscious of an inevitable mental attraction, in however vague way, to some deeper Reality which may be their eternal source and unity,— in fine, so long as man stays man, the religious sentiment must stay as a vital part of him; for it is the veritable life of ages pulsing in his consciousness, thrilling his organism with a sense of the majesty of its eternal purpose and law, and with a measure of its supreme calmness and joy.

THE TWENTY-THIRD PSALM IN THE NINETEENTH CENTURY.

I.

THE ETERNAL OUR SHEPHERD.

"The Lord is my Shepherd; I shall not want."

THE Twenty-third Psalm as a whole is a specially fine antique expression of religion; and in this series of lectures we are to consider the question, What does this pious utterance mean for us to-day, in view of the most enlightened and scientific ideas of religion which the nineteenth century has been furnishing? The Psalm divides naturally by its six verses, each of them presenting a special phase of the relation between religious sentiment and religious thinking. Hence the general theme will divide easily into six discourses, each with its specific form of the question just stated.

But before I proceed to the particular verse, the opening one, which will occupy our attention to-day, let me make two or three brief prefatory statements applicable to the Psalm as a whole.

First, the question of the date and authorship of the Psalm is of little or no account, as concerns our present purpose. The application of the modern method of scientific investigation to Biblical literature makes it one of the assured results of criticism that most of the Psalms attributed to David, and this among the number, must have had a later origin. And, for myself, I should prefer to believe that the picture of idyllic innocence and serene moral confidence which we have in the Twenty-third Psalm did not have for its author a man of so many villanies and crimes as are recorded against King David. But in these lectures we are to consider the Psalm for what it is in itself, without reference to its origin, except that we know that it belongs to the ancient Hebrew literature. Second, the Psalm presents, in an exceptionally pure and exalted form, an expression of the religious sentiment, an expression vivid with local and national coloring; yet its few sentences — for it is among the briefest of the Psalms — are so free from antiquated dogmas that there is nothing in it which must needs offend modern rationalistic thought when it is remembered that the whole form of the utterance is poetical. It is poetry of the religious sentiment with which we are here dealing, and not with theological prose, — with pictures and metaphors of the ideal realm of the imagination, not with logical syllogisms. Third, the common English version of the Psalm has become so fixed in the memories of people and so embedded with their strongest religious associations that I shall use it in preference to a more literal rendering, pointing out, however, when we come to them, the places where an exacter meaning might be given by a different version. The revised version of the Old Testament only ventures a change in two words in this Psalm, and those so slight as to be hardly noticeable. Of other changes which a more exact conformity to the original might require, I will add that they would not, as in some other Biblical passages, detract from the spiritual beauty and significance of the sentiment, but, rather, enrich it.

And now I ask you to consider with me the first verse of this little Hebrew poem of religious confidence and hope, querying with ourselves thoughtfully what it can mean for us.

"The Lord is my Shepherd; I shall not want"; so we read or repeat the words from our Bibles, and always, I think, with a tender reverence. But do we recall them merely for their tender sentiment, expressed by a picturesque poetic metaphor? Or do the words still stand for some very real truth to us, of which they have power to excite a vivid feeling? We are to remember that religious sentiment, like sentiment in general, has two quite distinct phases. A noble work of art, for instance,— a great poem, a great piece of music,— may affect us to the point of enthusiastic admiration and incidentally touch even deeper feelings simply through its high artistic power, irrespective of the ideas it was meant to convey; the ideas in such cases are merely a skeleton, which sentiment covers with its own forms of beauty and life. But, if the ideas and the excellence of the art both are able to strike responsive chords in our mental organism, then we have a correspondingly larger satisfaction. And this unity in an enlarged result is especially important in religious usage. Without it we may have the piety of an æsthetic ritualism and the cherished associations of traditional and liturgical forms of worship, but not that profoundest reality of worship which is in spirit and in truth. And this phrase, "in spirit and in truth," well expresses the desired combination of sentiment and thought which should be sought in religion as a preserver of sincerity. There is a mental perception of truth which is one of the characteristics of the understanding, or the reasoning faculty; but there is also a feeling of truth, which is the function of sentiment in its highest form. And this feeling of truth is a phase of sentiment which means a great deal more for man's nobler culture than can be wrought by any amount of emotion excited by a rare achievement in the forms of art merely, or by a tender affection for the beautiful in poetical expression.

So again I ask, when we repeat the old words, "The Lord is my Shepherd; I shall not want," do we cherish them simply for their poetic beauty and their venerable antiquity, or do we have a feeling of their truth? Here, in this first verse, the keynote of the Psalm is struck in the pastoral metaphor wherein Jehovah is pictured as shepherd; and the note is carried through to the end, in all the succeeding imagery, even though the metaphor is abruptly changed just before the close. If this first note does not ring true for us, then there must be for us falsity all through; beautiful words, but not, for us, the beautiful thought! Perhaps some critic may say that, however forcible this picture of Jehovah may have been to the primitive Oriental people among whom it was uttered so many centuries ago, and where one of the chief occupations of life was the care of flocks and herds, it can have little significance to the civilized nations of the earth in this nineteenth century. To the Hebrew, indeed, who was wont to conceive of Jehovah as a mighty monarch, a God of hosts and of battles, a leader of armies against the national enemies, a thunderer in the heavens, and a sender of plagues and of pestilence, in his displeasure, upon the earth, it must have been a comforting relief to listen to this confident description of the same supreme sovereign as a wise and tender shepherd personally leading his flock and supervising and securing the highest felicity of each one. But, our critic asks, are not both of these conceptions, that of the mighty monarch who was the leader of armies, and that of the tender shepherd who was the leader of flocks, equally obsolete as descriptions of Deity to-day?

Other critics may dispute the facts stated in the verse, as at variance with human experience. Could the starving Russians last year, it is asked, believe in a Deity who was a Shepherd to them and would not suffer them to want? The Russian peasants have been taught that the czar himself, as head of the church, is God's vicegerent on earth, having supreme power. Yet they found him able in their dire famine to lead them into no green pastures of plenty and refreshment. Or what truth was there in this sentiment, "The Lord is my Shepherd; he will take care of me; I shall not want," for those thousands of victims of the late earthquakes in Japan and Zante? or for those suffering and slaughtered by the recent rage of tornado and tide in Louisiana and on the South Atlantic coast? or for the hungry and famishing ones who, thrown out of employment, may be found in most of our large cities to-day, those who know not to-night where to-morrow's bread is coming from, and whose natural "want" of food is seldom on any day fully satisfied? Can any of these classes of people repeat with truth the pious phrase, "The Lord is my Shepherd; I shall not want"?

Yet such objections, it must be replied first, could just as legitimately be made in the Hebrew singer's own time. As to the first of these supposed querists,—and they are not merely imaginary persons, but represent real objectors to the conception of Deity as a Shepherd of the human race,—the first of our critics is treating this Psalm as if it were intended as a philosophical or metaphysical conception of Deity, whereas it is poetry, and not theology; and poetry, if genuine and lofty, never becomes obsolete. The Psalmists, whoever they were and whenever they wrote, were not logicians nor scientists: they were simply religious poets. Of science there was then nothing bearing that name in the modern sense. Nor were these writers engaged in producing such works as Calvin's "Institutes" or Barclay's "Apology." They had no concern with the metaphysical problems of religion which taxed the powers of those eminent logicians, and would not probably have appreciated those famous treatises even so well as you and I can. Our Psalmist was simply a poetical observer of nature and human life from a religious point of view, and then he put what he saw and felt into song. He would have made no insistence on the conception of Supreme Being as a Shepherd, as if that were a description of Deity excluding all others. On the contrary, he turned readily from one metaphor to another, according as he viewed for the time being one aspect or another of man's relations to the mysterious infinity of the world-forces. Now Jehovah was the tender Shepherd; but anon the same pen might characterize him as man's Fortress, his Rock, his King, his high Tower, his Sun and Shield, his Light, his Life, his Savior, Father, Law-giver, and Judge. Writers who employ in their work such picturesque conceptions and descriptions as these are no more to be judged by the rules of prose and logic than is Longfellow's poem of "The Building of the Ship," with its closing application to the "Ship of State," to be submitted to the same standards of criticism as the *Federalist* or the Constitution of the United States. The close of this poem, indeed, with its felicitous expression of ideal hopes and prophecies for the union of the States against actual inimical assaults and threatened perils and death, may be taken as a happy illustration, from our own time, of just what the poetical conception of Jehovah as their Shepherd meant for the Hebrews in the midst of their national troubles.

For, again, those commentators err who imagine that the writer of "the Lord my Shepherd" must have written out of the provincial experience of an idyllic pastoral life, and knew nothing of the terrific evils against which the human race as a whole has to struggle, evils which, these objectors think, overthrow the theory of a shepherding Providence. On the contrary, the Hebrews had experimental acquaintance with nearly every form of human woe. They were aggressive and ambitious as a nation. At first they were a group of discontented wandering tribes seeking a better domain for their homes, better pasturage for their flocks. They were, in consequence, almost continually at war with their neighbors. They became divided, too, into warring factions among themselves. There were rival and fighting claimants for the throne, with the customary Oriental incidents of intestine intrigues, strifes, assassinations. There were seasons of famine and pestilence. Nature, with all her friendliness, was not always friendly.

Her pitiless bitterness was a familiar foe. In the reign of King David himself, the reputed writer of "The Lord is my Shepherd; I shall not want," there was a fearful plague and a famine of three years, when David ordered some of the chief of his domestic enemies to be killed, as a sacrifice to appease the wrath of Jehovah, who was believed to have sent this calamity upon his people for their sins. Later the nation was conquered, scattered, carried into captivity. Yet, through all and after all, the national prophets and poets did not cease to preach and sing — in full confidence, in order to nerve the national heart and will — their ideal faith and hope in Jehovah as a good Shepherd, who would lead his flock out of bondage and want into plenty and peace.

It is evident, therefore, that even originally this conception of Jehovah as a Shepherd had for its germ a faith, a thought, which went below the superficial appearances of events, and was rooted in some deeper reality than outward prosperity and contentment. Mere freedom from calamity and suffering,— this was not what the wise, devout Hebrew meant when he sang of Jehovah his Shepherd. This might come as a consequence, but it was not the essential thing which in his inmost heart he craved. There he touched a measurement of want and of weal, in which purely outward treasures and pleasures, however much he valued them, did not count. The Psalmist was not a philosopher, like Socrates; yet he approached in this thought the wise Greek's prayer: "O all ye gods, grant me to be beautiful in soul; and may all that I possess of outward things be in harmony with those within." Nor did the Psalmist have the stoical nature of the Roman Epictetus; yet, though his hope was more buoyant and childlike than that of Rome's slave-philosopher, it was kindred in spirit to that confidence with which Epictetus declared his faith toward Zeus: "Though he set me before mankind poor, powerless, sick; banish me, lead me to prison,—shall I think that he hates me? Heaven forbid! . . . Nor that he neglects me; but to exercise me and to make use of me as a witness to others." And it was in one of the Hebrew books, by an author who was a philosopher as well as poet,—the Book of Job,—that this expression of implicit confidence in Deity reaches the climax of depreciation and sacrifice as to the things ordinarily regarded as necessary for the satisfaction of human wants. Out of the midst of his afflictions Job says to his vain counsellors, "Though the Almighty slay me, yet will I trust in him."

There is no occasion, then, to believe that, when the Hebrew thought of Jehovah as a Shepherd, he necessarily expected a cosseting care for individual human souls, which would save them from all pains, anxieties, trials, and personal efforts for themselves. This "Lord my Shepherd" Psalm itself contradicts such an idea. It speaks of dangers, terrors, darkness, enemies, to be encountered. Nor would the metaphor of the office of shepherd, drawn from the writer's personal knowledge or experience, convey the idea of escape from all encounter with the hazards and perils of life. The Hebrew shepherds at their best did not protect their flocks against all unhappiness. They could not make the grass to grow wherever they wished. The way to the green pastures was sometimes long and wearying. The refreshing fountains were sometimes dried. Violent assaults could not always be warded off. And once every year the shepherd himself led his flocks to the shearers' hands. And any one who has seen the plaintive pathos of entreaty on the face of a sheep under the shears, tied against struggling, and even though, according to the Scripture, dumb, will know that the operation to the poor creature is no pleasant experience, however needful it may be for mankind. The good shepherd was wise and tender, but his wisdom and tenderness had their limitations; and these limiting conditions the flocks could not always readily distinguish from hardness and cruelty. So, though Jehovah was believed to be a being of infinite wisdom and tenderness, the Hebrew devoutly acknowledged that his ways of showing his wisdom and kindness in the leadership of Israel might often be beyond the limits of man's vision and knowledge. Nevertheless, despite all apparent aberrations and delinquencies, he still trusted the divine leadership; and this was the highest test of the loyalty of Hebrew faith.

We are now prepared to see what were the essential elements of the Psalmist's conception of Jehovah as Shepherd. There are only two of them, but two which to him covered the whole infinity of the character of the Hebrews' Deity, however variously they described him by other forms of speech. The first of these elements will be made conspicuous at once by a more exact rendering of the leading word of the Psalm. Let us translate it thus: "The Eternal is my Shepherd." The word which is translated as "Lord" in the common version is the Hebrew word "Jehovah," more correctly, "Yahweh," and its literal meaning is "eternal existence." "I am that I am" is a Scriptural paraphrase of its meaning. Here was indicated the Being of all beings, Power of all powers, the mystery of supreme existence prior to and penetrating all finite existences. "The Eternal" appears to be as good an English phrase for the idea as any that can be found of equal brevity. And what the Hebrew meant was that, amidst all that was transitory, finite, changeable, perishable, confused, and uncertain in human affairs, there was an Eternal Power as leader, a Power working through and over all for some sublime and lasting end of its own. This is the first essential element of the Psalmist's conception of Deity as a Shepherd, or Leader, of his people. And the second element is that this leadership is accomplished and the sublime end of the Eternal reached through the law of righteousness. The devout Hebrew believed that the Eternal was himself the author and giver of the law of righteousness, and that amidst and despite all the moral disloyalty and disobedience, all the vices and wickedness and crimes and calamities of the Hebrew people, the Eternal would turn and overturn, check and punish, until Israel was established in righteousness; and that the prosperity and peace which the nation dreamed of as its ideal destiny could only be attained through the people's learning and keeping the ways of righteousness.

These, let me repeat, were the two essential facts to which the Hebrew held in his metaphorical description of Jehovah as Shepherd: first, the Eternal, through all change and transitoriness, is man's leader; second, the road of leadership is up the ways of righteousness, to safety, felicity, and peace. The Eternal Power that maketh for righteousness — to adopt essentially Matthew Arnold's oft-quoted phraseology — expresses well the Hebrew conception of Jehovah in its inner significance.

And now I ask whether the intervening centuries have rendered these two declarations obsolete and nugatory? Has the nineteenth century taken us past them? Have we any science that has controverted them? Is there any philosophy of the universe that does not use these two ideas, in some shape, for corner-stones? Is there any rational and ethical, not to say religious, action of man that does not in some way involve them?

Of course, the Hebrew gave other distinctive attributes to his Deity, generally clothing him with very anthropomorphic qualities and features, and representing him as personally and miraculously overseeing and arranging all the affairs of individual human lives. In this region we should certainly find many dogmas which have been outgrown and abandoned, many opinions which to-day's science and reason would deny. But these beliefs were merely subsidiary to the two points of faith just named and in no wise essential conditions of their soundness, and in the Psalm of the Eternal as our Shepherd these merely temporary beliefs have little place. In that poetic utterance, only those two central points of Hebrew faith — the Eternal as leader, and a leader Righteous and Good — are prominent.

What, then, does the rational and scientific thought of modern times have to say on these two points of the Hebrew faith in Jehovah as a Shepherd? On the first point, as soon as we give the literal translation, "*The Eternal* is my Shepherd," there comes at once to view a remarkable parallelism. "The Eternal" we may almost say is the phrase of science. Eternal power, eternal energy or force, eternal existence, — these are all expressions to represent that something, that original, uncreated, and unevolved substance of being which all science and all discussions about the universe have to assume as the basis of all phenomena. There is no blankest atheism, no form of philosophical materialism, which does not admit the existence of such a power. The great scientific doctrine of evolution, which is revolutionizing so many theories of philosophy and religion, demands an eternal evolving force or agency. Herbert Spencer, the prince of agnostics, calls it the "Ultimate Reality," and, more descriptive still, "an Infinite and Eternal Energy, from which all things proceed." This is "the Eternal" of the Hebrew, the very meaning of the word "Jehovah," the "I am that I am." These are all names or phrases demanded in the name of science or even of the crudest reasoning faculty for that primal Reality without which nothing that we see, or know, or that anywhere exists, could ever have been. When Spencer calls it "an Infinite and Eternal Energy, from which all things proceed," he describes it in the bare prose of scientific statement. Yet, when he speaks of man as ever, by an absolute certainty, in the presence of the mystery of this Infinite and Eternal Energy, we begin to have, even when thus expressed with logical bareness, that feeling of its truth which approaches religion. Now, add to the same thought the sentiment of poetry in the expression of it, with no added attribute of character whatever, and we have Wordsworth's

> "Sense sublime
> Of something far more deeply interfused,
> Whose dwelling is the light of setting suns,
> And the round ocean and the living air

> And the blue sky, and in the mind of man,—
> A motion and a spirit, that impels
> All thinking things, all objects of all thought,
> And rolls through all things."

This is only "the Infinite and Eternal Energy, from which all things proceed," depicted with no conscious intelligence nor purpose, but only as universal motive power; yet, in the guise of poetic sentiment, the conception rises into the realm of religion.

But the Hebrew poet went further. In describing God under the phrase "my Shepherd," he depicted the Eternal Energy as acting with intelligence and a good purpose. He meant to declare that the Eternal Power was to be trusted to guide man through all trials and perplexities to the happiest results, because it was united with attributes of infinite Wisdom and Righteousness. Can we say that modern scientific and philosophical thought as confidently indorses this second point of Hebrew faith as it indorses the first? Frankly we must admit that as yet it does not. Science here becomes agnostic. For settling questions of infinite personality and of an eternal, conscious, purposive intelligence apart from finite intelligence, scientists, for the most part, declare that they have no data. If they believe that the Eternal has these attributes, they will say they hold their belief on other than strictly scientific grounds. Philosophy, too, is hesitating, uncertain, and variant in its voices on these intricate problems; and even theology, once claiming that here was her special field of revelation, has lost a good deal of her old positiveness, has become apologetic. What shall we say, then? Is the Eternal merely blind, unintelligent power with no moral aim, no purpose wise and beneficent in its scope? If so, then we must part company with the Psalmist's thought of the Eternal as our Shepherd; and we may as well let the pretty sentiment of it go, too, if we cannot with mental integrity keep the thought. But, for one, I believe that we may rationally hold to the thought that the Eternal Power shepherds mankind and all creatures.

For proof of this belief I am not going into any questions, subtle and metaphysical, concerning Infinite Personality and Eternal Conscious Intelligence. I am ready to accept such beliefs as philosophical inferences, provided that I am not required to define these alleged attributes of Absolute Being too closely by their human and finite counterparts. But for proof of my belief in a wise and beneficent activity interfused with Eternal Power I do not begin at the infinite side of the universe. I begin just where science begins,— among finite things. Leave, if you please, for the moment at least, infinite intelligence out of account; and begin with the lowest terms of rational knowledge. What then? We find, first, that the world in all its knowable parts and operations is an intelligible world, part adapted to part and force adjusted to force, in an order and harmony productive of certain results, upon which our intelligence can certainly calculate. Were the world a mere medley of aimless forces, operating by chance and whim and at cross-purposes, human beings could not with all their intelligence adjust themselves to it, and life would become impossible. That the world is intelligible gives us all the effects and benefits of purpose and aim and law, whether we affirm or not an infinite conscious intelligence pervading and governing it. And in all practical accomplishment of the ends of his existence it is vastly more important for man rationally to adjust himself to a world of intelligible forces, laws, and activities than to try to conceive and adore a being of infinite intelligence in a vague somewhere above the universe. And, second, we find the known and knowable universe to be not only intelligible, but to be subject in its own activities and unfoldings to amelioration. It is an improvable universe. There is a mounting from low and crude forms of life to something higher and better. The very power of life itself tends to eliminate the evil, which resists its aims and destiny. That is the very meaning of evil,— resistance to the power and aim of life. Hence the law of life is from bad to good, and from good to better and Best; that is, ever toward fairer and nobler forms and organisms of life. And man, through his rational and moral consciousness and his consequent intelligent purpose and moral endeavor, is made a helper in this ameliorating and ascending process. Nothing is better established by the evidence of history than that the Law of Righteousness greatens in its authority and in its results both in respect to nations and individuals with the lapse of centuries. But, third, according to the doctrine of evolution it is the Eternal Power itself that is actively and organically manifest in the intelligible order, law, harmony of the world-forces, and in all the meliorating and ascending activities of those forces, and in the mind and heart, in the moral will and righteous deed of man. And, consequently, all this ascent which is open to us human beings into larger and richer realms of life above mere material existence, and the very impulse toward the ascent, as also that inward faculty of adjustment to circumstances, whether they seem favorable or unfavorable, so as to turn them into some kind of benefit,— all these dominant factors in the conduct of life we owe to the actual leadership of the Power Eternal. Therefore, I can say the Eternal is my Shepherd. And, with this present fact underneath me and expressing the innermost reality and meaning of my existence to-day, I have as little interest to prove as to deny that in the primeval eras, before the first whirl in the fire-mist whence our solar universe had its origin, this Eternal Power must have existed in a personal entity together with Infinite Wisdom and Infinite Beneficence. There you carry me off to a distant metaphysical question. It may have an interest for the logician, but I prefer to stay with present facts. It suffices me to know that the Eternal Power is now organized in the law, order, harmony, beauty, purpose, adaptation of force to benefit, and ever-ascending life and increasing righteousness of this world which I inhabit, and where I, too, am called to some harmonious service for the enlargement of its well-being. It is thus that the Eternal shepherds mankind and all creatures,— through the law of mutual and gradually lifting service. The shepherding function is no police supervision from the skies, but is organized in the very laws and forces and movements of nature and humanity. Hence the Eternal shepherds man in a higher way than the flocks of the field are shepherded, man being more largely endowed with the function of being a providence unto himself, adjusting himself to his changing environment and converting his very trials and misfortunes into spiritual and moral wealth. The Eternal Power, too, is creative of new and higher wants as the creatures ascend in organism and breadth of life; but along with the wants goes ample provision for their supply. "Demand and supply" is one of nature's primal laws. Dr. Holmes, in his poem of "The Chambered Nautilus," touches both the ante-human and the human forms of this organic amelioration. In the nautilus

> "Year after year beheld the silent toil
> That spread his lustrous coil;
> Still, as the spiral grew,
> He left the past year's dwelling for the new,

Stole with soft step its shining archway through,
>> Built up its idle door,
Stretched in his last-found home and knew the old no more."

But

> "Build thee more stately mansions, O my soul,
>> As the swift seasons roll!
>> Leave thy low-vaulted past!
> Let each new temple, nobler than the last,
> Shut thee from heaven with a dome more vast,
>> Till thou at length art free,
> Leaving thine outgrown shell by life's unresting sea."

So to this mystic, creative, ameliorating power of the Eternal I bow in reverence, to adhere to it and work with it in trust and love. It comes to me, bending under a past eternity of accumulated wisdom and beneficence, which it offers to me for the serving and refining of my wants. At my co-operating gesture toward it flow supplies from infinite reservoirs. I know that, if I am disloyal to it and disregard its behests, even though all the wants of my flesh may be satisfied and I may be rich in many things called wealth, I shall yet be poor in manhood and bereft in soul. But if I loyally follow and obey it, whatever other treasures and pleasures I may lose, I shall be possessed of all things most worthy of human attainment. In this Power Eternal is man's highest Friend, his Shepherd, his King, his God.

THE TWENTY-THIRD PSALM IN THE NINETEENTH CENTURY.

II.

GREEN PASTURES AND STILL WATERS.

"He maketh me to lie down in green pastures; he leadeth me beside the still waters."

In approaching the lesson that is couched in this refined luxury of poetic words, it will be helpful to bear in mind certain points of last Sunday's lecture on the Eternal our Shepherd. The first two verses of the Psalm have a peculiarly close connection. The writer evidently meant to intimate how impossible it is that the Shepherd should allow his flocks to suffer want, with such satiety of supply at hand in meadow and stream for all hunger and thirst. Hence, lest we go astray with the idea that the Hebrew poet was thinking only of a cosseting Providence that should shield the human race from all possible harms, and shelter it safe from the necessity of rugged disciplines, let us recall from last Sunday's discussion these conclusions: —

First, the Eternal shepherds mankind, not by miraculous displays of sovereign care, but through the fact that the Eternal Power is organized in the ordinary productive forces of nature and in the natural human faculties. The Eternal, indeed, leads us, but does it through the inward constraining force of reason and conscience, and the sentiments of affection, honor, and benevolence. Second, the goal of this leadership is attained through an educational process whereby human life is gradually adjusted to the great world-energies. This process of adjustment means that the Eternal Power which is organized in man as mental and moral perception and as rational and moral motive for action, places itself in vital relationship of practical concord with the Eternal Power that is organized in the vast energies of the universe outside of man; and hence man derives for his finite existence and purpose sustaining supplies from that infinite bounty. Third, the conditions of this educational process of adjustment by their very nature do not admit that man shall be provided for by a fondling supreme care, without effort or thought of his own to meet his wants; but rather they necessitate the putting forth of human faculty in a strenuous struggle with problems of difficulty, in order to attain the higher ends and satisfactions of human destiny. Fourth, in this educational process of adjustment, moreover, human wants themselves are enlarged, elevated, and spiritualized. They emerge from material wants and blossom into wants of a mental and moral nature, and material wants are refined from their merely animal grossness and made subordinate to nobler demands of reason and moral right. The wants of a tribe of Hottentot Indians are very different from the wants of any ordinary community of citizens in Massachusetts. And again, the wants of such a soul as Fénelon, or Epictetus, or Emerson, or Elizabeth Fry, or Clara Barton are not only far removed from the wants of a Congo negro, but almost as far removed from the dominant wants of many a person called civilized and who may live in the luxury of riches at the very acme of modern civilization, yet who lives chiefly for gratifying the propensity of covetousness and the passions of the flesh. It does not follow, therefore, because all our actual wants may appear to be satisfied, that it is the Eternal who is always leading us to their gratification. We may be under the lead of merely temporal desires and appetites. Man is subject to diseased, abnormal, and rebellious wants, which actually work against the Eternal purpose; and he is only led away from them to higher satisfactions, through disciplines of pain and retribution.

These points were all stated or implied in the previous lecture, and they have a direct bearing on our thought to-day.

For what kind of wants or satisfactions did the Hebrew poet mean to symbolize under the picture of nature's luxuriance of green pastures and still waters? Plainly here was something more than merely feeding and drinking, something beyond the bare necessities of existence, a suggestion of other than physical hungers and thirst to be satisfied,— a suggestion of ideal wants as well as the gratification of actual wants. The green pastures and still waters are beyond all the needs of present hungers and thirsts. The flocks are to lie down in the midst of this beautiful, bountiful greenness; and the Hebrew phrase for "still waters" is rendered, by one of the most literal translators, into "well-watered resting-places." The Hebrew phrase does, indeed, carry a finer, fuller idea even than that of "still waters." It means "waters of restful quietness." The eager appetites of the flocks are depicted as already appeased. The scramble for food is over. The tiring, dusty, hot journey to the pastures has had its reward. The flocks can now rest at ease on the lap of Nature's bounty. The grass from which they have fed offers a bed deliciously soft and fragrant. The air they breathe is sweet with the breath of the still waters, and invites their senses to repose. With such abundance close at hand, they can have no anxieties for the future. The Shepherd has led them to the very sources of Nature's plenty, and they are at peace.

But now consider for a moment the times and circumstances under which the Hebrew poet wrote this pastoral verse, and the purpose he had at heart. Of course, we understand that he was not merely indicting a pretty poem of nature. He had another flock in mind and other pastures in vision than any he saw among the sheep and hills of Palestine. To him Israel was the flock and Jehovah the Shepherd. And, whenever this serene poem was written, it could never have been written at a time when Israel had found all its wants and longings satisfied and was at peace. For Israel never came to such a time. Its land of promise, flowing with milk and honey, was always just before it. It journeyed toward that promise, struggled for it, prayed for it, fought for it, was sometimes just on the verge of securing it; but Israel never passed over the inexorable boundary which separated from it. The promised land was an ideal country,—always in promises, not in fulfilment. Yet the devout Hebrew did not cease to believe in it. Though far away from it, he saw it at hand. Though enemies resisted his advance, he saw them overcome. Though his people were in captivity, he saw them free and going forth to conquer and possess. And the Hebrew poets and preachers never ceased to appeal to and uphold this sublime, transcendent faith. To keep the faith was to help toward the fulfilment of the promise,— was, indeed, to insure it. Hence, while their national wants were still unsatisfied and they were in the midst of innumerable troubles, they pictured in perfect confidence the serenity and prosperity which would surely come, if Israel would but faithfully follow Jehovah's guidance and law. That outward serenity and prosperity, which they saw in prophetic vision as the fruit of faithfulness, already seemed to have settled inwardly upon the souls of seer and poet, so that they spoke out of a spiritual calmness which could not have been suggested by their present surroundings. Hence, our Psalmist saw the green pastures and restful waters which were before Israel as if close at hand, and he wrote as if he already breathed their atmosphere of ineffable peace. "As if" do I say? Nay, he did. For to souls such as his, that live in a spiritual atmosphere of faith and courage and hope, time and distance are elements which do not count. For Israel as a people, the green pastures and still waters may have yet been far away, with many troubled years between. But he who wrote "The Lord my Shepherd" had found them. Though troubles raged around him, his spirit rested in trust on the calm, bountiful bosom of the Eternal, and shared the eternal strength and repose.

And now let us ask what meaning this particular verse of the Psalm can have for us in this rationalistic age of the nineteenth century. Has the Oriental picture of the Eternal as a good Shepherd, leading mankind into green pastures and beside still waters and leading them beyond the bare needs of existence, no power to touch our hearts nor to stir within us any feeling of its truthfulness? Are we of this prosaic era,— an era of bustling material energies and enterprises,— when gifted minds are not poetizing so much about the universe as philosophizing about it, and when the philosophies and theologies do not begin so much as once they did with *a priori* assumptions about the perfect attributes of an infinitely perfect Being, but begin with observing the hard, bare facts of nature and of human life,— are we losing our sensitiveness for such an idyllic picture of universal harmony and peace? Science has, indeed, told us of the facts of an animal ancestry for mankind, of savagery in which human history everywhere begins, and of the animal propensities and habits still adhering by the iron links of hereditary law to our most advanced civilization; and only our own observation is needed to tell us of the wickedness and woe everywhere prevalent,— the bitter, killing toil, often for the poorest necessities, the gaunt poverty, the deadly famines and diseases, the frequent hardships of innocent souls, the cruel covetousness of mean and grasping souls, the stories of brutal crime which, reeking with blood and filth, the news-gatherers bring daily to our doors. Are we, I ask, so crowded and pressed by such facts as these close at hand that our minds are utterly unimpressible by any of the higher and more comprehensive facts of nature and of human life, which the Psalmist painted in those phrases, in themselves so beautiful, "the green pastures and the still waters"? Have we become such pessimists that we no longer see truth nor beauty in these words? Or, if we still see in them a certain artistic beauty of form, is the poetic sentiment but a bitter mockery for us, in view of the cruel facts of existence?

Even while my brain was busy, on an April day, with these sentences, I looked from my window, and beheld there before me, on the tender spring grass, two sparrows in terrific battle, one of them picking the very life-blood from the other's breast. And, as I looked, I thought of the tender, trustful words of Jesus: "One of them shall not fall on the ground without your Father." What do those words mean, with that fact of bloody sparrow-slaughter before my eyes? Yet that battle of the sparrows is but the most insignificant fraction of the great battle for conquest by blood that is going on in the world of nature, and that from time immemorial has been going on, and is still going on we must say, among men. What mean these terrible facts of conflict, battle, and blood, which seam with their horror all the strata of natural and human history? With our eyes holden by these horrors, can we anywhere descry the still waters and green pastures of the Psalmist's vision? Yet, as I watched the battle of the sparrows, I noted also the upspringing grass newly carpeting the earth with its beautiful green, and above the warring birds the tree-buds pushing out their colors; and I saw the crocuses in brave blossom where snow was lately banked, and all the miracle around me of the new spring-time; and I looked up to the sky's inimitable blue, arched over all, and to the white cloud-ships sailing across that upper main: and then my soul said to itself that, despite the ugly seams in its structure, this is a beautiful world, and despite the moral horrors the moral beauty overarches and overpowers them.

The Hebrew had to encounter the ugly and bitter facts of the same depressing nature as those which confront us to-day. Yet through them he caught glimpses of green pastures and still waters,— glimpses of an ideal destination toward which the Eternal was leading his people and against which no facts of present hardship would be able to prevail. The sublime interpretation which he thus gave to present facts was impervious to criticism. His faith rose above the facts, so that he seemed to ignore them. He believed that the Eternal was leading him; and would not he do all things well, and ultimately make the very enemies of Israel to praise him? Of course, our modern logician will say that the Hebrew here begged the very question at issue. And, regarding merely the small segment of human experience which he had in view, he did beg the question. The enemies of Israel as a nation were not conquered. Nationally Israel fell, fell pierced to death by its stronger neighbors, fell as the sparrow fell stabbed by its angered comrade. As a nation, Israel was not led into the green pastures and by the still waters of its promised land. And yet, when these questions are put to-day, What do these hard facts mean,— the cruel conflicts, the disappointments, the hardships and poverties, the bloody horrors, the sparrow's fall, the nation's overthrow, the crucifixion of Jesus by his own national kindred, the pressure of the poison to Socrates's lips by the hand of cultivated, classic Greece? I aver that enlightened reason to-day is in a better condition than Hebrew or Christian theology has ever been to overbalance all these dark facts of existence with brighter, larger, and higher facts, and to give to all life's facts a rational and ethical interpretation.

Science, with its doctrine of evolution, has given us the clew. The universe is a school of education, which has the Eternal for its leader and master, and eternity for its course. The Eternal Power is thus, through the new science, revealing its purposes in a grander scheme to sublimer ends than the Hebrews ever conceived or dreamed of in their dream of national glory. It is an ascending process and progress, leading on from one amelioration to another, all the way from the clay and the atom and the primal force to the intelligent consciousness of man, which enacts rectitude into laws and customs, creates States, and controls brute passions by reason and love. The brief suffering of a sparrow in its fall, the violent death of a man, the calamity of a nation, are throes incident to these higher births. Nor, in viewing this evolutionary process and progress from the point of view of science, are we burdened with the questions which have always embarrassed the theologians in debating the problem of evil, "Why does not the Eternal, All-wise, and All-benevolent Omnipotence prevent this, and do that?" It is ours only to note what the Eternal is doing, and to adjust our own lives thereto; to discover to what end and by what method the Eternal is moving and to make that our aim and way.

That with respect to man the movement is onward and upward there is no reason nor science that can doubt. The history of the ages is proof that man is slowly led, by the constraining power within him uniting with the power without, away from brutal degradations and childish errors toward greatening realms of wisdom and right, and toward corresponding experiences of felicity and peace.

Human adjustment to the Divine or Eternal Power,—that is always the one dominant duty. Whatever our surroundings, whatever the events that befall us, in whatever form the Eternal may here and now touch our dwellings, our lives, the primary question is, How shall we adjust ourselves to the Power so as to draw into ourselves somewhat of its strength, wealth of resource, and felicity? The Power is abundant, over and above all human needs: can we not connect with it so as not merely to find all our necessities supplied, but to feel also a sense of the supplying, creative, nourishing energy around us in such luxuriant bounty that we can have no longer present ailing, nor fear for the future, nor any sense of estrangement from, but only vital unity with, the very sources of Life and Well-being and wholesome Joy?

Consider even the lowest plane of life,—that of physical sustenance. "The green pastures and still waters" represent that provision for human wants which looks beyond to-day's boundary of meagre necessities. They may symbolize for us nature's fertile resources for meeting man's progressive wants. Whatever man himself can save from the product of to-day's toil, beyond the day's needs, for the morrow's or the next week's uses, that helps to emancipate him from the mere drudgeries of toil and opens opportunities for the supply of higher needs. It may be safely asserted that, even with the world as it is, nature's capacities for furnishing sustenance to mankind, responding to man's labor, would be more than sufficient to feed all the millions of mankind on the earth every year. Even now, with a more skilful adjustment of intelligence to improved methods of cultivating the soil and distributing its products and for preventing waste, there need nowhere at any time be starvation nor hunger. But by and by irrigation may convert the most desolate deserts into gardens and laugh at years of drought and famine. Last winter, in California, I saw vast districts of dale and hill, which three years before had been as barren of vegetation as Sahara, covered now with every variety of shrub and blossom, with grass and with groves of young orange and olive trees, and with forest shade trees thirty feet high and more, which had grown in that time from small twigs. Irrigation had done it all. The nutritive elements were waiting there unused in the soil, and there was the snow in sight on the mountains. And human skill had married the snow and the soil together, and hence all this fruitfulness and beauty. The great San Joaquin valley, once almost a desert from the Sierra Nevada to the Coast

Range of mountains, now by the same means teems with towns and cities, with vineyards and orchards and fields of grain, bearing wheat and fruit ample for millions of people. Thus by improved modes of agriculture man literally creates for himself green pastures, and waters which shall be still or shall flow at his pleasure; and thus he produces food in excess of the day's needs, and can turn his faculties to other achievements.

Man's progress in civilization and in the refining arts of life depends, for one of its essential conditions, on the surplus he is able to save from supplying the mere necessities of physical existence. This is true of nations and of individuals. The first-earned surplus above actual wants of the body is the opening gateway to the green pastures and still waters of life. As soon as that saved surplus can begin and the saving is persistently followed, whether it be a saving of material earnings or of time from physical toil, the road is entered that leads to better education, enlightenment, culture, to refinement of manners and the creation of the tastes which demand nobler than physical sustenance and pleasures. That saved surplus above daily uses or wastes is the seed of all these mentally nutritious and pleasant pastures, the fountain whence started the rills that have gathered in these inward waters refreshing to mind and heart. A dime or half-dime saved each week might mean a picture on the wall of the home, plants in the window, a plat of grass and flowers in the yard;

and these all have their civilizing influence. A dime or half-dime saved each day may mean a few books, a good newspaper, a brighter smile on the face of the wife, better clothed and happier children. The more dimes and nickels saved and put to such uses, the more rapidly will the green pastures and still waters come, to ornament life's hard necessities and relieve its toils. Yet there is many a husband and father — sometimes, alas, even a wife and mother — who drinks up his green pastures by spending the dimes and half-dimes for liquids that intoxicate. Philanthropy can do no better thing for the laboring poor who depend for their bread on their daily toil than to show them how, by saving a little money above their needs each week, they can throw around their toilsome, arid lives an atmosphere of comfort and even of a refining luxury, of which no one can rob them.

And, again, there is the ornament of a trustful and quiet spirit, exhibited in certain characters, which carries in itself all the blessedness of the best kind of outward possessions. Such persons may be poor in worldly goods, they may be forced to painful toils, their homes may have little of material beauty; but they have so adjusted themselves morally and spiritually to life's trials and duties that the green pastures and still waters appear in their souls. The beauty which graces their homes is that of their own holiness, the nutriment they offer is that of the spirit. You feel in their presence the refreshing, assuring atmosphere of open

spaces and clear skies. They keep their serenity
unmoved by life's changes, their trust undisturbed
by its trials. They are not merely led by the
Eternal, but they have within them the stability
and life and repose of the Eternal. Mr. Wasson's
fine poem, "All's Well," written from a bed of
broken health and pain and threatening poverty,
voices the feelings of those who have thus found
their green pastures and still waters in the realm
of mental and spiritual possessions.

> "Sweet-voiced Hope, thy fine discourse
>   Foretold not half life's good to me;
> Thy painter, Fancy, hath not force
>   To show how sweet it is to be!
>   Thy witching dream
>   And pictured scheme
> To match the fact still want the power;
>   Thy promise brave
>   From birth to grave
> Life's boon may beggar in an hour.
>
> "O wealth of life beyond all bound!
>   Eternity each moment given!
> What plummet may the Present sound?
>   Who promises a future heaven?
>   Or glad, or grieved,
>   Oppressed, relieved,
> In blackest night or brightest day,
>   Still pours the flood
>   Of golden good,
> And more than heart-full fills me aye.
>
> "I have a stake in every star,
>   In every beam that fills the day;
> All hearts of men my coffers are,
>   My ores arterial tides convey;

>   The fields, the skies,
>   The sweet replies
> Of thought to thought are my gold-dust;
>   The oaks, the brooks,
>   And speaking looks
> Of lovers' faith and friendship's trust.
>
> "Life's youngest tides joy-brimming flow
>   For him who lives above all years,
> Who all-immortal makes the Now,
>   And is not ta'en in Time's arrears;
>   His life's a hymn
>   The seraphim
> Might hark to hear or help to sing;
>   And to his soul
>   The boundless whole
> Its bounty all doth daily bring."

But even where there is less of spiritual experience and of moral wealth than this exquisite lyric voices, considering, for instance, quite ordinary routines of life's ties, toils, and duties, there is always ample provision, if we will but seek and accept it, for a softening fringe around them of grace and beauty, which may be compared to the green pastures and still waters lying beyond the naked necessities of existence. A happy marriage and home, — what refreshment and added vitality do they give to the treadmill routines of labor and duty! Friendship, good books, the beautiful in nature and art and the love that may be cultivated for the beautiful, and the stimulus and delight of intellectual companionship, — these all make a rich part of life's needful luxuries. Man can exist without them, can exist and work and have all physical wants as a breathing animal gratified. But without them he cannot live according to the full breadth and wealth of the normal measure of manhood. So, too, duty may be gracefully clothed beyond the legal requirement of the commandment. The same kind of duty may be done — is done — by different persons so as to produce very different effects. Let it be, for instance, a needed moral rebuke to another or an act of charity. One person will do it with such rigidness of law and frigidity of manner as to irritate and arouse resistance. Another may do the same action with such graciousness of spirit as to make the recipient feel all the breadth and sweetness of Nature's bounty.

But, whatever possessions we may hold in this broader and higher domain of life beyond the bound of life's primary needs, there is yet always a vision of finer fields and purer waters still before us. There is no attainment that seems permanently to satisfy as if it were the end. The Eternal ever leadeth us on to some further goal. Nourished in the green pastures, refreshed by the still waters, we are strengthened for another journey and prepared for nobler tasks. "Sweet-voiced Hope" is the enticer. The young man's or the young woman's toil to-day over books or music or accounts, or at some necessitated or chosen task of the hands, might become a wearing, degrading drudgery indeed, did not hope light up the future with some finer achievement as the result. The highest ideals of character, the highest ideals of society,— these are still disembodied. They invite us onward to give them body and power. With social weals the age is alive. Impracticable, fantastic, impossible, many of them may be; but beneath them is a divine discontent, because of present wants inequitably satisfied and of higher wants struggling for birth, a divine discontent which calls for a new adjustment of social rights and duties. So much of human vitality, on one side, is spent perforce in the mere labor of keeping soul and body together, and so much, on the other side, is wasted in needless and enervating luxuries, that the refreshing pastures and restful waters of social life are hardly yet in sight. Still, there is good reason from past experience for the faith that present iniquities will gradually be removed, justice be done between man and man, labor and capital join hands in friendship, and, in some happier century to come, righteousness and peace kiss each other.

I know that the fulfilment of this great hope is commonly adjourned to another world. The Christian Church especially, apparently despairing of ever finding the green pastures and still waters on earth, has put them among the promised pleasures of the redeemed in heaven. This world it has described as mainly given over to the wiles and woes of evil, as a vale of tears and griefs: only in the world to come could the hope for happiness and peace find its fruition. But it has not been my purpose to follow this teaching of ecclesiastical Christianity. Rather have I aimed to keep with the Hebrew, who believed that this world was not so bad that it could not be redeemed, and that its utmost desolations could be made to rejoice, and blossom as the rose. I have sought to show how even here, along the dusty, toilsome, and often sorrowful ways of earthly life, the Eternal has brought the green pastures and still waters close to our reach; aye, how he has caused them also to spring up in human souls themselves, ample with an inward bounty and beauty of spirit to compensate for outward trials and wants. The Hebrew believed in a Deity omnipotent for good on earth, but did not give time enough for the accomplishment. This thought allows all time for the grand consummation, which, through man's own help, shall show earth's deserts converted into gardens and its hells into rooms of heaven.

THE TWENTY-THIRD PSALM IN THE NINETEENTH CENTURY.

III.

PATHS OF SAFETY.

"He restoreth my soul: he leadeth me in the paths of righteousness for his name's sake.

IN this verse of the Twenty-third Psalm, the revised version ventures a single change from the King James translation. It substitutes the word "guideth" for "leadeth." The euphony is thereby somewhat improved, since we have the word "leadeth" in the preceding verse; and the sense is in no way altered. The original Hebrew, moreover, has two different words, and hence on this point the revised version is the more exact; while the change from the common version is so slight that an ordinary reader, even though familiar with the old form of words, would hardly notice the variation. And this, I may say in passing, illustrates one of the rules which appears to have been followed by the authors of the new translation; namely, to be faithful to truth in the rendering unless old and devout associations were to be too rudely shocked, but, when these were likely to be thus shocked, then exactness of truth must yield to the devout associations, even though the original utterance be believed to be a miraculous revelation of the perfect truth. But in this verse the revisers might have made still greater changes in the interest of exactness, and have thereby still further improved the poetic diction. Following in the main the version of Dr. Noyes, we should then have this rendering of the verse which is to occupy our attention this morning: "He reviveth my soul; he guideth me in paths of safety for his name's sake." You will note that the phrase "paths of safety," which the Hebrew allows, is in finer keeping with the metaphor of the Shepherd leading his flock than is the common version "paths of righteousness." And yet, as we shall see later, the final idea is not essentially different.

The meaning of the first clause, "He reviveth my soul" (or "restoreth," as the King James version has it) is that the Shepherd takes means to impart new life to the flock or to refresh their spirits, after fatiguing journeys, for instance, or hard pasturage, or exhaustion from heat. The effect of the resting in green pastures and beside the still waters is gathered up designedly by the poet in these first words of the subsequent verse, "He reviveth my soul"; and then a still further idea is added to the same thought in the suggestion of the Shepherd guiding his refreshed and reinvigorated flock onward in "paths of safety."

And this is a good place to call attention to a

unique feature which often appears in the rhythmical structure of Hebrew poetry. It is called "rhythm by gradation." The Psalms thus constructed are entitled "Psalms of Degrees," or "Steps." Perhaps they were originally used as chants in solemn processions. And their peculiarity is that "the thought or expression of a preceding verse is resumed and carried forward in the next." One of the best illustrations where it is simply the resumption and enlargement of the expression is the One Hundred and Twenty-first Psalm:—

> "I will lift up mine eyes to the hills,
> Whence cometh my help:
> My help cometh from the Eternal,
> Who made heaven and earth," etc.

And the Twenty-third Psalm presents a fine example of the resumption of the thought rather than the verbal form,— the resumption of the thought, with enlargement and heightening from verse to verse, from the first sentence, "The Eternal is my Shepherd," to the climax of the last words, "And I shall dwell in the house of the Eternal forever." Sometimes the relation between the verses is not so much a resumption of the thought as suggestion of thought. The "I shall not want" of the first verse suggests the abundance and refreshment of the "green pastures and still waters" of the second verse; and this bounty of grass and of "waters of restful quietness" suggests the refreshed and quickened life and its continual guidance in safe paths beyond both want and harm. In the next verse, again, the safe paths extend even into the valley of deathly shadows. Bearing in mind this peculiarity of structure, we are helped to a clearer perception of the delicate shadings and blendings of the thought as well as of the beauty of the poetical form.

Let us now return from this digression, explanatory of the peculiar connecting links between the verses of the Psalm as a whole, to the more special theme contained in this third verse. And our first inquiry is, What was the thought in the Hebrew poet's own mind, which he clothed in the poetic language of this verse? Possibly it may have occurred to some of you that, in the substitution of the phrase "paths of safety" for "paths of righteousness," the one most conspicuous ethical element of the Psalm has been swept away. But not so. The Hebrew word (*Tsaroq*) is capable of both renderings. It is a word rich in varied meanings, yet all of them branching from one root-thought. The primitive significance of the word as applied to physical things (and in that usage the word originated) is straightness, evenness. It was specially applied to straightness and evenness of paths, as opposed to crookedness, roughness, and deviousness. It meant rightness and fitness of physical things with one another. Hence, and still on a physical plane, it meant safety, felicity, deliverance from difficult places. But, with the intellectual development of the Hebrew people, the same word came to be applied to mental and moral attributes. It became one of their greatest words. It then meant mental and moral straightness, uprightness, integrity, justice, righteousness, which would bring national deliverance from difficulties, bring national felicity and prosperity and salvation. The Hebrews had other words for some of these ideas; but the ideas to them were so mutually related and dependent that they came to use the words interchangeably. The straight paths of righteousness were for them, individually and nationally, the only paths of safety and salvation. Hence the Psalmist, voicing in this song Israel's trust in Jehovah and comparing it to the assured confidence of a flock in its shepherd, would have in his thought both of these allied meanings. True to his metaphor, his poetic vision would see the flock led in the paths of physical safety; but in the moral application both he and his people saw that the very word he used meant that for Israel there were no paths of safety except those of righteousness. With regard, therefore, to the central thought of the verse, no deduction is to be made from the strong ethical meaning of the common version, "paths of righteousness," though we substitute for it the more metaphorically consistent phrase "paths of safety." To the Hebrew, safety, salvation, and righteousness meant for human beings essentially one and the same thing.

But this central idea of the verse is placed between two other ideas, which are also important in disclosing the poet's full thought. First he says, "Jehovah reviveth [or restoreth] my soul." The word (*Nephish*) here translated "soul" is the same word which the writer of Genesis used in describing the creation of man, where Jehovah is depicted as breathing into the nostrils of the clay image he had formed "the breath of life; and man became a living soul." The Hebrew word for "soul" signified primitively the breath of life, the animating principle of all living creatures, the vital essence without which they could not be sustained in existence. And this always remained the primary and leading meaning of the word. The derivative meaning, of a rational intelligent principle as something distinct from the physical principle of life, never had for the Hebrews so prominent and positive a place as it has had in Christian thought. The soul was literally to them the breath of life, as it was the breath of Jehovah's life, from whom it came. And the Hebrew poet's most natural thought in this first part of the verse is that Jehovah still revivifies and refreshes this principle of life which came from him. One of the most literal translators renders it, "He reviveth my life." Dr. Noyes, while retaining the word "soul," in a note paraphrases the meaning of the sentence thus: "He refreshes me when drooping and fainting with fatigue or distress." In all translations this idea of renewal of vitality is evident.

The other subsidiary thought, on the other side

of the central idea, is contained in the familiar Scriptural phrase "for his name's sake,"—"He leadeth in paths of righteousness for his name's sake," which means simply that he does it because of his own nature, or from the impulses of his own being and for ends involved in his being.

These three elements, then, constituted essentially the thought of the verse as it sprang from the Hebrew poet's mind, but disrobed of its poetical dress: first, Jehovah — the Eternal — is the continual quickener and sustainer of human life, as he was its creator; second, he is guiding human life toward and in ways of righteousness and safety; third, his doing, both as to motive and end, is because of the nature of his own being. Now put the three parts together into prose thus: "The Eternal Power is the producer and sustainer of life, and in and of its own nature is guiding life onward to righteousness." Is there anything in that statement which the human mind to-day can rationally deny? As we approach the twentieth century, are we outgrowing the convictions here expressed? Has science as yet even offered anything to displace them? So far from it is the fact that we may say with confidence that the doctrine of evolution, which is at the basis of modern science, involves necessarily these convictions. As in the discourse on "The Eternal our Shepherd," so again let us use Herbert Spencer's propositions to illustrate this. I refer to him not because I am an accepter of his philosophical system, though I recognize his great ability both in research and analysis, but because he is the acknowledged head to-day of that large school of philosophy which takes as the basis of its reasonings only such phenomena as science would accept. Alongside, then, of the foregoing translation of the poetry of our verse into philosophical prose,— "The Eternal Power is the producer and sustainer of life, and of its own nature is guiding life onward to righteousness,"— let us place Mr. Spencer's now familiar declaration concerning what he commonly calls the "Ultimate Reality," "the Unknowable," or the "Great Enigma" of the universe: "There remains the one absolute certainty, that man is ever in the presence of an Infinite and Eternal Energy from which all things proceed." That tallies sufficiently with so much of the Hebrew thought as refers to the relation of human life to the Eternal and to the action of the Eternal Power from its own nature. And as to the other part, the guidance in righteousness, consider this passage from one of the earliest of Mr. Spencer's works: "Man may properly consider himself as one of the myriad agencies through whom works the Unknown Cause; and, when the Unknown Cause produces in him a certain belief, he is thereby authorized to profess and act out that belief. Not as adventitious therefore will the wise man regard the faith which is in him. The highest truth he sees he will fearlessly utter; knowing that, let what may come of it, he is thus playing his right part in the world — knowing that if he can effect the change he aims at — well; if not — well also; though not *so* well." Mr. Spencer wrote this particularly of intellectual truth; but he would say it equally of ethical truth, and it would apply equally to the conditions of moral progress. The Eternal Power, we can say, is guiding man in righteousness, because the Power is itself organized in human beings as the sentiment of right and as the impelling authority of obligation to do the right. Even ordinary men and women have this much of the Eternal within them directing them toward right paths. And in extraordinary men and women, in saintly characters, in heroic actors for the right, in martyrs and prophets, it is nothing less than the veritable power and presence of the Eternal that in and through them is leading and lifting the world to higher righteousness.

Of course, I am not claiming that the Psalmist himself had the slightest intimation of these ethical results of the doctrine of evolution or any conception of that doctrine. Nor am I making any attempt to rationalize his words in order to fit them to modern beliefs. That is always a vicious mode of interpreting the Bible or any other book. I am not in these lectures seeking Biblical authority, but only a possible harmony between the suggestions of poetic religious sentiment and scientific fact. The Psalmist accepted, doubtless, the belief of his time and race that the relation between Israel and Jehovah was of a supernatural kind; that God had mechanically created man, as the Genesis writer said, from the dust of the earth, and then breathed into the frame of flesh the breath of life; and that, all along, the divine guidance of Israel was miraculously attested. But, though doubtless holding these theological beliefs, they do not appear in this song of confidence and hope. Nothing appears there that, considered as poetry, is at all inconsistent with the most rational belief in the natural order and unfolding of the universe as explained by the most recent science. Like all great poets, the Psalmist was a seer as well as poet. He had an insight into deeper truths than those which the theologies express,— into truths which underlie all forms of statement and abide, though the verbal forms may change and disappear. The important thing for us to note in respect to this verse is that the poet here expressed a sublime faith in the Eternal as the power that from its own nature and life produces and sustains life in individual human beings and in nations, and is guiding life on to moral consciousness and moral deeds. This is the great and abiding truth which this verse has brought down to us; and this truth is of infinitely greater moment to us than to know what kind of theological explanation the writer might have given of it. And it is of infinitely more consequence to us to-day to grasp this truth of vital relation between man and the Eternal,— to grasp it not merely in its intellectual but in its practical bearings,— than it is to hold this or that philosophical theory concerning the mode of the relation. And should any one still object that the poetical imagery of the verse is anthropomorphic, pointing to an external relation between God and man rather than to an inward organic relation, I should answer that a similar objection might be made to Emerson's "Song of Nature," whose motive is to depict the creative process according to the philosophy of evolution. That is, he personifies, as the Hebrew poet did.

> "I sit by the shining Fount of Life
> And pour the deluge still"

suggests a venerable personal figure, mixing the creative elements which are finally to result in man. These are matters to be settled by the canons, not of logic nor metaphysics, but of poetry.

But there is another point where the underlying truth of this verse comes into wonderful accord with the rational and scientific thought of the present day. It is one of the recently discovered principles of the science of ethics, which may now be regarded as established, that the law for distinguishing between right and wrong had its origin in the instinct of self-preservation or of physical safety. I do not mean that it is settled that the entire moral sentiment thus originated. There is a part of the moral sentiment, and a most important part,— as the intuitive sense of justice, for instance,— which I do not think can be thus accounted for. That part of the ethical faculty I should define as an intuitive perception of the equation of rights between human beings in their relations to each other. At first a man said to his neighbor, You have no right to kill me, you have no right to take away my food. But by and by there dawned a day when he saw that, if his neighbor had no right to rob or kill him, he for the same reason had no right to rob or kill his neighbor. That is, what was good for him was equally good for his neighbor. Then dawned the idea of justice and the Golden Rule. And this is a perception that was as sure to come with a certain stage of mental development as was the perception of the mathematical relations between numbers. But, long before this stage of development was reached, there came to primitive man from the instinct of self-preservation the first crude perception of a division of things or acts into those that were right and those that were wrong. Actions and things which favored life were regarded as right: they were to be sought as good and fitting. But actions and things which were hostile to life, threatening or assailing it, were regarded as wrong: they were to be shunned. And they were instinctively shunned, in fact, as their opposites were instinctively sought. And this primitive attempt at moral classification of things on the line of the separation between things according as they favored or did not favor the instinct of safety for one's own life remains to this day the bottom line of the distinction between good and evil. Only the definition of life has now become for man so enriched and heightened that that original dividing line is mostly concealed or obliterated. Still, to-day it is the things which favor life that are right, and the things which oppose life that are wrong. But for civilized and enlightened mankind life means vastly more than it could mean for the primitive savage, who was simply bent on finding supplies for his physical instincts. Above the physical life are now whole realms, another order of life,— intellectual, moral, affectional, philanthropic, spiritual,— of which our barbarian ancestors were wholly ignorant. Yet it remains true that things which favor these higher and highest phases of life are the things which we are to seek as right, and that things opposing are to be shunned as wrong; so that now it happens that the mere physical instincts, even the instinct for saving one's own bodily life, must often be denied and sacrificed for the sake of holding to the things demanded by the higher life. There are many things which a highly moral man will die rather than do. He will let go his physical life in order to keep untarnished his moral integrity, his honor, his convictions of truth.

> "Though Love repine, and Reason chafe,
> There came a voice without reply,—
> 'Tis man's perdition to be safe,
> When for the truth he ought to die."
> *Emerson.*

Now, whence has come all this varied and wonderful development of the function of life, ascending in man from the lowest grade of fleshly instincts, through realms of intellectual sagacity and enjoyment, and of affectional activities, and through all the grades of moral perception and deed, up to the hero's self-sacrificing action in defence of the right, and to the beauty of holiness shining in some woman's character and face, whom you may find unhonored and little known on your own street? Whence comes it all? all this abounding richness, power, and beauty of moral life? Whence but from the mystery of that "Infinite and Eternal Energy, from which all things proceed?" Whence but from that Power Eternal which the Hebrew conceived as breathing into man the breath of life, as ever invigorating that life from his own nature, and continually leading mankind on in ways of righteousness to higher and nobler life? If the Hebrew conceived the action of the Eternal as outward and miraculous, while modern science regards it as inward and organic, the difference is not as to the substance of the fact, but as to the method of explaining it.

Life itself, then, under the impulsion of the Eternal Power, develops and advances in the human race on the lines of righteousness. In other words, the paths of righteousness are the paths of preservation, safety, increasing vitality, and growth. The right is organic, organific, life-sustaining, and life refining and greatening. Evil is inorganic, disorganizing, disintegrating, noxious, and deadly,— in the end suicidal. The late Professor Kingdon Clifford, the premature cutting off of whose remarkably acute and sincere intellect the philosophical and scientific world can but still lament, was fond of touching upon this scientific natural distinction between right and wrong. "My actions," he said, "are to be regarded as good or bad, according as they tend to improve me as an organism, to make me move further away from those intermediate forms through which my race has passed, or to make me retrace these upward steps and go down." This organic power which appears in right action he personifies as "the mother principle of Life." He was very chary, you know, about recognizing or naming any power that theologians have called God; but this phrase, "the mother principle of Life," may remind us of Theodore Parker's frequent descriptive name for the Eternal Power, "Our Father and Mother God." And to this "mother principle of Life" Professor Clifford's fine poetic instincts led him to apply, still further personifying it, Mr. Swinburne's rich hymn, which aptly illustrates our theme: —

> "Mother of man's time-travelling generations,
> Breath of his nostrils, heart-blood of his heart,
> God above all Gods, worshipped of all nations,
> Light above light, law beyond law, thou art.

> "Thy face is as a sword smiting in sunder
> Shadows and chains and dreams and iron things;
> The sea is dumb before thy face, the thunder
> Silent, the skies are narrower than thy wings.

> "Thine hands, without election or exemption,
>   Feed all men, fainting from false peace or strife,
> O thou, the resurrection and redemption,
>   The godhead and the manhood and the life."

The phrasing of this hymn is more modern, more colored by scientific thought; but in essential idea and sentiment there seems to me no great difference between it and the Twenty-third Psalm. And the poetic metaphor is fully as audacious and anthropomorphic as was that of the Hebrew singer. Indeed, the Hebrews' conception of Eternal Power and of its relation to human life on earth was more in accord with the modern scientific view of the universe than the commonly accepted Christian theology has been. We may almost say that the Hebrew thinkers anticipated that scientific view of the law of right being the organic principle of life which we have been considering. They saw at least the vital connection between righteousness and life and the successful attainment of life's ends, whether in individuals or in the nation as a whole. This truth was a central article of the Hebrew faith. Israel's prophets preached it and his poets sung it. The Hebrew had a glowing vision of national prosperity, power, and happiness; but he saw the realization of the vision always at the end of the paths of righteousness. It was righteousness that would exalt the nation. The national kings, in fact, were not very righteous; yet in righteousness was the king's throne to be finally established. And the sacrifices which the people brought to the altars — that is, their forms of worship — were declared to be worthless unless with them they brought the sacrifices of righteousness.

And these truths have lost none of their force with the lapse of centuries. There are weak points in our own national life where they apply to-day with special aptness,— points where party success is sought rather than the country's welfare, or self-seeking demagoguism is raised to places of power which should only be filled with wisdom and integrity, or wealth buys its way into official position where only honest votes should be the electors. At all these points and others which might be named lurks danger. At every national act of injustice there is a fracture of the nation's armor. Every species of wrong-doing, every kind of wickedness, whether on the part of a nation or an individual, falls back with devastating effect on the doer. We cannot wrong the negro, nor the Indian, nor the Chinese, without wronging our country by retarding its possibilities of progress in real greatness. It was one of the ancient wise men of India who wrote: "Justice, being destroyed, will destroy; being preserved, will preserve: it must therefore never be violated. Iniquity committed in this world produces not fruit immediately, but, advancing by little and little, it eradicates the man who committed it. He perishes at length from his whole root upwards." Thus our doctrine comes back from the far East: it is only paths of righteousness that are paths of safety.

Wrong is a crime against the universe. Right is the law of unfolding and ascending life for personal man and for mankind.

Illustrations of this pregnant truth in individual experience we should not have to seek far to find, — men and women who, because of some wrong committed against the body or against conscience or against the higher aspirations of heart and soul, lose not only the high successes which their faculties might have achieved, but lose the very power of achieving; while persons of smaller natural gifts, by keeping to the paths of right, advance steadily in mental and moral wealth and in all the satisfactions that are worthiest of human attainment. The paths of rectitude, of purity, of temperance, of kindness, of love, of honor and honesty, these are also the high and straight paths of safety. They are the ways of the Eternal, the highways which the Eternal Power has been preparing through the ages whereon man may walk. Into these ways and on them the Eternal is still striving to guide mankind. Manifold are the solicitations and constraints which would hold man to the high paths of rectitude and holiness. Alluring hope beckons. Fear of the natural retribution of pain, which follows every departure from the way of right, urges. Conscience, with its august authority, commands. Reason, by its persuasions, invites. The heart, through its kindly sympathies and loves, its generous affections and spiritual ideals, offers the gentler leading-strings for keeping human feet and faces turned toward the better future. Thus the Eternal, with man and in man and through man, has, from the beginning to this day, been guiding him onward in a pathway of material and moral amelioration and ever toward some larger, purer, and richer good. But this guidance is for mankind, and for individual man as a part of mankind. The aim of the Eternal is not to gratify selfish, individual passion as an end in itself,— not to grant a purely selfish pleasure, or safety, or prosperity. The principle is, not what is good for me singly or you singly, but for us and all together. And the same majestic yet tender Power is at this moment soliciting each one of us to come willingly, docilely, with our whole heart and soul and mind and strength, under this wise and benignant leadership, as active helpers in the ameliorating work. The ameliorations both social and personal may be slow, but they come. To what great consummation even on this earth they tend, our finite understandings may have little power to descry. But, where the understanding cannot see, the spirit can dream and yearn and impel. The Hebrew poet pictured for Israel at the end of the paths of righteousness a land "flowing with milk and honey,"— a national era of undisturbed power and prosperity. England's laureate has voiced the nineteenth century social dream,—

"In the Parliament of man, the Federation of the world."

And, to show that this principle is no mere philosophical abstraction, let us note a few of the familiar practical exhibitions of its working. Not far-fetched, but every-day illustrations they shall be, and briefly sketched. Two men are making a business bargain with each other. It is for goods or labor or skill on one side, to be paid for in money on the other; or it is some kind of exchange of service or of property. On the ground of purely selfish propensity each strives to get the better end of the bargain, the utmost possible for himself, leaving to the other the shorter part of the exchange. But there comes in a third party to this contract, demanding equal and honest measure between them. This demand is made by the Eternal that is in them,—the voice that pleads in each of their hearts, however much they may attempt to confuse and silence it, for honesty and honor. These, it says, are the pathway of the Eternal: make room for them in your contract if you would have it hold before the moral tribunal of mankind and your own conscience.

Questions of great public moment arise,—questions affecting the interests, the physical and moral welfare, of large numbers of people; questions of social and political reform; questions pertaining to the relations between capital and labor. Here, too, it is some form of selfish interest that is the cause of strife. One man's or party's selfishness pulls this way, and another's selfishness pulls that way. "Follow the paths of the Eternal," cries a voice above self-interest or party interest, "which are ways of justice and equity." Find them, and they will safely bridge the gulf that separates you. Or it may be a strife between nations. National selfishness, a false pride, a false patriotism, high, giddy-headed arrogance and boastfulness, and even selfish individual ambitions, help to foment the terrible passions of war. But in the midst of all such international strifes there enters another power that demands justice and magnanimity,— a Power that is the arbiter among the nations, and declares that only by adhering to these ways of the Eternal Righteousness can strife be allayed and peace preserved permanently.

A young man or a young woman reaches the age of discretion and responsibility. Youth with its tasks and its training is over. They are about to take their places in the striving world of business, or of professional or social achievement. They are elate with anticipation and the sense of freedom, eager for the new tests of their powers. They can follow some of the manifold ways of selfish pleasure and pursuit; they can live for social success, make fashion a god, regard wealth as the chief end of existence, and covet the material luxuries and enjoyments which wealth can purchase. They may be ambitious of high position and distinction without much concern about the means. They may be free even to follow the beck of false pleasure to lower levels of folly and vice. But there is no young man or maiden who has had the fortune of a home education of even average worth to whom, at such an era in their lives, there will not come from their own hearts a protest against all the grosser of these forms of self-indulgence, and a summons to higher paths and pursuits, for a nobler success. There are high fields of honor and duty and usefulness, of noble culture and unselfish service to others' good, which also invite their fealty and their consecration; and this is the invitation of the Eternal. In brief, it is an hour when the ways of the carnal self and the ways of the moral self are alike soliciting their hearts; and they must choose between them. The earnest appeal of the nobler self is, Bar out the tumult of the selfish ambitions and passions, the revelry of carnal desire and ignoble pleasures, and follow the highways of the Eternal.

Again, the passion of love enters the heart, that kind of love which is Nature's special way for the preservation and progress of society, through the founding of the family and the home. This instinct of love, in itself, is literally the constraining power of the Eternal in the human organism, so that the old religious tradition is right which represents marriage not merely as a civil contract, but as a divinely ordained institution. Indeed, it may be in this sense, as the Catholics claim, rightly called a sacrament. Yet how often marriage is degraded to merely a union of self-interests, or, following the sexual instinct alone, may even be debased to prostitution and cruel sensualism! The flesh itself then, in protest against the profanation, cries out for the higher law, for the Power whose ways are manifest in Reason and in Conscience as a law for the effective control of the instinct. Thus, and thus only, can marriage be lifted above the physical bond to a vital union in heart and soul, to the end of increased intellectual and moral productiveness. In every marriage relation, lest passion should become selfishly extortionate, and the parties be too exclusively absorbed in their own joint interests and pleasures, let husband and wife take their vows to the law of righteousness as well as to each other, and through that bond in the Eternal be joined together. Then shall marriage become, not the debaser, but the sustainer of purity, holiness, moral growth, and genuine love.

There is, in fine, no personal relation in life, whether it be between neighbor and neighbor, between citizen and citizen, between husband and wife, between teacher and the taught, or among the various members of the household, where the voice of the Eternal does not proclaim the law of righteousness as the way to unity and mutual helpfulness in the upbuilding of character. It is the voice of that mysterious, unseen guest who makes the third in every human transaction, calling for justice, honesty, and honor, who enters noiselessly every company, to silence the slanderous tongue and to command courtesy, candor, kindness, and truth. It is the voice of the One over all and through all, who has the right to say: —

> "They reckon ill who leave me out;
> When me they fly, I am the wings.
> They know not well the subtle ways
> I keep, and pass, and turn again."

Man may follow the ways of the lower self, which end in disappointment and ashes; or he may follow this higher guide, whose ways, even when difficult, are lined with pleasantness, and all whose paths are toward peace.

THE TWENTY-THIRD PSALM IN THE NINETEENTH CENTURY.

IV.

THE VALLEY OF SHADOWS.

"Yea, though I walk through the valley of the shadow of death, I will fear no evil: for thou art with me; thy rod and thy staff they comfort me."

I HAVE named the topic suggested by this verse of the Twenty-third Psalm "The Valley of Shadows." The phraseology of the common version has tended to associate the verse very deeply and almost exclusively with the human experience of death,— with bereaved hearts and darkened homes, and the mysterious passage of familiar friends to some other and unseen sphere of existence. But to the Hebrew the structure of the language suggested a much broader meaning; namely, any perils comparable to the dark mystery of death. The key-phrase of the verse is "shadow of death"; and in the Hebrew idiom "shadow," or "shade," is the leading noun, and the adjunct "of death" performs the service of an adjective. The Hebrew language is very poor in adjectives, and nouns habitually are used for descriptive epithets; and the common version too often follows the Hebrew rather than English idiom in this respect, and hence frequently leads to misconception of the original meaning. A more exact rendering of the meaning of this phrase would be "deathly shadow" rather than "shadow of death." It is not an infrequent phrase in the poetry of the Old Testament; and the context, as well as the structure of the language, shows that the general idea is that of death-like darkness in opposition to the light and cheer of life. There is another word in the verse which may be improved in the interest of exactness; namely, the word "rod." It means here the shepherd's crook. But it has another meaning in the Hebrew as well as in English, by which it becomes an instrument of chastisement and terror. This, of course, cannot be the meaning in this verse. Making these changes, so as to get nearer to the actual thought and imagery of the Psalmist, we should have: "Yea, though I walk through a valley of deathly shadows [or, still stronger, deathly darkness], I fear no evil: for thou art with me; thy crook and thy staff, they comfort me."

This translation, while more literally exact than the common version, gives us a phraseology equally poetical; and, you will note also, it is a rendering that harmonizes much better with the metaphor of the shepherd guiding his flock. For the common version here, as in the phrase "paths of righteousness" of the preceding verse, has the defect of passing from the metaphor to the human side of the comparison, which the metaphor should vividly suggest to the imagination, but not express. Nor, it may be added, is it probable that any Hebrew poet would have ventured to assert of a dumb animal that it could be led into a pen of actual slaughter, with the sight of death-struggles before its eyes and the terrorizing smell of blood in its nostrils, and show no signs of fear. It could be led through dangers and darkness, confiding in the shepherd's care, but not without terror to the extremity of death. This is a victory over the animal instinct of life-preservation which is reserved only for rational and moral beings.

Following, then, the changed translation I have offered (which is very nearly that of Professor Noyes, and of which, let me say in passing, the moral lesson for mankind would remain essentially the same as that conveyed by the common version, only enlarged), following this changed translation, what was the idea imaged to the Hebrew poet's mind in this verse? We can present it as a picture, for doubtless it was pictured before his mental vision. He had imagined the flock led by the shepherd from the green pastures and still waters where all their wants had been more than supplied, and as then gathered and guided, with their refreshed animal spirits, along paths of safety as if bound homeward to their folds. But the homeward paths of safety suggested the further thought that even these safe paths must often pass through ways of seeming danger. For his people, to whom his song was to carry its moral lesson, the poet knew that the safe paths often thus lay through imminent perils. His thought of a safety full and complete, therefore, in order to reach its climax must be tested, not merely by ways of comparative smoothness and ease, where all was light and cheery, but by ways of difficulty and darkness, where unseen dangers might lurk and life be menaced by secret foes. His metaphor was adequate to the need. It is not unlikely that there came to his mind and to his poetic vision the vivid remembrance of some actual valley which was known to him,—a narrow defile, with rocky but wooded heights looming precipitously and darkly up on both sides; a valley of shadows even at noonday, damp and deathly with its malodorous atmosphere, but at twilight, with its deepening darkness, a place of terrors, suggesting wild beasts watching in ambush for their prey; a place ghostly with the mystery of evil, and hinting every imaginable form of it. The poet had probably seen a flock following their shepherd through such a defile. He had seen the sheep of the flock, as they struck the dampness and darkness of the valley, instinctively huddling closer together, as if for mutual protection, and crowding closer upon the heels of the guiding shepherd, no one of them there lingering to nibble a tempting blade of grass, nor to quench thirst at any wayside spring, yet the flock moving onward in perfect order, without panic, as if massed in one bodily organism, only with a little quicker and more regular step than elsewhere, and with animal spirits subdued under the darkening shadows, moving steadily onward after their shepherd and apparently with entire confidence in his power to lead them safely through, either to the morning light and the joy-giving pastures or to the sheltering folds of their nightly rest. Very literally, perhaps, by some actual experience they may have learned that his crook and his staff could be trusted for their defence against foes along this way of dismal shadows.

Some such scene as this was probably pictured to the Psalmist's mental vision; and the Hebrews, for whose inspiration to patriotic faith and heroism he sang this song of trust, could not fail to understand the lesson, however little they may seem to have profited by it. In this verse, especially, the poet's phrases were rich in meaning for them. Well they knew that their actual ways were not often ways of pleasantness, nor their paths peace. Well they knew that their national road was often narrow, devious, and difficult; that it was beset with perils and lay under great shadows of mystery and darkness. Secret and open enemies awaited them on either hand. Battle and death had to be faced. Their pathway was marked with a trail of blood. Jehovah they trusted as their God, and that they were his peculiar charge was their faith. Yet Jehovah's purposes were sometimes veiled from them in thick clouds of darkness, when he seemed to have left them to their fate. But the

Psalmist sought to inspire his countrymen with the assurance that, amidst all trials, darkness, and perils, Jehovah was still their guide, and that he was not afar off,— a distant Deity,— above the clouds and beyond the valleys, but a leader there with them, under the clouds and in the valleys, with them. Therefore, with such a leader and protector, what evil could they fear, even though they walked among the dark shadows of death? The shepherd's "crook" was emblem also of authority and power. It carried to the Hebrew mind manifold meanings. It represented kingly sovereignty. Sceptre was one of its synonymes. It stood also for the united strength of a tribe. And the shepherd's "staff" meant not only a stick to lean on, a stay, a support, but it had another meaning signifying the means of physical sustenance,— kindred to the English phrase "staff of life." To the Hebrew, therefore, Jehovah was here depicted not merely as Shepherd and Guide, but as Sovereign Defender and King, as the Bond of tribal union, as Stay and Supporter of human uprightness, and as Sustainer of Life against the powers of darkness and death.

Not that the average Hebrew mind distinctly held together all these attributes in his conception of Jehovah as a Shepherd. Perhaps the poet himself did not have them all clearly in his thought as he wrote. Yet his words imply them; and all these qualities, and more, were continually affirmed of Jehovah in the best Hebrew literature.

The writers resorted to every kind of noble appellation, yet could not find epithets of excellence enough to match their ideas of his greatness in power and in righteousness, so that, after all their rhetorical endeavors at description, they humbly acknowledged that, "Lo, these are but a part of his ways." And the poets and prophets were ever aiming to stir into effectual motive these higher and deeper elements of Hebrew faith. Hence our Psalmist, while he would still declare that Jehovah was a leader of Israel, by the way of righteousness, into paths of safety, yet saw and also declared that the ways of righteousness and salvation often led downward, through trials and dangers, to seeming desolation and death. Nevertheless, let Jehovah's leadership be followed, and even that way, he proclaimed, might be trod with serene fearlessness. With the Eternal Power as leader close at hand, there would surely be victory for the right at the end of the way,—victory for light and for life over desolation and darkness and destruction.

Now the essential elements of belief couched in this verse (which has itself been a comfort to millions of souls), when translated from metaphor to plain prose, are simply these: Human experience is not all bright and joyous, but has its trials and sorrows, and always present before it is the dark problem of death; but there is an Eternal Power with man, working with and in and for him, amply adequate for meeting all problems and all trials and for allaying the fear of them, — a Power working for Righteousness through all tribulations, and for Life in the midst of death. Nor has any one of these points been gainsaid by the rational thought or science of the nineteenth century. The first of them, that man is subject to trials and sorrows, and stands ever in the presence of death, is merely a fact of common observation and knowledge. The second, that there is an Eternal Power working with him, is one of the affirmations of science in the doctrine of evolution. The third, that this Power is an ameliorating force, working, amidst human conditions, towards personal and social Righteousness, and ever higher forms of Righteousness and of Life, is amply based on the testimony of human history. And even though it be said that the ameliorating power for mankind is displayed wholly in and through man's own faculties, nevertheless, according to scientific doctrine, the power must be derived from and be a manifestation of "the Eternal Energy from which all things proceed."

But these several propositions have been sufficiently considered in previous lectures, and need not detain us to-day. Beyond anything I have been able to say, they may be regarded as having received, both from philosophy and science, abundant justification. The more important question which remains for us now is, Are these truths receiving, or can they receive, practical justification in present human experience? To put the question still more definitely, Is this verse, which gives us our theme to-day, true to the experience of human beings whose lives have come within the compass of our own knowledge? Is it true to our own experience? Now possibly we may not have realized the truth of it in our own experience because of not having observed the right conditions; and yet it may still be true. And possibly we may have observed a similar seeming failure in the experience of other persons for the same reason. But, in a larger survey, taking in all our varied experiences and those of other persons within our knowledge, do we find that the comforting assurance of this verse is practically justified? And, it should be added, a negative experience, for the reason above named,— that is, failure to meet the hard experiences of life in the right way,— might be positive evidence of the practical truth of the verse.

In seeking an answer to this question, two points definitely present themselves which can be best considered separately: first, the common perplexities, trials, and hardships which beset human life and which make a large part of our "valley of shadows"; second, the dark fact of death, which has caused human life on earth to be called "a vale of tears."

First, as to the trials, hardships, difficulties with which human life has to contend. We must here revert, primarily, to what I have called, in these lectures, the universal plan for the education and civilization of mankind by a gradual process of adjustment of human life to the great world-energies. We saw that, by the very conditions of this process of educational adjustment, man's wants could not be provided for by a cosseting Providence outside of himself, with no effort or thought of his own; but rather the conditions necessitated the putting forth of human faculty in a strenuous struggle with difficulties. We saw, indeed, that the Eternal is leader, a provider, whose sources of supply are to be depended upon, an Energy from which all finite energies are derived, but that for man the leading is through the inward constraining force of reason and conscience and the moral sentiments, and the provision largely through his own disciplined ability to care for his own life and destiny by adjusting himself to nature's forces and laws. It is not for us, using the methods of science, to ask why things pertaining to the education and progress of mankind are thus and so. We have simply to note the facts and follow the law of their trend. And among the most conspicuous facts of human history we cannot fail to note that, in order to gratify his desires and even to maintain his existence, man has had to grapple with difficulties, to contend against obstacles, to fight often, with hand and brain, against nature's forces threatening to quench his life before he can subject them to his service. He has been compelled to labor, to self-exertion, to the agile use of physical and mental faculties by the very conditions of life. And, as a result, we must note the enlargement of his life, the increased development of his faculties, the growth of physical skill, of brain power, and of moral enlightenment; in a word, the result is man educated from animalism into a civilized and ethical being. The obstacles, the hardships, have been the anvils on which his faculties have been sharpened and shaped to larger uses, and personal character has been hammered to a firmer strength and tempered with spiritual refinement.

All this history tells us. Adverse circumstances — that is, seemingly adverse — are not man's enemies, but may be his friends. It depends on how he adjusts himself to them. But, leaving history, do you not know of men and women, contemporary with yourselves, who have harmoniously and successfully made that adjustment? men and women who have converted the very obstacles in their careers into stepping-stones to some higher success? men and women in whose experience trial and tragedy may seem to have had a larger place than joy, but who from all their conflicts, from their baptisms as if with fire, have only come forth stronger and purer for useful deeds, the serenity of their faith unshaken, their humane sympathies quickened, their goodness heightened and glorified? How can such persons have any fear of evil circumstances? They know the Eternal to be with them, a Power stronger than circumstance or fate; and the Eternal is, indeed, with them, the very sustenance and life of their goodness and of their noble serenity and spiritual beauty. Again I ask, Have not you known such persons? And have you not at times been conscious of the same Power moving and working within your own minds, to transform some hardship or sorrow in your experience into moral goodness and a deepening of character? The way of life, which is the way of righteousness, often must pass through a valley of shadows, dark, dispiriting, deathly. Yet it is the way of life still, and the way of safety, for all who have learned faithfulness to the law of life, which is righteousness. For them the very difficulties create in the soul a more robust fibre, and they emerge from the valley of darkness into light with a clearer vision and a firmer step for ascending life's heights. In their hearts they carry the very presence-chamber of the Eternal, with his sceptre and his staff; and their lives are adjusted to organic unity with his ways and for arriving at his high results.

It would be easy to fill large space with special illustrations of this truth of the transformation of hard circumstances into noble character. But I must limit myself to two or three that are freshest in my notice. And I retain those that were freshest at the time of my writing. The morning paper of the day on which I wrote brought two despatches, which in opposite ways hint the lesson. The first is a telegraphic despatch from Texas telling the story of four suicides there, in the same town, on the same day. Two young women and two young men, their lovers, had done this desperate act. One of the four lived long enough after the suicidal deed to say that they had taken a pledge to one another to end life together at their separate homes, but within the same twenty-four hours; that they had tried to live true and honest lives, but the world was against them, and the harder they tried the worse things became; that they were too poor for marriage, yet felt that life was not worth living apart, and so they resolved to end it all, together. This was a case of lamentable failure to make right adjustment to life's conditions. These young people lacked those qualities of high courage and confidence which are able to convert failures into success and to wrest from calamities the materials of moral victory. Instead of facing difficulties and conquering them, they slipped unsummoned ignominiously from the field. The other item was the story of the painful catastrophe which has befallen a young professor in Michigan University. Bending over a chemical experiment he was conducting in his laboratory, an accidental explosion so injured his eyes that both of them had to be removed at once. Only twenty-eight years old, with already a high reputation as a chemist and a brilliant promise before him! We can hardly conceive of a greater calamity befalling an eager student of natural science. Yet he is likely to prove himself of the stuff from which heroic character as well as science comes. He has before him for inspiration the noble, well-rounded life of England's late postmaster-general and distinguished political economist and reformer, Henry Fawcett, who at twenty-five years totally lost his sight by an accident, but who thereby turned his retirement into studies which have blessed his country and the world. Yet the greatest blessing of his life comes from the example he has left of a man undaunted by such a catastrophe, pursuing his life-purposes firmly and calmly against such difficulties, and, withal, achieving a character as beloved as his abilities and usefulness were honored. Our own honored countryman and brilliant historian, Francis Parkman, against similar almost insurmountable obstacles, followed unswervingly a purpose formed at seventeen years and achieved his world-famous life career.

Another illustration is brought to my memory. Some of you here may recall that touching incident which happened at the visiting committee's reception at the Massachusetts Kindergarten for the Blind last year. Helen Keller, a girl of then eleven years, whose name is becoming as well known in Boston and Massachusetts as was that of Laura Bridgman,—a girl who is blind and was a deaf-mute, but who has been taught to speak, though she hears no sound, and who has a genius for sympathy and love,—was the most impressive speaker of the occasion. She had taken a most active interest in the forlorn condition of Tommy Stringer, a little fellow of five years, a deaf-mute and blind like herself, who had recently been brought to the institution, but whose parents had no means to provide a special teacher for him. Helen has taken it upon herself to raise the funds for his education; and, in her little speech appealing for his needs, this girl who hears no sound, who sees no object in this fair world, said: "Life is sweet and beautiful when we have the wonderful key of language to unlock all its secrets. Educate Tommy, and give him this key." But this was not all. Dr. Edward Everett Hale followed, saying, at close, "Let every man and woman, every boy and girl, give something." Then there was a pause, broken by a sob from a little boy, one of the littlest of them all, who could not repress his feelings. A teacher, who was his shepherding crook and staff, gathered the little lamb in her arms to comfort him. He buried his blind eyes against her neck, but he was only blind. He had heard the speeches, and he could tell his trouble; and, when the teacher coaxed it from him, it was that he "had no money to give for little Tommy." Thus this blind baby, scarcely able to talk plainly, made the most eloquent appeal of all. When the meeting broke up, and it was told from one to another what was the cause of the child's grief, his sob was converted into subscriptions; and one lady from a distant Western city, a stranger to most of the people there, a Hebrew woman, asked the privilege of being an annual subscriber to the kindergarten in behalf of Tommy Stringer, and in response to his still smaller companion in blindness, whose heart had broken into a sob because he couldn't help Tommy himself. For those of us who have all our senses it seems as if there could be no valley of shadows deeper in its gloom than that through which these little blind children are doomed to walk all their days. Yet what a light of sympathetic love streamed from their sightless eyes through all that company! a light and warmth of love which revealed strangers' hearts to each other as of one blood and kindred, and touched a sentiment within differing creeds and faiths which melted them into one religion. Thus the calamity that afflicts these little children becomes the nurture of humane and spiritual life in the mature men and women who are drawn to care for them; and the ennobled life of these benefactors is again reflected back as the light of love, which penetrates even under the dark shadows of blindness, so that those whose eyes see not and whose ears hear not can yet feel that "life is sweet and beautiful" for them. To have effected this interchange of human sympathies, to have lifted life up to this level of unselfish love and devotion, I had almost said it were worth while that the calamity should come. Yet that I will not say. This, nevertheless, is true: the calamity having come, the dark and the tragic intermingling everywhere with the good in our human lot, we can see how, in this and in other of life's hardships, the great world-purpose takes them up and weaves them into the world's benefit. Wonderful is that power of compensation in nature by which one of the senses adjusts itself, by increase of scope and refinement, to do the work of other senses that may be enfeebled or disabled! And wonderful, to the height of the miraculous, is the educational skill which, working with this facility of nature, can give to the sense of touch, as it were, sight and hearing, and cause the blind and deaf-mute to articulate, to speak, and rationally converse! It is as if the Eternal Power had said: "My intent shall not be balked by any calamity that may close the eye or the ear. I will give eye and ear to the sense of feeling, and so cause the tongue of the dumb to shout for joy; and thus shall my blind ones see and my deaf hear and my dumb speak. Only I want men and women who are wise, loving, and patient, to be my agents for working this miracle of scientific skill and philanthropy, whereby I may guide and comfort those who walk in the lonely valleys of darkness and desolation."

So, too, of that more special calamity which our verse in the original does not name, yet suggests, — the fact of death. Death is one of the mysteries which has made the whole world akin. Strangers elsewhere, around an open grave we join hands as brothers. All nations, ages, faiths, are linked together by this bond of our common humanity; and it is a bond of humanity in the finer sense of that word as well as in the sense of a common physical nature that is mortal. Whether in palace or in hut, death is the same mysterious, solemn messenger, before whom all alike must bow. A world watched at President Garfield's death-bed, and again at the Emperor Frederick's of Germany, and at General Grant's. And in General Grant's great career there was no soldierly heroism which so ennobled his fame and endeared him to mankind as did that self-controlled, serene, and masterful march in his last year against the forces of Death, in order that, before the inevitable hour when he must surrender his pen to the advancing foe, he might see his self-imposed task complete, and leave to his family and to the historic annals of his country the rich legacy of his Autobiography. The sympathetic interest of a world surrounds such deaths. But the same regardful anxiety watches somewhere, though confined to one room and a few neighbors, the slowly wasting life of some poor sewing-woman, whose heroic combat for life no fame tells to the world. Death equalizes all, despite unequal monuments in graveyards. "The small and the great are there together, and the clods of the valley shall be alike sweet to them."

The Hebrews appear to have had no such terror of death as certain Christian theologies have cultivated. Their system of rewards and retributions was practically limited to this world. For the greater part of their national history they manifested no specific belief in immortality. Not until their contact with the Persians, in the time of their captivity to these people of the old Zend religion, did they imbibe that doctrine. The doctrine appears in the Apocryphal Old Testament, written after the Captivity, but not, except by a few vague intimations, in the canonical Hebrew Scriptures. As a substitute for spiritual and personal immortality in another world, the Hebrews seemed to have faith in a national immortality for Israel in this world. And that kind of immortal existence, like the present life of the nation, they associated with righteousness. Long life was one of the promised rewards of righteousness. Death they regarded as an evil, not for any torments that would follow it, but because it was antagonistic to life; and, as the enemy of life, they associated it with unrighteousness. Sometimes it seems as if they believed that, if they could attain to perfect righteousness, they would overcome death and then have power to live forever.

But, so far as this verse of our Psalm is concerned, deathly things and death itself were put with other mysterious trials and calamities as not to be feared, since the Eternal was present to guide safely through them. That Power could be trusted to make all things, if not clear, at least right and sure. And in its essential features this belief finds practical justification to-day. Let death come into our homes when and in what form it will, and, however deep may be the grief that comes in its train, it is yet one of the inevitable facts to which we are to so adjust our characters and lives as not to sit in dismay and lamentation over the evil of it, but to draw forth all the compensating moral and spiritual good which may be hidden in the sad experience. It is no fable, no myth, that the Eternal is with us in those hours,— with us in the silence and under the shadows,— and with us, as rational thought to-day assures us, not so much as a far-off celestial guide and a mysterious, overseeing Providence, as the old theologies have been wont to teach, but veritably within us as a form of strength, sharing and enduring with us our burden, and nerving us with courage to meet the new responsibilities and the strange and bereft condition of life. We know, too, in this modern time, that death in itself is no calamity, that it is no abnormal intrusion into nature's order, but a natural stage in the unfolding of that order itself, at one with nature's organic law and with all her maturing processes. Death, when it comes in old age, in accordance with natural law, is like the harvesting of ripened grain. Cicero likens it to the gentle touch of the fingers on perfectly ripe fruit, which requires no violence to pluck it. It is then one of the beautiful, orderly mysteries in the great procession of the occasionally resting, but all-abounding and never-ending forces of life. Nor would it be an entirely visionary and irrational expectation to look forward to a time, centuries and centuries hence, when mankind shall attain to a height of civilization so enlightened and moral, and shall have so learned and obeyed the laws of life and health, that disease will be practically conquered, and death will come painlessly as the natural limit of the physical organism in old age. There is actually some scientific ground for such an expectation in the fact that the tables of longevity, computed for the business of life insurance, show a perceptible increase in the average length of human life with the progress of civilization and the better observance of sanitary laws. Death, so considered, would be no catastrophe, but one kind of culmination in nature's order. But premature death — death in youth or in early maturity — is a calamity usually to surviving friends, and may be a calamity and loss to the world. Thus coming, death may plunge bereaved families from the fairest heights of hope and happiness to the depths of despairing agony. But even then the tragedy may be met so as to draw from it those higher ministries that may transform grief, not into joy, but into noble service and chastened beauty of character. Have we not all witnessed such transformations?

In every such company as this are likely to be those who have recently been walking in the valley of death's shadows, and are still gazing wistfully after the forms of beloved ones who have passed through it. Others among us may be watching with even a more anxious tenderness the tremulous steps of friends and kindred who may be entering it. All of us, day by day, are approaching that valley, and none of us can evade it. Yet, whichever be our case, let us not look on death as "the king of terrors," nor think that our valley of shadows is only a blot of darkness on the universe;

but rather may we see how it connects outward and upward with a world of everlasting light and life and beauty, with bright mountain-tops and clear skies.

The monk, Francis of Assisi, as the end of his life came near, addressed Death as his "sister." This amiable and accomplished saint lived in such close, familiar intercourse with nature that he was wont to call all natural objects his kindred: the sun, the moon, the grass, plants, water, and light and fire and air were his brothers and sisters. They were all forms of the Eternal; what could he fear? So, as his eyes grew tired and dim, he welcomed his "sister Death," and put his hand trustfully in hers, that she might lead him in his darkness; but down into his darkness shone the eyes of his brothers, the stars, and over and around all was spread the light of the Eternal, undimmed: and, lo! his darkness was day.

THE TWENTY-THIRD PSALM IN THE NINETEENTH CENTURY.

V.

THE OVERFLOWING BOUNTY.

"Thou preparest a table before me in the presence of mine enemies: thou anointest my head with oil; my cup runneth over."

ON reaching this verse our Psalmist abruptly changes his metaphor. He abandons the imagery of a shepherd leading his flock for that of a host serving his guest. Yet the poet's thought goes on, rising toward its climax with such perfect consistency that an ordinary reader, not thinking of critical analysis, is not likely to notice the sudden rhetorical transition. It seems as if the pastoral figure was no longer adequate to the emotion which stirred the poet's soul, as he thought of the bountiful provision made by Jehovah for human needs and happiness. After the pastures with their tender grass and refreshing waters of quietness, after the journeyings, whether by safe and plain paths or by ways of menacing and deathly dangers under safe guidance, there was for a flock no other natural conclusion than the sheltering folds for rest. But the dangers which had been safely passed suggested to the poet's imagination a more demonstratively triumphant issue. The hostile difficulties depicted in the preceding verse gave the cue-thought to that victory over enemies which this verse celebrates; and the happy exit from the valley of shadows was cause for a scene of festive rejoicing for which the narrow conditions of the sheep-cot and the small wants of dumb creatures now seeking only rest and sleep furnished no materials. Hence the figure of a hospitable householder caring for guests occurred to the Psalmist's poetic vision as offering more ample conveyance for his enlarged and heightening thought.

This was a favorite figure of speech with the Hebrews, as the New Testament, as well as the Old, bears witness. Hospitality was, and still is, one of the supreme Oriental tests of religion and humanity. No finer metaphor was available for carrying to the Hebrew mind an idea of Jehovah's devoted and inexhaustible care than to present a picture of the head of a household caring with impartial and lavish generosity for his guests. To such a picture the poet turned — perhaps unconsciously — for continuing his parable. The flock of dumb creatures was displaced by a vision of tired and needy human travellers. They, too, may have had to journey not only by fatiguing but by dangerous roads. In narrow and dark defiles enemies may have waited in ambush for them, and may have even harassed and pursued them beyond the perilous pass and out upon the open plains to the very gates of refuge which opened to welcome them. Once within, the sentiments of honor and humanity were their protectors. We may imagine a Hebrew patriarch, with his numerous household around him, as the host. The law of Moses bade him to treat with equal justice the native-born and the stranger within his gates. He was even to love the stranger as a brother, and the law of hospitality bade him quickly to supply the stranger's needs. His hospitality was unstinted in profusion and untainted by suspicion. Even in actual sight of pursuing enemies a table might be spread with all needful and bountiful viands. If it was a time of feasting, the traveller became as one of the guests. After the Eastern custom, the host might even anoint his head with perfumed oil, for refreshment and honor and in token of hospitable welcome. In the midst of such a banquet the weary and harassed traveller, safe from his perils, surrounded by such friendly protection, might indeed exclaim that the cup of his felicity was filled to overflowing.

And the overflowing bounty of Jehovah's provision and care for Israel was what this verse of the Psalm said to the Hebrews. Remember that the whole Psalm was a song of patriotism, a song of religious, spiritual patriotism, not a celebration of the sentiment, "Our country, right or wrong," but a song intended to inspire the highest patriotic hope and courage, and faith in the law of righteousness as the basis of national prosperity. The theme all through was trust in Jehovah as guide and protector, as supplier of wants and rescuer from dangers; and in this verse the thought ascends to the contemplation of Jehovah's overwhelming resources for meeting every possible strait. Whatever might be Israel's needs, dangers, or distresses, there was One at hand, so preached this prophet-poet, whose power and good will were manifest as even more than ample to carry the nation safely through any emergency. Jehovah was described in Hebrew poetry not only as a Being eternal in power and awful in majesty, but as one whose works superabounded in goodness and gladness. He was said to make the very earth rejoice, to crown the years with goodness, to cause the valleys to stand so thick with corn that they shout and sing for joy, to make the ground soft with showers, and to bless the increase of it. His very steps dropped richness; and the fields of the wood rejoiced before him, rejoiced because he cometh to give justice to the earth and to judge the people with his truth.

In such picturesque language did Israel's poets try to impress their idea of the character of Jehovah as the all-bountiful giver of good, and this verse of the Twenty-third Psalm is an illustration of the same attempt. By its structure the verse concentrates attention on three points of the all-dominating Bounty. Under the figure of a hospitable and beneficent householder, supreme in power as in goodness, Jehovah is represented, first, as revealing his abounding friendliness and munificence, even in the very sight of enemies, as if defying their pursuit and annulling their power. The singer had doubtless in mind, as his hearer would have, the actual and almost omnipresent armed foes by whom the Hebrews were surrounded, and whom they had to meet, and, it must be admitted, were not reluctant to meet, in stratagem and in battle, in order to preserve their national existence. The verse was designed to inspirit and nerve Israel for the hard tasks of war by presenting a picture of the abundant rewards of peace at the end of the conflict. The bountiful table spread in the face of the foe was a symbol of the coming national prosperity and wealth,— a vision which poet and prophet never ceased to hold before the eyes of the people, however hard-pressed the people were by actual distress. And, indirectly, the phrase "in the presence of enemies" might stand for any difficulties and obstacles that hindered the realization of this vision, for any kind of hostility or terror which had been met in the "valley of shadows" and triumphantly vanquished. The same Power that had led safely through those dangers now turned the dangers into a banquet of rejoicing. This was the purposed result of the struggle and its interpreter. The feast represented that bounty of good things which the overcoming of every kind of antagonism had made possible; but, lest it should be said that the Hebrew idea of prosperity was too exclusively material, it must not be forgotten that one of the essential conditions — the fundamental condition, indeed — of arriving at this goal of national felicity was obedience to the law of righteousness. Only paths of righteousness were the paths of safety, which led finally to this great salvation and joy, of which the feast was emblematic. Thus did the Hebrew poets and prophets teach in their highest moods.

Second, under the metaphor of the host of a hospitable house, the Psalmist represented Jehovah as specially honoring Israel as his guest, in picturing him as observing the Oriental custom of anointing a guest's head with oil. This was a service which a host might commit to the hands of a hired servant. But, if he wished particularly to do honor to any guest, the host performed this office himself, not in the spirit, however, of condescension and patronage so much as in the spirit of friendly equality and fraternal fellowship. He brought forth his costliest ointment, spiced and perfumed with the most precious substances, and with his own hands both honored and refreshed his guest by this menial service. This anointing of the head was the same ceremony which was in use as a prominent feature in the consecration of a king or a high priest to his office. In its generic meaning it simply signified a high token of honor and regard. In its more specific meaning it symbolized the bestowal of the highest human authority upon those who received it. The language of the poet here was bold — bold almost to the point of audacity — when we consider that it was Jehovah, the Eternal Power, who was from everlasting to everlasting, and whose throne was regarded as established above the heavens, and whose majesty was unapproachable, who was also described as a host hastening to do honor to a guest and personally serving his wants. But to the Hebrew there was little or no incongruity between the two ideas. His Deity, it is true, in the most abstract conception, was a far-off inaccessible sovereignty; but he was also conceived as very human, even more so than would accord with the ordinary Christian conception, and, in his human aspects, as coming very close to man and serving him, though in miraculous ways, yet in very humble capacities. He it was who was believed to have corralled quails for the Israelites when in their hunger they cried for flesh, and to have kept the poor widow's barrel of meal and cruse of oil replenished while she harbored the fugitive prophet Elijah. A Divine Being who was believed to do these things would suffer no loss of dignity in Hebrew eyes, though he should be described as a host honoring his guests as if he were their servant.

Third, the Psalmist's comparison of Jehovah's bounty to an overflowing cup meant that the provision made for the Hebrew people by their eternal care-taker was not limited nor measured by their actual wants; that the divine resources so overflowed all present needs that there should be no anxiety as to the future. This point is so simple that it requires no further explanation. True, the Hebrew believed that miracle was one of Jehovah's resources for eking out the shortcomings of nature, or for resisting nature's disasters when they pressed too hard. But to the Hebrew mind — to the mind of every primitive people, indeed — it was more natural to believe in miracle than in unvarying law. The verse, however, makes no suggestion of miracle. And, in any case, the main lesson of this point was the fact that Jehovah's bountiful provision for Israel was overflowing and immeasurable, and not how the beneficent power was exercised.

Now remember that Jehovah, the most familiar Hebrew name for Deity, may be rendered by the phrase "The Eternal" better, perhaps, than by any other English expression. It means Eternal Existence and the power therewith implied. A good paraphrase of its signification may be found, as I have already in these lectures pointed out, in Herbert Spencer's phrases, the Ultimate Reality, with its infinite and eternal Energy. Hence, denude our Hebrew poet's thought of its metaphorical dress, and he was saying something like this: "Though I am continually in the presence of forces which are inimical to life, thou, O Eternal, art my bountiful provider; thou honorest me by serving me; yea, thy bounty lavishly outruns all my needs." This is personification, it is true. But every one of the three things here asserted, the doctrine of science might and does say to-day of the Eternal Energy from which all things proceed. When Science turns poet, as it sometimes does in the fervid utterance of such a man as Professor Tyndall, it personifies and says these things to the Eternal Energy.

But, again, as in the preceding lecture, it is not so much philosophical justification for these statements as practical justification that needs at the present time to be most set forth and illustrated. The enemies of human happiness and life, even in the midst of our most advanced civilization, are so many and so persistent and strong that it sometimes seems very hard to believe in any bountiful provision for human needs. The enemies, the hostile forces, are present and very close, while the supplying bounty may seem far off, beyond reach and call, so distant as not to be realized. Just now, especially, is a most opportune time to consider the first of the three statements of our verse from a practical point of view. The casualties from natural causes, the devastations to property and life, within the last year have been appalling, to say nothing of those catastrophes in which human agency has been more apparent. Floods and tornadoes, mine explosions and drownings, earthquakes and conflagrations, have been casting human beings into the abysses of death by the thousands. And where, many persons have asked, amidst such scenes of terror, devastation, and destruction, is the careful and bountiful Provider? Why does not the Eternal Power intervene to save human beings and human possessions from such fearful disasters?

In attempting an answer to this question, we must again remind ourselves that the Eternal Power may shepherd and beneficently provide for mankind, though not on the cosseting plan of a special Providence which would intervene to snatch us from this or that danger. It is the ground plan of this universe that human beings should become a providence to themselves; that the Eternal Power works within and through their own faculties by natural law; that thus it provides and cares for them, while all around them, as well as within them, are the mighty forces on which they are to draw for sustenance and benefit. Whether the sustenance and benefit will be formed in individual cases depends on the measure of adjustment to these great world-forces. That the welfare is found in the experience of mankind at large there can be no question. For this process of adjustment of finite life, through finite perception and effort, to the infinite resources and forces that pervade and surround it, is the school of education for the human race from savagery to civilization, and to all the power, prosperity, happiness, and well-being which an enlightened and moral civilization implies. And all the time, while mankind are staggering under the difficulties which confront them, in presence of the very enemies of their prosperity and peace, this infinite bounty of natural resource is offered, awaiting and soliciting man's adjusting effort to partake of it. While we may be reading, every spring-time, of destruction and death by flood and gale, Nature weaves around us, alike under storm as under sunshine, her yearly garment of life and beauty. And, when the desolating winter storms come, Nature is not dead. In the tiny, strongly cased buds on yonder leafless trees are safely garnered all the vital hopes of next year's bounty of foliage and fruit. Dissect if you can a single snowflake of the storm, and you will find it a house of perfect crystals of amazing beauty. Seed-time and harvest arrive in their order, not with such certainty of measure as to make man careless on his side of the needed mutual service, but by laws that never fail. Somewhere the earth produces, or may be made to produce, enough for all who anywhere live upon it. Under the ground are stored treasures of wealth, ready at man's transforming touch to be converted into heat and light and motive power. And in what secret cells of earth or of air is hidden that mightiest and most marvellous of nature's forces, which, wherever hidden, man has discovered, but is only just learning its vast capabilities of service? The thunderbolt, drawn from that secret chamber, is becoming man's right hand. The lightning's spark is steed for our loaded cars. And the same power, under a surgeon's scientific skill, has removed a tumor from a baby's lip as painlessly and tenderly as if done by a mother's kiss. It seems as if everywhere the Power of the

Eternal in nature were appealingly saying to man, "Learn how to use me, and see how I will bless you!"

For the truth of these lessons of our Psalm I like to find the most recent illustrations possible; and there came to me, as I wrote, an apt illustration of this point we are now considering, in the number, just then at hand, of that little newspaper called the *Southern Letter*, which is printed by the colored students at the Tuskegee Normal School, Alabama, a school where the president and teachers are also all of the colored race. The little sheet comes to some of you, perhaps; but it is so very small and modest that I suspect it is quite likely to go into the waste-basket unnoticed. But, humble as it is in appearance, I always find in it some suggestive hint of the way in which good is gradually overcoming evil in this world. First, at the head of it, there stands the excellent motto, "Devoted to the Education of the Hand, Head, and Heart." And this is what that school is doing down there for the colored people, right in the presence of their old enemies, who once held them in the ignorance of slavery, but who are now being converted into friends. But the thing which specially struck my attention in that particular number of the little paper was the story of the experience of one of the graduates of the school, which he sends back to the principal in a letter. The young man went out into a country region in the autumn to begin a school where there was no school-house nor school organization. For several weeks the teaching was done in a room which was a dining-room and lodging-room and kitchen, yet sometimes there were fifty scholars. But in six weeks he had managed, with a little help, to build a school-house, for which the forests around furnished ample material. And this is the way he tells the story of the building and its uses: "I had to skin most of the logs myself and help lay them up, help get out the board timber and get the boards, help buy the lumber, and had to pick nearly one-fourth of the nails out of an ash-bed, where a cotton-gin house had recently burned down. The house was without heater or chimney; but we made a fire in the yard, and gladly turned first one and then the other side to it, when it got too cold in the house. I spoke to the people there one night in each week last month, and feel satisfied that much good was done. I have organized a Sunday-school there, which has about fifty members, most of whom are in earnest. Many of them are parents. We have had singing, too; and I have talked to them on Sunday afternoons, when sometimes nearly a hundred people would turn out. I have thought of you and your Commencement address to us very often. I thought of [what you said of] Emerson's looking for himself. But I found it necessary for me not to look for, but to lose myself. To do this was a hard task. 'Tis not a perfect accomplishment yet. With this one thing accomplished, I can climb above any other barrier."

There is a man who has learned how to adjust himself to nature's provision and laws for human needs; and so he has got at the heart of the Infinite Bounty. He does not sit down to lament over the afflicted condition of his people, he does not stop to ask why the Almighty does not do this or that for their relief; but he takes hold of the forces of the Eternal himself, and wields them for his people's good. In the presence of obstacles that would daunt the spirit of most of us, he finds a way to the Infinite Beneficence and makes himself its agent for his people's redemption.

Abundant justification may also be found in human experience for the modern lessons of the remaining parts of our verse. The parable of a host anointing his guest with oil signifies, as we have seen, the bestowal of something beyond the needful supplies for physical existence. It means the rendering of honor and regard by personal service. It recognizes among the obligations of hospitality not merely the satisfaction of bodily wants, but the sentiments and amenities of affection. It means something that touches the heart and solaces the spirit and honors the person. These are the refinements of hospitality, like the perfume and beauty of flowers. They may be costly, but there are needs of human beings that are higher than the stomach's appetites. Jesus, notwithstanding his ready rebuke for all insincere and ostentatious display, and his compassion for the wants of the poor, allowed the woman to break the precious box of ointment to express her personal regard, though the ointment might have been sold and the price given to the poor. There are other hungers besides that of the flesh, — hungers of mind and heart, which measure the advance of the higher civilization. And these, too, the Eternal Power, under which they are developed, supplies. The Infinite Bounty covers the needs of heart and soul no less than those of the body. Nature serves man's physical wants; but she does it with an infinite beauty and grace, that gradually charms the savage in him into civilization, and causes the brute instinct to blossom into soul.

Nature, indeed, in this and in manifold ways, is man's constant servant; and hence we are literally correct when we say that the Eternal Power, which works in and through nature, is man's servant as well as educator. A few years ago a scientific man wrote an essay to show the probability that at some time the sun's heat might be mechanically applied for the pumping of water from underneath the sands of the great deserts of Africa, thus fertilizing them into rich productiveness. And thus, he added, that great luminary that has been worshipped as a god would become man's servant. A god transformed into a servant seemed a startling suggestion. And yet the Eternal Power whom all enlightened minds worship as Deity, the God of reason and science, is now and constantly the servant of man. If the earth in any way serves our human wants, if the sun, by which we live and move and have our being and exert all our power, serves us, if the forces of nature, through the air we breathe, the electricity we put to use, and the gravity that holds us to the globe, serve us, then *a fortiori* must the Infinite and Eternal Power, of which earth and sun and all nature's forces are but a partial manifestation, be our servant. "A serving Deity!" This thought which our verse suggests may well command our attention a little longer. And, if there be apprehension lest this conception of Deity shall be wanting in the attribute of "parental love," where, let me ask, shall we find the highest expression and demonstration of love? In that effervescence of passional emotion which, within the breast of its possessor, self-regarding, bubbles and sings of its own felicity? or is it in that other-regarding feeling which at once goes forth in acts of service for the being that is loved? When does a mother show the supreme devotion of her affection? In those moments of rapture when she hugs her children and devours them with kisses and wants to lavish sweetmeats upon them? or is it in the long hours and wearying days and lengthening years, when, forgetful of self, she is spending her energies, her very life, in serving their manifold wants, on her spent care and strength carrying them safely through the various crises of their ignorance and weakness, though often having to exchange the rapture of personal tenderness for the disciplines of that larger, wiser law which is no respecter of persons? "Love," said the old writer, "is the keeping of the laws of wisdom." Nor should this proposition of science startle Christendom, which, through all its centuries, has been taught that the infinite God humbled himself and came down to earth, and took the form of a servant in Jesus of Nazareth, who washed his disciples' feet. Only the service is not through one man only but through manifold men, and not through humanity only, but through nature. Service and honor are rendered to man by the Eternal, to the end that in man there is created a being who, in turn, honors and serves and carries forward the Eternal purpose. Sang another of the Hebrew poets: "When I consider the heavens, the work of thy power, and the stars which thou hast ordained, what is man that thou art mindful of him, and the son of man that thou carest for him? Yet thou hast made him little lower than the gods; thou has crowned him with glory and honor; thou has given him dominion over the work of thy hands." What the Psalmist here says of man being invested with dignity and honor as a sub-ruler in the affairs of earth, holding a responsible part of the divine sovereignty, a rational philosophy and science would indorse to-day.

And, finally, the bounty of nature overruns all actual needs. The Eternal measures out its supplies by no stinted hand. Man may regulate production and distribution, but Nature will fill his cup to overflowing if he will let her. He himself must watch against her wastes in some parts of the globe, and in other parts his skill must do the work of climate. But Nature's storehouse of various bounty for man's use is inexhaustible. What luxury of power and of life on which he may draw! What wealth of mineral and chemical resources! What teeming fields and forests in the vegetable world! How the seeds are scattered on the winds and storms! Even the birds of the air are their carriers and sowers. They may fall by the wayside, or among thorns, or on stony places; but Nature provides against disaster by the extravagance of her sowing. Beneath the sea, on Alpine snows, over hoary rocks, is wrought the miracle of the all-abounding principle of life. I picked flowers last June which were wedged close between the rocks at the top of Pike's Peak. Make a ruin; and, let it be her own or man's, Nature will gradually weave her green mantle gracefully around it. Go into wilds, where man's foot has seldom trod nor his eyes gazed, and behold there, unseen before, unknown, richness on richness and beauty on beauty, of the living wonder. "Beauty is its own excuse for being," and life ever transcends the powers of death. It is the overflowing cup of the Infinite Bounty which in wilderness and on plains, by the roadside and in our gardens, spills and scatters the seeds from which comes the beauty that charms our eyes and gladdens our hearts. This world has much of darkness and evil. It has storms of rough trial, and many foes of happiness and enemies of life. Yet the Eternal welcomes and honors this little storm-tossed earth as a guest and friend, and provides for it such a bounty of all the things which make for life and light and goodness and gladness that these finally may master all their foes, and overcome the trial and the evil and the darkness. The word "bounty" is apt to suggest only material good things. But the Eternal Bounty covers all realms, all needs of human life, in its highest ranges. What inexhaustible riches of truth to reward and delight the eager intellect! What joyous æsthetic gratifications for the eye with a cultured mind behind it! What opportunities for affection and goodness in which the heart may revel! Have you not seen some persons whose characters have an inexhaustible radiance of goodness, like the sparkling of perpetual fountains, and whose daily life is an overflowing bounty of sunshine from the soul?

When I wrote, a disappointing spring day turned to a cold, heavy rain. But the rain had not wholly ceased when I heard the sparrows bravely chirruping, and the robins singing their evening hymns. Despite the rough storm they found the joy of existence. So the human soul, through the stress and storm of life, may so adjust itself to the ways of the Eternal as to learn the harmonies of beneficent service, and thus break into the harmonies of joy and of song.

THE TWENTY-THIRD PSALM IN THE NINETEENTH CENTURY.

VI.

THE ETERNAL GOODNESS AND HUMAN DESTINY.

"Surely goodness and mercy shall follow me all the days of my life: and I will dwell in the house of the Lord for ever."

IN this exalted rapture of perfect confidence and hope, the sentiment of the Twenty-third Psalm reaches both its logical and poetical climax. Each successive verse of the six has expressed some definite expansion or rise of the poet's emotional thought; but thus far everything has been included within the limits of actual experience. The present tense has prevailed. Jehovah is the good and all-powerful shepherd. He leadeth into the green pastures and by the restful waters. He guideth in the straight paths of safety. In the deadly valley of shadows it is his power that supports and comforts. And, in the very presence of hostile forces, his friendly service overflows in bountiful provision. The Psalmist has spoken from the basis of experience, and not, so far as appears in the text of his song, from any *a priori* theological assumptions. His appeal has been simply to common facts for testing the truth of his patriotic and assuring declarations. "Look around you," is the implied injunction of his words: "Behold how Jehovah is doing all these things for his people." And then, from this basis of experience, the poet turns, with serene and perfect assurance, to face the future; for (this is his inference) the same bountiful guidance and care can certainly be depended on for continuance. That is his sole reasoning. It is the simplicity of the child's logic. And yet it is the solid foundation on which all science rests: the order of things observed in the natural world in the past can be depended on in the future. The sun in the glory of its power may be expected to rise to-morrow because it has risen, by calculable law, in innumerable yesterdays. It is by a similar mental procedure that the Psalmist rises, in this triumphant ending of his pæan to Jehovah as a Shepherd, to the exulting exclamation: "Surely goodness and mercy will follow me all the days of my life: and I shall dwell in the house of Jehovah forever."

I may say in passing that the common version stands in no urgent need of revision here for the sake of accuracy, except that it would be better to transpose the auxiliaries "shall" and "will" in the two divisions of the verse. The Hebrew word translated "mercy," I may add, is the same word that is often rendered by the richer phrase "loving-kindness"; and the word translated "goodness" carries from its primary root a meaning of outward prosperity and good fortune. And this latter idea is one of the rhetorical links which connects the verse back with the immediately preceding verse depicting Jehovah's bounty. Another and more obvious link is in the expression "house of Jehovah,"— "I shall dwell in the house of the Lord for ever." The preceding verse had given a picture of the gracious and bounteous hospitality of a householder to a guest. That thought is now expanded and carried forward to the security and beneficence which must be enjoyed by one who is to dwell, not transiently, but for all time, in Jehovah's house. (I have previously explained that the Psalm is one of steps or degrees, each verse rising upon some suggestive thought of the preceding.) And these two heightened thoughts, to which I have just referred, make the steps by which the poet ascends to his final and sublime contemplation of a beneficent Providence unbounded by time and including the whole future of Israel in its scope. To generalize the lesson of the verse, we may say that it consists of these twin ideas: the Eternal Goodness and its assurances for human destiny.

But neither the Hebrew poet nor the Hebrew theologian was accustomed to regard such ideas as these in any abstract or metaphysical fashion. The Hebrew religion kept close to nature and close to this world. Even in its childlike faith in the supernatural, the supernatural agencies were conceived in very human and earthly form. If the Hebrews talked of eternity, it was an eternity not severed nor distinguished from but including time. If they thought of the continuance of human existence, it was existence lengthened out indefinitely on this earth. In the very verse we are considering the phrase translated "for ever" meant literally "length of days." It was only a more intensified form of the expression rendered in the first part of the verse by the words "all the days of my life"; and a literal rendering of the last half of the verse would be "I shall dwell in the house of Jehovah to length of days." It is the same term which occurs in Proverbs as representing one of the gifts of Wisdom: "Length of days is in her right hand." Yet this phrase seems to have come nearer than any other in the canonical Hebrew Scriptures to taking the place of the word for eternal duration in the Christian Scriptures. In truth (as shown in the fourth lecture), for the greater part of the time of their national existence, the Hebrews manifested no specific belief in the doctrine of immortality, at least in the Christian sense of it.

To the Hebrew, moreover, the earth was a goodly world; and he had no unwholesome, impatient desire to depart from it. Its evils, which he by no means ignored, were, he believed, the consequence of human departure from the law of righteousness. Its destructive forces, its afflictive ills, its deaths and terrors, were to him the penalty for violating Jehovah's commandments. Thus the garden of Eden, he believed, had been lost, and all after woes had fallen on mankind. But still Jehovah was regarded as no implacable ruler. Let the people only return to his commandments and keep them, and he would abundantly pardon. With long life would he satisfy them and show them his salvation. He would deliver them from all their distresses, and cause them to bless his name forever. It was not, therefore, because the Hebrew was blind to the evils of the world, and did not suffer his full share of earthly troubles, that he still thought this earth a goodly world. In fact, he was always under the harrow of some trouble. Yet despite all the evil he could sing, "Oh, that men would praise Jehovah for his goodness and for his wonderful works to the children of men!"

It is quite certain, too, that, when the Hebrew spoke of the "house of the Lord," he was not thinking of a "mansion in the skies." The house of the Lord for him meant the holy temple of worship. This reference to the house of the Lord is one of the evidences which modern criticism has pointed out for proof that the Twenty-third Psalm was not written by King David, and could not have been written by any one until after David's son, King Solomon, had built the great temple. Before that event the ark of the sacred covenant had been sheltered and protected in a tent (or tabernacle), which was transported from place to place. But when Solomon built the costly temple, that became by pre-eminence in Israel's view Jehovah's house. The sacred covenant was deposited there, in a place of safety, as it was believed, for all time. There was the innermost Holy of holies of the Hebrew faith. To the devout believer the solidity and magnificence of the temple became symbolic of national stability and prosperity. The patriotic sentiments of security and dominion mingled with and enhanced the joys of worship for those who entered there for that sacred service. To the faithful ones of Israel the act of worship in this great temple was the transcendent act of human life. There as nowhere else they came into the immediate presence of Jehovah,— or so they believed and felt. There they acknowledged his power and received assurances of his aid and blessing. Felicitous, indeed, they thought, must be the lot of those who dwelt there as chosen servants of Jehovah for performing the manifold offices of the sacred place. Some such picture as this of the grandeur of the outward temple and of its holy service doubtless presented itself to the Psalmist's poetic vision. Yet, doubtless, also, it symbolized to him, as it would to the most spiritually intelligent among his contemporaries, not, indeed, all that finer culmination of the worshipful attitude which is "in spirit and in truth, without reference to any technicalities of place and time, but at least an idea of a constant nearness to Jehovah's presence through acts of righteousness, and of that service of him which is rendered by the clean heart and the just deed. For, however magnificent in its surroundings and formalities was the outward worship of the Hebrews, they had prophets who denounced the oblations and prayers and praises, even of this sacred temple, as an abomination and mockery, unless the worshippers brought justice and mercy and a contrite heart among their offerings. And no religion, more clearly and strongly than the Hebrew, has ever set forth obedience to the law of righteousness as a requisite condition, individually and nationally, of acceptance with Deity and of achieving all the most desirable objects of human existence. In righteousness, and in righteousness only, was the way of salvation, of individual and national health, of prosperity and confidence, of strength and peace: yes, righteousness was the very law and condition of life itself and of all life's noblest felicities. This is the constant injunction of Hebrew Proverb and Prophet and Psalm. And the connection of righteousness (or right conduct) with the forces of life is one of the prominent points in modern science and scientific ethics, as was specially shown in the third lecture.

These two great thoughts of the Hebrew faith unite, then, to make the final climax of this Twenty-third Psalm: first, Jehovah, the eternal power, is a good power to be depended upon perpetually; second, in that Goodness is full assurance of a good destiny for man through a life allied with the very life and power of Jehovah.

Now, in this statement of these two root-thoughts I believe I have put nothing which the Hebrew singer would not himself have accepted. Into what details of theological or mythological belief and expression, fitting the intelligence of the time, he might have carried these thoughts, or how he might have dressed them in the fashion of his age and race, is another question, and one which we have no occasion now to consider. Our question is whether these root-thoughts themselves can be justified in the light of modern intelligence. What has the scientific philosophy which is in vogue in this closing decade of the nineteenth century to say with regard to the validity of these two ideas? That is the question with which we are most concerned.

And, first, it is remarkable how little change is needed in the statement of these ideas, as just made, to make the statement itself seem modern. In the place of the Hebrew appellation "Jehovah," let us (as I have before asked you in these lectures) put the English phrase which is its nearest equivalent, "The Eternal," and we have a statement which might be taken from a religious treatise written from the standpoint of the most advanced scientific philosophy. Put still more succinctly, our statement might then stand thus: "The Eternal is to be depended upon as a power for goodness, and in that goodness man has assurance of a good destiny."

And, in the next place, you will not fail to note

that here are precisely the two great modern problems of religion,— the problem of God and the problem of immortality. For it is no secret to the reading and thinking portion of mankind that these fundamental problems of religion and philosophy have been opened afresh to-day as the result of advancing science in every direction, and it is not rationally probable that questions thus opened will ever be settled again in precisely the old way.

Not in the old way; and yet I maintain that these questions will be rationally settled in a way that will vindicate and confirm these two great and essential points of religious faith,— the Goodness of the Eternal, and for man a good and worthy destiny. And these are the two important points now to be considered.

As to the first, I frankly admit and affirm that, unless it can be legitimately maintained that the Eternal Energy of the universe, which science recognizes as the Source of all phenomena, is purposive in its action and toward results intelligible and beneficent, we shall have no Deity left worthy of human adoration or capable of imposing or being the source of any law, intellectual or moral, which man could or should obey. If the Infinite and Eternal Energy from which all things proceed, and in whose presence we ever are, is merely power,— power working blindly, wildly, recklessly, at mere chance and hazard, unconditioned by anything corresponding to intelligence and benevolence,— then it is not a Power which man's intelligent and moral nature could or ought to regard with feelings of admiration and affection. Nor, if the Infinite Energy manifested an intelligible aim, but no moral quality, could it attract the worship of the human conscience and heart. If it were to manifest an intelligible aim directed by positive malevolence, then we should have a world governed by diabolism, but no Deity to whom man would have any occasion to sing praises or direct his aspirations. Man might fear such a being, and try to evade his malevolent power; but he could not count it a blessing to dwell with such a being forever. The only Deity worthy of the name, the only Deity, in fine, whose existence is worthy of belief, must have the quality of goodness. If the Eternal and Infinite Energy of the universe, of which science talks, does not have that attribute, let us have done with it forever as a name or substitute for Deity. If the Eternal Power cannot be seen and believed to be a good power, then let us candidly confess that the world is orphaned of its God.

The question, then, is, Can the conception of Deity furnished us by the scientific philosophy of the day meet the test of this requirement? And I answer, unhesitatingly, confidently, in the affirmative. I make this affirmative answer, fully aware of the long and tragic list of evils which may be drawn up against the world of nature and against mankind. I remember John Stuart Mill's terrific indictment of what he calls nature's acts of demonic cruelty,— acts of torturing, maiming, and killing, for doing the like of which society imprisons or hangs human beings. Our popular journalistic reporters to-day write of the cruel waves which suck down to death in our harbors a man or child, and of the merciless tornado or the demon of fire or flood, that are somewhere slaughtering our fellow-creatures by the scores, in every month of the year, even doing it in the season when Nature is most active in weaving her "coronation robes" of living beauty. Thus even the very terms of these newspaper writers are accusations of pitiless cruelty against the power of Nature. And considering her smiling aspects even while she slays, they might compare her to Rome's bloody tyrant, who played music while his imperial city burned. But, despite all this which can be charged against Nature's forces, I can still say, with the Hebrew Psalmist, that the Eternal Power is not power only, but has the moral attribute of goodness. I could not, however, say this if I regarded material nature alone. I might admire and stand in awe before the sublime process of the evolution of the natural world, as science declares it, from the primal nebulous fire-mist to the sun in the heavens and the rose in your gardens, or to the last chrysanthemum blossom of the season, that lingers to kiss the snow. My imagination would be entranced by the beauty everywhere manifest, and often springing from the transformation of the ugly and disgusting. In the orderly adjustment of part to part, in the grand sweep of the forces, in the unchangeable stability of the laws, in the slowly evolved, mighty product and spectacle such as our eyes now behold in the heavens and on the earth, my intellect would certainly acknowledge the wondrous evidences of a power infinitely greater than, but kindred to, its own intelligent activity. But, if nature stopped there, if there were nothing further, I might hesitate to affirm a moral aim of the Power within and behind it, or might even deny to the Power a moral quality. But nature does not stop there. The material world is not the whole of nature, nor does physical science cover all the manifestations of the Power within and behind nature. In a large, scientific sense, man is a part of nature. He sprang from her loins. By the same great process of evolution whereby the material world came into existence man also came,— man, indeed, with his early brutalities, his primitive savage degradations, his still degrading vices and crimes, but man, also, with his moral consciousness, with his as yet unmeasured mental and moral capabilities, with his sublime ideals of rectitude and benevolence, with his pure, unselfish aspirations and affections, with his capacity for unlimited moral and mental progress,— in short, man so endowed with mental and moral gifts as to be able to take up nature's work and carry it forward to ideal aims, such as material nature alone, without him, would never have achieved. We are not, therefore, to separate man from nature, as if they belonged to two different and antagonistic worlds. This was an ancient view, from which sprang the theory of a dual universe fought for by two supreme principles, or deities, a good and an evil. But to-day it is not a question of two deities or more, but of one or none. If science has made any deliverance that is generally accepted, it is that the Power within and behind all the manifoldness of phenomena is unitary. It is not many, nor two, but one. Hence, we have a right to say that, whatever of goodness and the possibilities of goodness appear in man, these reflect back their glory upon nature's dark ways, and show the whole process of evolution to have a moral purport, and disclose, moreover, that the Eternal Power within and behind the process is working toward a beneficent result. Whence, indeed, can come the moral consciousness of man, with all its sublime actualities and possibilities, but from that Infinite and Eternal Energy from which all things proceed? By the highest standards of man's moral faiths, aims, achievements, and hopes may we find suggestion of a measure, though finite and inadequate, for the Eternal Goodness. As these are only products, in that must be their Source and Cause and ancestral Kind.

But this argument would be rounded to better completion were the further points made which have been developed in one or another of the previous lectures, and which I will here only allude to; namely, that the Eternal Power, as a rational philosophy gives us the conception to-day, is not to be thought of as a being in the skies, policing human affairs from a seat of sovereign authority there, and saving human beings from disaster by a dispensation of special providences, but rather as a power organized in the very laws and forces of nature itself and in the mental and moral capabilities of the human mind; that the conditions of life are such that man must adjust himself to the eternal energies and laws, and thereby become a providence unto himself, wielding the eternal power for his own and others' welfare; that this process of adjustment is educational, developing human faculty and character, and making man a responsible agent in repressing evil and evolving good in his world; and that the Eternal Power, working in and through all things, is justified as good because evolution itself, which is the process of its activity, proceeds by the law of amelioration and ascent from simple to complex forms of organism, and from low to higher and ever higher and fairer realms of life. Man, regarded through the long ages of history, has advanced in moral perception, capacity, and conduct, and is still advancing; therefore the Power that has been man's central and vital impulsion must be good and not evil.

At this point I may be asked: "But what of the evil impulsions in man? Do not they also come from the Eternal Energy from which all things proceed, and hence reflect back their dark character upon it?" To this I answer, In their original germs these impulsions, like everything else, do spring from the Eternal Energy; but in their original form they are void of moral attributes. They appear first in the lower animal creatures as instincts merely of self-nourishment and self-perpetuation and preservation. And there they are as normal as they are necessary. In primitive man these instincts were little removed from their brute stage; and in individual man to-day, as in primitive man, these instincts of self-interest and self-gratification have a normal function, especially in the earlier years of life. But, since man is also a being of rational and moral consciousness, these instincts in him come into rightful subjection to the higher laws of reason and conscience. And they become evil impulsions in him when they refuse this subjection to the larger and higher law of life which the Eternal Power, through the very conditions of his creation, has wrought out for man. Self-interest is never normally an end in itself. It is only an instrumentality for the accomplishment of some universal good. And it is of the very essence of the religious and ethical consciousness, when it is awakened, to annul all interests and gratifications which are bounded by self, and to subject all the self-seeking propensities to the service of the general benefit or of some universal aim. In his capacity as a free agent, free within certain limits, man can pursue the ends of sheer selfish gratification. But, so far as he does so, he is irreligious, immoral. He unmans himself, and resuscitates in his nature the cast-off brute, only in worse form, from which the Eternal Power had been lifting him for a higher possibility. So far from acting under an impulsion of the Eternal, he has transmuted what the Eternal once made good into evil, and for consequence loses the conscious power of the Eternal and the godlike from his nature, and sinks back under the sway of carnal and material law, toward the meagre existence of the brute and the clod; and thus he subjects the Eternal Goodness to another effort to lift his existence again to the capabilities of manhood.

There is, moreover, one additional consideration on this phase of our theme on which I wish to dwell for a moment or two. Our verse says, "Goodness and mercy shall follow us." Perhaps the writer would have said "attend us" or "lead us" just as readily. Yet, in the use of the word "follow," there is a peculiar suggestiveness. In the midst of life's ills, they are sometimes so dark and distressing that, at the time, we cannot see nor feel the overshadowing goodness and mercy. There are calamities in which we cannot say, and are not called to say, that all is for the best because Eternal Power has so willed it. The Eternal has not willed to drown your child, nor to sweep away a city by flood, nor to make a holocaust of a town's population. The Power has simply not interfered; and it is better, on the whole, that the great natural laws of cause and effect, which are pregnant with benefit for man, should take their course than that a life should here and there be saved from violent death, and you and I be spared from grief. Yet even then the goodness and mercy of the Eternal are not wanting, though often they may follow so far behind our suffering that we may fail to see them. They are never to be looked for in the suffering itself, but in the way we meet it. The substance of character is such that it may be nourished from sources which seem most unpromising. Trials that threaten to destroy may strengthen its fortitude. Temptations resisted, vices overcome, may be converted into moral vigor. Sorrow and tears, however bitter to bear, may beget a tenderer humanity and a more spiritual loveliness. There is no distress which can befall us for which there is not a following mercy in the very laws and forces whereby character grows and is ennobled; no wound made in our natures, whether by moral transgression or outward calamity, but that from the greater nature that holds us and of which we are born there begin to move toward us, and toward the very place of bruise, the forces of healing and restoration. Only we must hold our minds and wills in readiness to receive and co-operate with the good intent. We are free, within certain natural limits, to walk our individual ways and to open or close the avenues of beneficial influence to our hearts; yet, on whatever way we walk, and whatever evils we encounter, there is in the very laws of being and life a reserve force of goodness and mercy following us, ready at our first beckoning gesture to come up to our side, and to help us transform the ills into some kind of moral benefit, and to lead us ever toward larger vision and higher attainments of character.

And this same Power that has been patiently working during a past eternity and through all kinds of conditions for and toward goodness may be trusted to have in store for man a worthy moral destiny. Whether that destiny is to include a personal immortality there is no science as yet, using that word in its common acceptation, which either affirms or denies. We are here left to the argument of the most rational probability. And sometimes, when there comes over me an impression of the inconceivable magnitude and orderly grandeur of this universe, of its indescribable splendor and beauty, of the eternity during which it has been in process of creation, of the infinite transformations and interactions of its forces, of its manifold realms of life, material, mental, affectional, moral, spiritual,— organism rising upon organism and life upon life to ever complexer nature and finer consummation,— and when I think of man as the crown of this ineffably sublime process of creation on this earth, and as endowed with the faculty and responsibility of carrying the creative task forward in this world to some nobler issue, he being a veritable and conscious incarnation and agent of the Eternal Power that

> "Step by step lifts bad to good,
> Without halting, without rest,
> Lifting Better up to Best,"—

when I think of man, honored by such a capacity, mission, and service, I am almost ready to say: "That is enough: to fulfil that function well is adequate dignity and destiny; no other immortality can be asked for than that which accumulates from personal goodness in the aggregate welfare of the race, and which seemed to suffice even the womanly heart of George Eliot, when she wrote of

> 'The choir invisible
> Of those immortal dead who live again
> In minds made better by their presence;
>
> . . . .
>
> In thoughts sublime that pierce the night like stars,
> And with their mild persistence urge man's search
> To vaster issues.'"

Were that to be all, it would yet seem a worthy destiny for individual man. He must then live so well as to greaten and gladden the mind and heart of the human race for all time after him. His rectitude would be a necessity for continuing the unbroken and beneficent succession of the all-abounding and ascending life. The individual might perish, but even then the life that was in him would go on. The old leaf on a tree, which the new bud pushes off, we may imagine even to welcome the new, since the same life has gone into it to serve a perpetuated purpose. So man might die with serenity, happy in the ripeness of years to give up his own vitality to feed the never-dying vitality of his race. And even,— if I may make a most daring hypothesis,— even if the human race were at some remote period to become extinct, even if, as astronomy now says, a world may become dead, a sun or star go out of existence, we may yet conceive of a universe so vast and majestic in its proportions that the death of a man or of a world may have no more effect on the vast and ceaseless procession of beneficent life than does the fall of a leaf from its tree when it has fulfilled its function in serving the unfolding, ceaseless, vital Law.

But, again, when I think of the countless æons which were spent by the Eternal Power in producing a being capable of such service as this which man at his best can perform, when I think of the world-struggles and birth-pains of which he is the product, I am reluctant to believe that the consummate flower of creation on this planet, the moral personality of man, is after a few score years of existence to be extinguished forever, blown out like the flame of a candle by a whiff of your breath. And then there rises before me, with massive strength the more rational conclusion that somewhere, somehow, this responsible vicegerent of the Eternal Power will continue consciously to live and work in this universe, which is the house of the Eternal.

Nor am I troubled by the problem of the how and the where. The old mythological heavens and hells and stories of physical resurrections we may regard as outlawed by modern criticism. Nor do the alleged claims of Spiritualism, though I have no prejudice against them, appear to me to have so sifted facts from personal illusions and mercenary frauds as to avail much before the tribunal of science. But there is no more difficulty in conceiving of a new and more ethereal body for the human personality after the death and hopeless dissolution of the present body than there would be in conceiving *a priori* of hundreds of things which science has made familiar facts. We should never *a priori* believe it possible for the butterfly to come forth from the grub, nor for the sun's heat to be motor of all energy and life on the earth, nor for a tiny seed, almost invisible, to possess within it a principle of life capable of drawing elements from earth and air and moisture, and translating them into a gigantic tree, with all its beauty of foliage and blossom and its bounty of fruit. Just consider, for a moment, that unique kind of matter, the ether-atmosphere, which, as science assures us, interpenetrates our denser air and all the interplanetary and interstellar spaces. It is not visible, yet makes for us all other things visible. It is not tangible nor measurable. No chemical skill has resolved it into its constituent elements. Science has nevertheless inferred its existence as a necessary condition for transmitting light and heat from the sun to its planets. It is the highway of communication between the worlds. But it may be more than that. Here is one kind of matter actually occupying to some extent the same space with another kind of matter. Why, then, may we not here have the material for another body developing within this body of flesh, which may be the cause of some of the strange psychic phenomena now seeking explanation? Here may be the fabric for the shining garments of our dead,— our beloved ones literally rising from death clothed with bodies of light.

Of course, I am not pressing this hypothesis for belief. It may seem to most persons wildly visionary. My only point is that, however improbable an hypothesis may seem *a priori*, it is not therefore to be dismissed as impossible. Wonderful as such a consummation of human life would be, I aver that in itself it would be no greater marvel than is the scientific fact that not a breath is drawn by any living creature on this earth, not a blade of grass grows, not a flower blooms, not a movement is made nor any kind of power exerted here, but that the engine which does it all is in that sun up yonder ninety-five millions of miles away. And the connection between the engine there and its work here is by the waves of this invisible ocean of ether! I am only urging that, on this great problem of immortality, it behooves us to be very modest not only in our affirmations, but in our denials,— very modest, yet very expectant. There is a theological dogmatism which greatly obstructs the way of truth; and there is a credulity that is the root of superstition. But there is an incredulity which is as hostile to truth's progress as is superstition or dogmatism,—an incredulity that is the dogmatism of negation, and closes the avenues of the mind to the very approaches of truth.

But, in whatever form this problem of man's future destiny is to be settled, his present duty remains the same. In some shape our lives and their results must survive death. Somewhere in the house of the Eternal, our influence, our work, our spirit, or our still living personality will continue for helping to shape eternal issues. In either case our duty now is to do the best service possible for this world's good, and to attain the utmost possible nobility of character and conduct, and then to wait serenely and patiently, and also, if it be possible, with the glow of large expectancy in our eyes, for death to lift the veil and reveal the after destiny. And in either case, too, we shall dwell still in the house of the Eternal, to "share," as said our greatest American prophet and psalmist, "the will and the immensity and the immortality of the First Cause." No rightly living soul need ever fear to be exiled at death to an utterly strange country. Moral realms are not separated by space nor time nor outward condition. Whoever lives a life of righteousness on whatever planet dwells now in heaven and inhabiteth and enricheth eternity.

THE TRINITY OF EVOLUTION.

THE modern scientific doctrine of Evolution, in its teachings and implications concerning world-formation, has given us a new trinity, which, I venture to say, will play even a more important part in the religious thinking of the future than the theological doctrine of the Trinity has played in the past history of Christendom.

The three constituent elements of the Trinity of Evolution are Power, Intelligence, Goodness; considering the various manifestations of the creative World-energy, we are in a condition, I think, now to affirm on scientific grounds that there can be no adequate explanation of all the phenomena of the world without implying that each of these three elements must be an inherent attribute of the creative Energy. Of course, there is hardly need to-day to add, in any intelligent assembly, that modern science does not allow us to conceive of creation as beginning or ending six thousand or even six hundred thousand years ago, or as being at any time a finished process. The scientific theory is that creation is a continuous process, that productive forces which were operative in the universe six thousand or six hundred thousand years ago are operative to-day, that the book of genesis in nature is an unending one, and, further, that all finite existences known to us, from atom to animalcule and from animalcule to man, are linked in one organic creative process,—

> "A subtle chain of countless rings
> The next unto the farthest brings;"—

so that we cannot scientifically or logically separate man from the process of cosmical creation, nor, in determining the attributes of the creative World-energy, leave the attributes of humanity out of account. Whatever is in the product must exist in some elemental form in the Source or Cause. Hence, in any question concerning a world-plan or world-purpose, man, with all his immense moral capacities and possibilities, must be included as a most important part of the answer.

There have been some philosophers, as well as common people, who are not wise philosophers, who doubt whether the world of nature below man gives evidence of any moral law, of any beneficent purpose. They count up the internecine strifes among the animal races, the bitter struggles for existence, the sufferings, cruelties, and destructions everywhere rife in nature; and then they ask in a tone of triumph, If there be a just and merciful Deity, why does he not stop this painful and merciless animal conflict? And why does he afflict human beings with unavoidable cruel calamities from nature's violence? But all these objectors seem to me to be still entangled with the old conception of Deity as an almighty artificer, who created the world by a few original strokes six thousand years ago, and set it in motion as something apart from himself. They have not really grasped the scientific conception of a continuous World-energy, which has not yet ceased its creative work nor reached its goal, of a World-energy that is involved and identified with all present forces for organizing and sustaining life, and is revealing its attributes and aims in all the manifold phenomena, movements, and progress of human thought and conscience as well as in the world of material nature. These objectors are really sitting in judgment on a being who is the creation of human brains in a past and ignorant age,—a mere fragment of a Deity. But whence, I ask, that very sense of mercy and justice which boldly judges nature's violence? Whence that human pity and intelligence which attempt to improve on nature's work? They are born with man of the very power that is the mainspring of nature's movements. Man is himself nature's child. He fulfils her aim, reveals her purpose; and all that he has of intelligence, conscience, goodness, all that he has of moral faculty and hope, is to be credited back to the motive-power that connects man with nature in one continuous process of creation. No evidence drawn from any isolated portion of the known universe, nor from a limited section of time, nor from any mere fragment of a creative process which even we see to have neither beginning nor end, can be adequate for a decision against the character of a sovereign Energy admitted to be eternal in its dominion and work.

It is from these large premises that the problem of the character of Deity must be approached; and it is from a survey as nearly universal as human knowledge will admit, it is from a study of the great trend of things from the beginning of man's knowledge of the forces of the universe and of human history up to the present moment,— comparing forces with results, seeing the character of causes in their consequences, tracing the evidences of advance and ascent along the courses of life from the primitive organic cell to the brain of a Plato and the heart of a Jesus,— it is from such a comprehensive survey as this that modern science enables us to affirm of the world's creative process that trinity of attributes which I have named Power, Intelligence, Goodness.

Of these attributes there is one of which no sane human being ever doubts. The evidences of power — of power above human power — are omnipresent. They are conspicuous on every side. They press upon the human senses in overwhelming array. These evidences of power in the universe above man and before man we can never escape. By day, by night, in joy or pain, in life or death, we are made conscious that we intimately touch and depend upon some Reality of existence mightier and older than ourselves or than the human race. It was the sense of this Power that first bowed primitive man in worship. It is the consciousness of this Reality above and more than ourselves that founded religious institutions, that built this house, and that has brought us to this house this morning, or that formed the habit of coming thither. Of this first constituent of the Trinity of Evolution, therefore, there is no need I should speak further. The evidence of it is almost too convincing, for it comes not always gently. It not only charms us in the rose and the grass and the orderly procession of the seasons, but it rushes in the deadly tornado, it heaves the ocean to destructive fury; it sends a tremor through the solid earth and bursts it asunder, burying in its yawning chasms cities and their inhabitants; it belches fire and ashes and death from the volcano's mouth.

But mere cosmical power alone could not hold intelligent man in the attitude of worship. Primitive man might have prostrated himself before nature's violent forces in sheer terror; but, as soon as the human mind developed an intelligence sufficient for controlling and using such natural forces as came within its dominion, only Power intelligible in method could receive its real homage. The human mind may stand in awe before the destructive calamities which sometimes ensue in this era of civilization from the breaking away from human control of those natural forces which have been harnessed to the service of man; but the very awe leads him to inquire by what act of omission or commission of his own that intelligent guidance was lost, and then how he may supply a remedy against a repetition of such disasters. What the human mind renders its homage to is not sheer power with no guidance but chance, not blind, reckless fatality, but power that works in the grooves of law and method to a calculable end. And this is true not only of the natural forces which man has learned to control to his own uses, but of that omnipresent World-energy which is the force within and behind all forces. Sometimes this almighty energy may seem to us to have escaped all grooves of method, and its end may be unintelligible to us, but, in the main, it works and has ever worked in ways of orderly sequence which respond so fully to man's own intelligence that he has a right to assume that the rule controls the apparent exceptions. Indeed, in view of the intimate connection between life and the constancy of nature's methods, it is safe to say that no race of intelligent beings, no species like mankind, could ever have been developed in a universe whose powers and forces were subject to infinite chance and caprice. Man has risen to his own intelligence, and developed a civilization which means largely a progressive, intelligent control of the forces of nature, only because he had an intelligible world to deal with.

I stood one day last summer on a lofty mountain-top, with still loftier peaks all around me and fertile valleys lying at the mountain's foot. On every hand were evidences of mighty Power.

What gigantic primeval force has lifted those rocky heights and scooped those valleys? Rough Titans of power they were that there laid the foundations of the earth and dropped those huge granite bowlders down the mountain slopes and over the hillsides. Nor man nor beast was there to see, nor had any tiniest form of life begun. But modern science has read for us the story, and told us that that primeval titanic energy is of Protean form; that the Power which lifted those mountain heights and shaped their sides to the line of beauty and impelled those granite bowlders to their lodgement is the same Power which, in other phase, clothed the mountains with forests and carpeted the valleys with grass, and brought in orderly sequence every kind of ascending life, the same Power which on that Sunday morning, when I worshipped on the mountain-top, was still all alive and active around me, making the very glory that held my vision, the same Power that was blossoming in the roadside asters, striving to cover the wounds of mountain slides and chasms with verdure, sparkling in the waterfall, crowning Mount Washington with a silvery cloud, bordering my very footsteps with the charms of color and form in the lichens, mushrooms, and mosses.

This story of nature's creation and movement and life, from the time when the earth first solidified into continents up to the present moment, is a history; there is a regular sequence of events, activities, living things and creatures, an orderly ascent of species with increasing capacities and functions, and throughout the whole history an advance in fitness of relationship, in symmetry of form, in harmony and beauty. Now, wherever there are fitness, order, method, harmony, beauty, cause joined to its own consequent, there are the marks of intelligence. These are the qualities that make the world an intelligible world, and render it inhabitable by intelligent beings. These are the qualities that attract the admiration and reverence of intelligent minds. I care little to prove that these qualities must be attributes of a supreme personal consciousness. It is the qualities themselves that win my trust and become my support and refuge. Somehow, because of the very orderliness of their working, I believe, they join in the unity of one Power. But it is not the power of a mere personal will more than mere material energy that I can rationally worship. I can only rationally worship those attributes that guide personal will to intelligible results. It is before the evidences of Intelligence presented in the universe that my own intelligence bends in homage.

But the doctrine of Evolution does not stop with a dual Deity. Power and Intelligence do not exhaust the attributes of the World-energy. The Evolution doctrine discloses to us a world which rises from power, through intelligence, to moral life. Power intelligibly proceeding to good ends, — that is Evolution's motto for the world. I do not mean by this that it is legitimate to repeat to-day the old argument of beneficent design in the realm of material nature. That argument dealt in petty details, and would now not always stand the test of facts. With regard to individuals, and even whole species, the beneficence of natural law is not always apparent. In the world of nature below man we need not look for any complete evidence of moral aim. The design in nature which science discloses is of a large style. It is adaptation, tendency, organic movement toward great and often distant ends. It means strivings, even though unconscious of any aim, that result in ascent and enrichment of life. It means finer species, nicer faculties, more delicate organs, increased facilities and better modes of living, truer intelligence, keener perceptions of the intelligible order of things, and more power to cope with and use nature's resources. After long ages of these upward struggles and strivings of material nature, man appeared as their resultant,—a being to a large extent self-governing, self-elevating, capable of improving upon his own nature both individually and in the species. In man the World-energy blossomed into moral consciousness; into perceptions of a right and a wrong, and into ability to choose and to do the right; into that voluntary rectitude and the love of it which is goodness; into pity for error and badness, and into effort to make the bad into good and the good ever into a better and best; into spiritual aspiration, which seeks ever to subordinate material means to intellectual ends and selfish pleasures to universal good. All this part of man is the World-energy itself in its moral aspect. Whence, otherwise, could the moral consciousness and moral law have had their source?

> "Out from the heart of nature rolled
> The burdens of the Bible old."

From Power to Intelligence, from Intelligence to Goodness, — so has the world-process revealed the world-purpose. Power, for its own conservation, necessitated an intelligent and intelligible order. A system, or rather medley, of chance-forces would be mutually destructive. And Intelligence, for the same reason, must rise to moral rectitude in order to hold the line for the best and permanent ascent of life. Intelligence itself, as soon as adequately developed, makes declaration of the principle of justice as the equation of rights between men, just as it declares the laws of beauty or the unalterable relations between numbers in mathematics. So came the Golden Rule, wherever and whenever intelligence rose high enough to perceive the moral equation, as in China, Persia, Palestine, and Greece; and so, too, the "Love thy neighbor as thyself," and all the recognized obligations, in religion and ethics, of fellowship and fraternity between man and man as the basis of society. Thus man himself is the proof that the universe, at least so far as concerns our existence, has a moral character and aim; and Goodness is to be added to Intelligence and Power, to complete the Trinity of forces in the world-process which Evolution teaches.

But I may here be told that man himself is not good, that he is a violator of his own moral consciousness, that he continually breaks the commandments which his conscience declares, that a very large portion of mankind is sunk in wickedness and moral degradation. To this objection I reply that we are here talking of aims and aspirations, of the world-purpose and strivings; and we are not to confound these with any present accomplishment. It is enough to prove a moral character and purpose in the universe that out of its own heart it has given birth to a moral guide, and that it has set in the spiritual sky of humanity an ideal of moral perfection to be followed after. Creation is not finished with man. Man himself has not completed the pattern of manhood. In most of us survive still some relics of the brute and the clod. But the ages are patient, and the world-purpose is to be judged by man's gradual success in overcoming animalism and enthroning intelligence and rectitude over brute selfishness and force. Says our Emerson: "The age of the quadruped is to go out: the age of the brain and of the heart is to come in. And, if one shall read the future of the race hinted in the organic effort of Nature to mount and meliorate, and the corresponding impulse to the Better in the human being, we shall dare affirm that there is nothing he will not overcome and convert, until at last culture shall absorb the chaos and gehenna. He will convert the Furies into Muses, and the hells into benefit." There is man's aim; and in man's aim Nature works toward her purpose.

In considering, therefore, the character of the world-purpose, we are bid to take man, not at his poorest, but at his best. We are to take him, not as he is, but as he may be and aspires to be,— not in his wickedness and degradation, but in the moral shape he is slowly rising to assume. We are to take him in his highest achievements and his noblest possibilities. We are to take him with his moral ideals even more than with his achievements. We are to think of the highest illustrators of manhood, of the saints and martyrs who have gone to their death rather than deny the truth, of the philanthropists who have lived self-denying lives for the good of their fellow-men, of the men and women who in quiet, inconspicuous stations or in the stress of life's conflicts have stood firmly for the right at whatever cost to self, of such lives of faithful affection, of stainless probity, of duties well discharged, as we have all seen in some realm or other of this common human life we share. We are to think of those in whose faces shine the Beatitudes, who are of humble spirit, who are peacemakers, who are merciful, who hunger and thirst after righteousness, who are pure in heart, who go about doing good. These are our patterns for the fashion of human life, and not they who still live in the company of base passions, and are still of the earth and the beast, earthy and animal only. And all these are revealers and apostles of an Eternal Goodness. Not only do they reveal the moral purpose of the universe, but they are sharers and sustainers in its accomplishment.

> "For Mercy has a human heart;
> Pity, a human face;
> And Love, the human form divine;
> And Peace, the human dress.
>
> "And all must love the Human form,
> In heathen, Turk, or Jew;
> Where Mercy, Love, and Pity dwell,
> There God is dwelling too."

Thus we have our Trinity, as science permits it. Power, Intelligence, Goodness,— these are the threefold manifestation of the creative World-energy. Power, Wisdom, Goodness,— these make our triune God. Nor is there a merely fancied resemblance between this idea and the philosophical trinity of the later Platonic school in Greece, which the early Christian thinkers transformed into a theological Trinity. Out of the mystery of Eternal Being, the vague Source of all power and life, came, these ancient philosophers taught, the Logos, or Creative Word, the Word of Wisdom of which the Old Testament apocryphal writer loved to discourse, the "Word made flesh" which makes the theme of the proem of the Fourth Gospel. And this old doctrine of divine incarnation is true, only (as it has become one of the commonplaces of liberalism to teach) it is not exceptional for one man, but is the law for humanity. This Creative Word, of Power, of Wisdom, of Love, incarnates itself in human character to-day, full of grace and truth; and we may behold its glory. Through human lives, bent on the errands of truth, justice, mercy, and love, it is striving still to lift the whole race of humanity above the sway of ancestral animalism into the higher life of self-controlling reason and moral law. The Power is from everlasting to everlasting, ever before our eyes; and a measure of it is organized in our human brains and hands. But Wisdom, too, reacheth from one end to another mightily, and "it enlighteneth our eyes." Power is only executive, Wisdom is creative; and Goodness, even our human goodness, completes the threefold creative work on this earth, and has been compared to the Holy Ghost of the ancient Trinity, whose "white wings stoop, unseen, o'er the heads of all."

RELIGION AS THE AFFIRMATION OF GOD IN HUMAN NATURE.

ONE of the best definitions of religion I have ever seen I met recently in a printed discourse by a minister of the Swedenborgian church. It was this: "Religion is the affirmation of God in human nature." The dialect of the discourse was somewhat technically theological, of the style peculiar to the disciples of Swedenborg; yet, in the main, the thought contained in this definition was developed simply, rationally, and naturally. The quickening of the soul to the perception of truth, the purification of the heart from all evil impulses and lusts, the instinctive action of conscience in denouncing wrong and approving the right, the consecration of the will to carry out into external deeds the behests of these inward perceptions of truth and rectitude and disinterested love,— these were depicted as the essential conditions and evidence of the influx and indwelling of the life of God in the human soul. The writer, for instance, further said that "the spiritual church of God is no other than the indwelling and irradiation of truth and mercy and justice and peace in all man's nature, coming from the centre, the temple where abides the Lord, throughout the whole earth of man's consciousness that silently listens and willingly obeys."

This definition of religion as the affirmation of God in human nature seemed to me peculiarly suggestive at this time, as offering possibly certain meeting-points of enlightenment and reconciliation amidst the religious doubts and controversies which agitate the mental atmosphere of the present age. The contents of the definition, it is true, present no new thought. To affirm God in human nature is that doctrine of the immanence of God in humanity which Theodore Parker made so familiar in his preaching, and which has now become one of the commonplaces of liberal religious thinkers, and is not even a stranger in more evangelical writings. But "the affirmation of God in human nature" is an expression of the same truth in less scholastic, simpler, and therefore more impressive phrase. Let us, then, consider this new aspect of our old and familiar doctrine, "Religion is the affirmation of God in human nature."

The subject, as it presents itself to my thought, divides into two parts: first, as a doctrine of enlightenment and reconciliation among current criticisms, doubts, and disputes concerning religion; second, as a doctrine of practical reconciliation and applicable to the exigencies and struggles of personal life.

If we apply the method and results of science to the various problems of religion, and if we interpret the proposition contained in this definition of religion thereby, it seems to me that light will be thrown where there is now much darkness, and a unifying principle be discovered for resolving certain antagonisms in religious thinking, and for bringing discords into harmonies. There is, for instance, the old idea of God as a being external to the universe, making and ruling it from his seat above the heavens, and communicating his will to man by supernatural inspiration and miraculous agencies,—an idea that has become thoroughly discredited by science, and finds little support among philosophical thinkers to-day, but which keeps its hold, though a hold becoming more and more precarious, among the mass of uncultivated people, if they have any religious beliefs at all. On the other hand, there is the wide-spread disbelief in this kind of Deity, both among cultivated and uncultivated people, combined with a professed incapacity as yet to attain to any other and rational conception of God; and this kind of denial calls itself atheism. And, again, there is another type of belief about Deity which denies the old theological conception of a God outside the world, making the world in six days, and ruling it from a throne of sovereignty above the heavens, but which yet recognizes, within and behind all the changing activities and phenomena of the world, some power from which all things proceed or depend,—a power, however, which it declares an inscrutable mystery: this is the agnostic position,—a mental position frankly confessed by a large class of people at the present day, and the penumbra of whose doubts overlaps a very much larger class, including a multitude of persons who still keep their connection with churches. Now, to what does science lead us for belief on this great primal question of Deity? Of course, science — physical science — does not profess to have the problem of Deity for its object. It is investigating the forces, forms, organisms, creatures of the finite world. But, in pursuing this investigation, it has necessarily come into contact and conflict with the old religious conception of the creation and government of the universe. And it has not done this without furnishing materials for at least a partial new conception of a Power corresponding to and taking the place of that Sovereignty to which the old theologies gave the name of God. If science has not made this new conception so complete in particulars and so definite to the human understanding as was the old, this is not because the scientific conception is smaller than that of the ancient theologies, but because it is vastly larger and more truly infinite in its comprehension.

Now, keeping within the limits of scientific allowance, what kind of conception of Supreme and Divine Being is permitted to us? Herbert Spencer answers for agnosticism thus: "There remains the one absolute certainty, that man is ever in the presence of an Infinite and Eternal Energy from which all things proceed." That gives us the essential and original idea under the Hebrew Jehovah-conception, "The I-am-that-I-am," or underived Eternal Being and Power. But, through the doctrine of the gradual evolution of the worlds and all their forms of life, combined with the doctrine of the conservation and correlation of forces, we are scientifically permitted to clothe this Infinite and Eternal Energy, in whose presence we ever are, and from which we ourselves proceed, with a certain history and attributes. In this part of the universe with which we are acquainted, we know that this Eternal Energy has manifested itself in the orderly development of finite forces, structures, organisms, and life; and on this planet, in the gradual ascent of life from the lowest and simplest forms of sensation to organisms more and more complex and expressive, until finally man appeared, and the Infinite and Eternal Energy in him broke into self-reflective thought and moral sensation, into speech and song and free co-operative volition for furthering the Eternal aim and process. Keeping strictly in the pathway through which science leads us, where could these human faculties of reason, of moral sense, and of moral volition, have had their source, and whence can they derive their continual being and validity but in that Infinite and Eternal Energy from which all things proceed? We can scientifically give no other account of them than that they are finite manifestations, vital organic forms and expressions, of that Eternal Energy itself. But what is this Eternal Energy but the scientific name for the Power which religion has called God, or Jehovah, or Brahm, or Deity? The name matters little: each nation or language has its own. But they are all attempts to denote the one Great Reality, the "one absolute certainty" of a Power eternal, in whose presence we ever are, and that not only comprehends but penetrates us every moment with its law and life, and is the substance of our mental, moral, and affectional being. If science tells us truly of the orderly sequences of life through which the Eternal Energy travelled until it appeared in the human consciousness, what escape is there from the conclusion that those inward perceptions of truth and rectitude and disinterested love that manifest themselves in the human consciousness are part and parcel of the very substance of that Eternal Power? or, in more religious phrase, are the manifestation and life of God in human nature?

And, to my mind, it appears both reasonable and credible that all thoughtful minds now holding the various and antagonistic beliefs to which I have referred should come gradually into accord on this central truth, the resultant of science, that the Infinite and Eternal Energy, or God, has its embodiment and revelation in human nature, and that ultimately it should become a generally accepted fundamental principle that religion is the affirmation of the Eternal Divine Law, Purpose, and Life in the intellectual and moral nature of man. The traditional adherent of the old theological conceptions would come to see that he has not thereby lost his God, as he may now fear, but that, in lieu of his localized distant Deity, he has found an infinitely larger and grander conception of God, bringing him infinitely nearer, a literally omnipresent and vital Helper in every act and moment of life. The sceptic and atheist, seeing that the ecclesiastical types of Deity had become obsolete and were relegated with their kindred to the shadow-land of mythology, could bring no logical objections to a conception of Deity suggested and substantiated by the science which they profess to take for a guide. They would see that their criticisms, many of them just, have been directed, not against this eternal root of the Deity-conception, from which there is no logical escape, but against the superstitious fancies which man's infantile imagination had fastened upon it. And the Agnostic, while still holding that the Infinite and Eternal Energy cannot be absolutely comprehended by man, and that it is vain that the human mind, by its metaphysical theologies, should attempt to analyze and elucidate all the attributes of Supreme Power, would nevertheless be logically compelled to confess that the being and character of a Power, whose gradual unfolding in nature and humanity is the one field where all our science makes its researches and discoveries, cannot possibly remain a wholly unknowable and inscrutable mystery. Why should not the agnostic, the sceptic, the atheist, the theist of all types, Christian and other, come thus to unite in the reverent pæan, which even the sciences now sing, to the Power that was and is and is to be, and that organizes its august purposes and high behests in the rational and moral consciousness of man?

A similar ground for amity may be found for bringing together the old disputants in the Christian Church about the doctrine of incarnation. The affirmation of God in human nature is, as we have seen, only a statement, in the more familiar phraseology of religion, of the scientific doctrine that the Eternal Energy, working its way upward through various orders of organic life, finally produces and embodies itself in the organism of man, in whose capacities of rational thought, of moral perception and volition, and of disinterested love, it reveals its own purpose and secures a finite helper of its own kith, in the execution of its aims. And this is, essentially, the doctrine of incarnation. Man is the offspring of the Eternal Power in a larger, higher sense than are the lower creatures which have come from the all-producing Energy. Man is the moral offspring of the Eternal Power, and revealer, therefore, of its moral nature. Man can thus legitimately claim conscious sonship and heirship to Deity. The rational and moral character in him, since it can have no other source, is of the same substance and character with the Eternal Power whence it proceeds. Not all men, indeed, give evidence in their lives of this great fact of legitimate kinship to Deity. They who give high and full evidence of it are very few.

But the germinal possibilities of moral character are in the human race and, in a measure, in all individuals. It is but natural, however, that those who have incarnated in their lives most of the Eternal and Divine should have been regarded in ages of the world's simplicity of thought as having been miraculously endowed and born. So we even speak to-day of exceptionally great intellects as "godlike." And thus the doctrine of incarnation as a process exceptional and supernatural arose. In Christendom it was only Jesus that was the Son of God; in a large part of Asia, only Buddha. But science to-day is teaching a larger fact, that comprehends all exceptions and belittles all alleged miracles,—the fact that man, in his mental and moral capacities, is the veritable incarnation and responsible vicegerent of Eternal Power on this earth. "The history of Jesus," as Emerson said, becomes in this view "the history of every man, written large."

Still again the various religions, with their conflicting claims and bitter contentions, may find terms of peace in the recognition of religion itself as the affirmation of God in human nature. Now the religions each have their founders and prophets and scriptures, each claiming to reveal the one true God. But the one true God is not provincial, but universal; not tribal, but of all races and nations; not now and here, but everywhere and of all time. When science says that the Eternal Energy has embodied itself in humanity and disclosed necessarily its own character and purpose in the rational and moral faculties of human nature, it points to the path of reconciliation among the now antagonistic religions of the world. They all claim rightly to be in legitimate connection with the Power Eternal and Divine. They all claim rightly to have some revelation of that Power, which, though they may claim for it supernatural origin, has actually come to them through the natural utterances of the rational and moral consciousness of human nature. Here then is their ground of unity. They are but different developments and manifestations of the same Power, branches from one common root, or, as Paul phrased it, "There are diversities of operations, but it is the same God who worketh all in all."

But it is more than time that I turned to what I named as the second division of my topic,—the practical application of the definition of religion as the affirmation of God in human nature to individual and personal needs, or its reconciling power in the actual struggles of life. And I touch here a subject, a central and fundamental truth of religious life, let me say, so momentous in its bearings, so solemn in respect to the responsibilities it devolves upon every one of us, that I know I can only treat it very inadequately. Though I have touched it or treated it scores of times in the course of my ministry, I have never yet been able to treat it to my satisfaction in the depth and breadth and height with which it sometimes presents itself to my mental vision. This subject, the Life and Power of God in the Soul of Man, was the subject of the first sermon I ever wrote; and, if in the last sermon I shall ever write, I could rightly deliver the message on this great theme toward which my thought aspires, I should deem it the highest crown my life work could receive. Here in this truth I am convinced is the gospel which this doubting, troubled age most needs,— this age of material prosperity and ambitions, this age of many threatening and perilous evils, but of noble moral and humanitarian aspirations. Amid these conflicting aims, here is the mediatorial motive needed for guidance, health, safety, and genuine progress. Could it be given to me to go through our land to proclaim with adequate power this gospel, I could ask for no higher mission. Here is the reconciling, atoning, saving religion of the future,— the gospel that is alike needed in the marts of trade, in the halls of politics, in the industries and professions, in homes and churches and social life.

Religion as the affirmation of God in human nature; religion as the proclamation of the veritable incarnation of the Eternal Power, with its attributes of intelligence and moral purpose in the human faculties, not by supernatural, exceptional inspiration, but naturally and inherently there in the very substance, fibre, and organism of the faculties themselves; religion as the organized presence, power, and life of God in the human soul,— how can any one of us so bring this truth before ourselves that we may actually comprehend it and behold it and feel it in all its mighty import? That capacity within you to discern truth from error; that mental loyalty to truth which will not let you betray her when the highest motive controls you; that conscious drawing of your hearts toward the highest rectitude, which only gives you ease and joy when you follow it; that sense of moral purity which shrinks instinctively from all uncleanness of thought and conduct; that impulse of disinterested love which summons you humbly to serve rather than selfishly to enjoy; your gifts of reason; your abilities to overcome difficulties, to transform nature's blind forces into benefits, to conquer vice and triumph over sorrow; your aspirations after knowledge; your domestic affections; all your noble enthusiasms for right and duty; the law laid upon all your faculties to do the utmost service with them for human good,— these are all not merely channels into which the Divine Life flows as if from an outward source, but they are the very energies themselves of the living power of the Eternal, vitally organized in the very substance of your being, and energies that are ever striving through you and in you and in all human beings toward the production of nobler forms of character and life, and of social welfare. This is the momentous import of our doctrine that religion is the affirmation of God in human nature. With this sovereign majesty of responsibility for the well-being and progress of the world, if I interpret the lessons of our latest science aright, is man literally and actually invested.

Nor does the critic have any valid ground for his question who asks, Since human nature proceeds from the one Infinite and Eternal Energy which we now identify as God, why must we not call human nature wholly divine in all its impulses, motives, and doings? The Eternal Energy itself takes care that no such consequence can follow. The God within is his own witness, and testifies clearly what parts of human nature are temporal and earthy survivals of material and animal law, and what parts are vital with eternal and moral purposes. Our doctrine does not teach that God is human nature, but that God is in human nature. Individual man, like the primitive human race, must subsist for a time through the various motives that spring from self-interest and self-gratification. But self-interest is never normally an end in itself. It is only an instrumentality for the accomplishment of some universal good. It is only for universal and eternal purposes that the Eternal Energy can care. Its high law can have no part in providing for personal partialities, nor demean itself to offices of purely selfish gain or pleasure. It is of the very essence of the religious consciousness, when it is awakened, to annul all interests and gratifications which are bounded by self, and to subject all the self-seeking propensities to the service of the general benefit. In his capacity as a free agent man can pursue the ends of selfish gratification; but, so far as he does so, he is irreligious, he loses the godlike from his nature, and sinks back under the sway of carnal and material law toward the meagre existence of the brute and the clod. But, obeying the God that is within him, man rises ever upward into successively larger and richer realms of mental, moral, and spiritual life.

Our faculties thus clothed with this majesty of Divine Sovereignty, how great the profanation and crime, and how overwhelming should be our shame, if we put them to base uses, if we harness them to the pursuits of selfish avarice and cunning and to the appetites of the flesh! For all such debasement and defilement, the hells open at our feet with ample retributions. The very faculties will dwindle and perish under persistent misuse and abuse. Yet heaven, too, is no distant place nor time, but lies level with the true mind, the pure heart, and the consecrated will. The God that is within human nature is a Power ever ready at hand in all the storms and stresses of life, and needs not to be invoked from afar. Prayer is the excitation of the higher and heavenly faculties of our own natures to take and hold dominion over the impulses of the heart and the conduct of life, and to redeem us from the sway of our own temptations and sins. The Divinity does not have to be waited for, but waits itself, at the very spot of need, for man's soliciting gesture and effort. If men will draw the lightning of the skies to do their daily errands, or harness fire and steam for their steeds, and the power comes also sometimes to kill and to maim, man must know that the Deity to whom he is to pray for averting the peril is the Deity enthroned in the intelligence and skill of the human faculties. If we are summoned into the valley of the shadows to part there with companions whom we have cherished, in the hushed chambers of our own hearts and in "the work of our hands" shall we find the rod and the staff that are waiting to comfort us. The cure for earth's distresses is committed to man's keeping. The elements of Divinity are within him, the elements of heaven are right around him. To his intelligent and consecrated will is given the task to transform the errors and ills of earth into the moral prosperity and gladness of heaven. Who of us will not with renewed alacrity enlist in that godlike service?

RATIONAL GROUNDS FOR WORSHIP.

In calling your attention to the question, "What is worship, and are there any rational grounds for it?" I wish to say at the outset that I use the word "worship" itself with a rational discrimination. It is one of the old religious words which, because of errors and superstitions surrounding them, have fallen largely into disuse among liberal thinkers as damaged phraseology. I am not myself accustomed to employ the word without explanation expressed or implied. In the ordinary ecclesiastical sense it means, of course, some specific act of adoration or homage to Deity or deities; and this act may be performed by a Christian or pagan, by a Jew, Mohammedan, or Buddhist, according to their respective beliefs, by every kind of idolater as well as by an enlightened devotee. It may be the turning of a prayer-machine, as among some of the Asiatic Buddhists, or the counting of beads, as in the Roman Catholic church, or a dance of ecstasy, as among the dervishes, or an act of silent aspiration, as among the Quakers, or a great burst of music by voice and instruments, as in many Christian and other churches. All these and any other acts, under any kind of religious faith, which are believed to give the participants special access to the Deity or deities of their faith, are rightly classified in religious history under the term "worship." Yet, into whatever empty and meaningless formalities many of these acts have fallen, and however superstitious, idolatrous, and corrupt they may seem to any of us,—and the idolatries are not all among the so-called pagan faiths,—the word "worship" has, when we analyze its origin, a very excellent meaning; and at the root of the practice there is a vital truth which is not yet outgrown, and which is capable of enlightened and beneficent interpretation. In itself, etymologically considered, worship means "the condition of attaining worthiness." The word is of Anglo-Saxon origin; and the first syllable of it means "worth," and the second syllable signifies "means," or "instrument," or "condition" (literally, "vessel," it is probable) for bringing the "worth." In this sense, certainly, it is a very good word to keep. And it is with this underlying sense that I use it in this discourse, with reference to the religious usage of the assembling of people together for some kind of specific and public expression of religious thought and feeling. It is of this kind of usage that I propose to consider whether it has any rational grounds of continuance. Not a few liberal thinkers to-day are disposed to doubt, or even to deny, that there are such grounds. And, in contending that there is a rational basis for worship as thus defined, and as such public services may be conducted, I want to make two or three definite preliminary statements.

First, I do not believe and have never taught that Deity dwells more in any edifice called a church than he does in our homes; nor that we can ever set apart any place, and make it by any verbal formula of consecration a divine temple; nor that genuine worship of the Eternal depends on special place or time or form of speech, or architectural structure. The universe is God's temple. In nature around us he both reveals and hides himself. He may be found on the mountain-top or by ocean's shore. The Eternal Power smiles for us in the beauty of the roadside flower and of the orchards, or may meet our thought as we gaze upward to the overarching blue sky,—that all-embracing, bending vault of the heavens, where our Aryan ancestors in Asia, centuries before the Christian era, found their highest symbol of Deity and named it "Heaven-Father." Looking, therefore, at outward nature alone, we cannot go outside of God's temple. We cannot find the smallest spot in all space, nor contemplate a single force in the whole realm of existence, but that Deity is there.

Further, and in a still deeper sense, the human soul is God's temple. The Eternal dwells and lives and moves in humanity. In human character, true, loving, beneficent, is his highest revelation. This is what one of our hymns says:—

> "God is in his holy temple:
> In the pure and holy mind,
> In the reverent heart and simple,
> In the soul from sense refined."

So we shall not find Deity in any church unless we have brought him with us in our minds and hearts; that is, unless we find him through the pathway of some desire for a better perception of truth and for purer life, through sincere desire for nobler thinking, nobler loving, nobler doing. Nor, again, do I forget that this "pure and holy mind," this "reverent and simple heart," this enkindling of a solemn purpose to live more uprightly, more unselfishly, more nobly and purely, this aroused devotion to high objects of beneficence, may occur elsewhere than in a so-called house of God. It must come most surely to the earnest mother, as she sits thoughtfully by the cradle of her new-born child. It comes whenever the young man and young woman take each other in the holy vows of a true marriage. It comes in many an incident of home life where heart touches heart to the awakening of new hope and firmer resolve for the good. It comes whenever a great temptation in the conventional life of business or fashion is overcome, and the soul is rescued to live henceforth upon its own integrity. Whenever and wherever the human soul is thus uplifted to see and to grasp for a higher good, there is worship, there is devotion, and there is God. And the soul that in any spot, by any means, thus finds him becomes his choicest temple. The grandest cathedral, the most beautiful temple, that human art ever built is not so amiable (to use the quaint Bible phrase), is not so fascinatingly lovely, so wonder-inspiring, as is the human soul when livingly consecrated to the service of truth and goodness.

All these things I firmly believe and teach. Yet I also believe in the great usefulness of a fixed place and time for special religious services. I believe in the Church as an institution which human society still needs for its highest good. Whether the Church is ever to be outgrown, whether this need is ever to be supplied in some other way, is a question which may be asked, and which some rationalistic thinkers do ask, but which seems to me to be a question that does not loudly call for present discussion. As to the future, it will answer it own questions. For the present, as I look around me and study the wants, the aspirations, the mental and moral condition of society, I am convinced that the Church as an institution is not yet outgrown, — in other words, that established religious usages and instrumentalities are serving humanity in a way which nothing else has yet been found able to supplant. Did I not believe this fully and thoroughly, I could not have faced a congregation Sunday after Sunday for more than thirty years, with the religious words on my tongue.

Of course I know that the Church, regarding it in the light of instituted religion as a whole, has tolerated and taught great errors and committed great wrongs. The saddest chapters of history, and some of the cruelest, are those that describe deeds that have been done in the name of religion.

I know that there are great sections of the Christian Church to-day which, by their doctrines and ritual, keep the intellects of their adherents in gross darkness and delay human progress. The Church needs vast transformations to fit it to do the work now demanded of it. But those transformations are coming. I see the beginnings of them even in churches that are still far from me in respect to beliefs and forms of worship. I believe, therefore, in the Church, not as it has been in the past, not as it is in the present, but as an institution capable of reformation and growth. I believe in it as having its origin in a vital human sentiment and idea, but as having become malformed through gross errors. But the sentiment and idea are genuine, and are still an organic part of the human mind demanding expression; and, when duly enlightened, they will convert the Church and its varied instrumentalities into an institution in full harmony with rational thought and humanitarian objects. That is the hope which animates my heart as a religious believer, and that is the purpose which has impelled me to cast my lot with radical religious reformers.

And it is from this position and point of view that I feel moved to speak these words to-day in behalf of the Church as it may be liberally organized. There is a significance and value in religious institutions which a large class of liberal thinkers seem to me seriously to overlook. This class of thinkers regard religious institutions as fatally involved with superstitions and false beliefs which must inevitably pass away; and so they are iconoclasts. They would sweep the Church out of existence or, at least, leave it to a process of natural neglect and decay as the increasing light of reason and science shall show it to have no valid basis in truth. But I claim for religious institutions ample validity on the ground of reason,— yes, on the ground of science and of a scientific philosophy of human nature; for the Church, not with its errors and superstitions, but reformed and elevated to its own ideal possibilities.

And my first reason for the continuance of the Church, as thus defined, is that it stands for the moral and spiritual interests of mankind, for the higher life of man as distinguished from those pursuits which are devoted to gain-getting and to the feeding and clothing and sheltering of the body. Now I believe that it is a historical fact that religion, notwithstanding all its corruptions and false teachings, has always in essence stood for this higher life, for an ideal beyond and better than the actual, for something more than the pleasure of the senses and the satiety of physical appetite. It has stood for a law of mental and moral restraint upon the body and its desires. It has stood for high commands of right and duty. It has held out the promise, either for this world or some other, of a better and happier life for mankind, when the evils and sins of their passing existence should be conquered and known no more. The literature of all the great religions testifies to this sense of a higher life. All the great prophets of all faiths have sought to kindle and strengthen these aspirations for higher than physical satisfactions. And to-day there is no question among people whose testimony is worth consideration that there is this higher life; that is, a life not given over to uncontrolled physical license or to the amassing of material wealth, but a life following the high leadings of mind and conscience and heart to felicities that are of a mental and spiritual order. This will be admitted even by those who hold a materialistic philosophy. It will be asserted by aggressive iconoclasts in religion like Ingersoll. There is a lower life, devoted to the physical senses and pleasures and to material ambitions; and there is a higher life of mind and heart and conscience. Now I say that religion represents and has always in a sense represented, even under its false creeds and strange practices, this upper and aspiring side of human life. It has taught that man may live by immortal principles and for a deathless destiny. And the Church, taken at its average at the present day, expresses for human society at large, though but in poor, pitiful, and stumbling fashion, this upward look and aspiration, this belief in and reverence for the higher law of life. And, if the Church in the average has this signification now, even encumbered as it is with false doctrines and with traditional usages which have lost their meaning for the present age, how much more effectively might it express and serve this purpose, were it emancipated from its blind thraldom to outgrown creeds and traditions, and brought up abreast with the growing light and truth and humane endeavors of this new time!

And no one, surely, can deny that a powerful influence on this upper and better side of life is needed in this age. It is especially an age given to material hopes, enterprises, and pursuits, an age of commerce and mechanical ambition and wealth-getting, an age when man is struggling with the material world to master its forces and drain to himself, for his own acquisition and enjoyment, its riches. All this is well, if kept controlled for serving the higher acquisitions of mind and heart and soul. But, as yet, this higher control does not to any mastering extent disclose itself. It is an age of Mammon-worship and of the power of Mammon. The amassed and quickly accumulated riches show themselves too often in pandering to the lower and animal life, in increased comforts and luxuries for the body, in multiplying every sort of means of self-indulgence, in pampering physical appetite and every form of desire for physical pleasure, in ostentatious parade of dress and equipage and costly festivities, and, alas, in the more positive vices of gambling and other dissipations that attach themselves to vulgar wealth and fringe the borders even of reputable society in all our large cities and at the fashionable places of pleasure resort. There are persons of wealth who have learned how to use their wealth for noble objects. But these appear to be the exceptions. The majority seem not yet to have learned that high art. These know no way to show their wealth except on their persons or their houses or their horses, and in devising a round of festive excitements for every season to fill up the year. And this spirit has infected nearly all classes of society. Families of smaller means ape, in narrower way, these false methods of the rich, and actually stint themselves in respect to some of the higher satisfactions of life which are within their reach in order that they may put on the appearance of vulgar fashion. Thus moral earnestness in all grades of society is very much at a discount, and shines with a beauty all the greater in the cases where we do behold it. The old-fashioned virtues of simplicity and self-denial in respect to the material pleasures of life, for the sake of a high aim which the mind or the conscience has set, are becoming too rare; and young people are bred too much under the idea that they must be having "a good time,"—their conception of "a good time" being generally some form of pleasurable excitement for the senses,— or else they are not getting their share of life's satisfactions. Thus, all through society, the aims of people are set upon the lower, material objects of life, and the actual standard of conduct is self-indulgence rather than self-consecration. The power of Mammon, too, with its selfish greed, is fatally corrupting our politics, so that it is often said that an honest poor man, though well fitted for the duties, cannot afford to enter political life, or is not allowed to enter it by the political rings. And business has developed a code of conduct of its own, on the plea that it cannot live by the ordinary moral code of honesty and sincerity.

Now, against this prevailing lowness and practical materialism of human life, this pampering indulgence of the flesh, these strong forces of selfish greed and cunning and sensual pleasure, the Church stands proclaiming for humanity higher hopes and nobler satisfactions, or should so stand. Though it does its work very imperfectly, it is to be honored for the attempt to do it. It is its function to recall to people the fact that there is a part of human nature which is capable of loftier themes than the rise and fall of stocks or the fluctuations of trade or social festivities or a neighborhood's gossip. It is its high office to summon people to a place where one moral law is to be declared for all sorts and conditions of mankind,— for the rich and the poor, for politics and trade, for the home and the street. It should hold up before bewildered and stumbling consciences the attractiveness of the virtues of purity, temperance, self-control, sincerity, mutual justice and beneficence between man and man. Above all, it may point out the value of those priceless and immortal possessions which, whatever may be the outward lot, even though it be one of deprivation, hardship, and sorrow, are the inalienable property of the pure heart and the upright mind. In a word, the Church stands, when it fulfils its mission, for the life of the spirit and for the joys that are the fruit thereof, as against the life given over to the sway of material passions and objects. Matthew Arnold summed up his characterization of Ralph Waldo Emerson by classing him as one to whom after generations would resort as "the friend and aider of those who would live in the spirit." So would I claim the continuance of the Church, rationally organized and open to advancing truth, because it is, and may be vastly more than it now is, the friend and aider of those who would live in the spirit.

But I go farther than this. I have another and still deeper reason for my belief that religious institutions will in some shape continue for supplying a need of human nature. This reason is that they express, as nothing else does, man's sense of his relation to that Supreme Power in the universe which science calls the Eternal Energy in all things, which religion has called, in simplest phrase, the Most High, but which is really beyond and above all our definitions and names. We in our English tongue say "God"; yet the word only hints at an Infinite Reality which outrides all our powers of thought. But, because this Supreme Power is more inconceivable and more fraught with mystery than some of the old creeds represented, it is none the less a real power, and one with which we daily have to do. If any think to construct human life without this factor, however much they may quarrel with the theological representations of it, they certainly have cast off as well all logical reckoning, having given up that which is not only the Highest, but the basis of all,—

"Path, Motive, Guide, Original, and End."

Religion may be defined, in its strictest philosophical sense, as the human consciousness of relationship to this Power and the effort to practical harmony therewith; and religious institutions, including the so-called services of worship, are an organized expression of this relation and effort. Their function is to deepen and strengthen the consciousness of the relation and to keep actively alive the sense of human obligation to Divine Law. And, by the new interpretations of Divine Power which science is giving us, I believe that the obligations of mankind thereto are strengthened rather than weakened. On this point I am compelled to take issue with the current teaching of some of my radical friends and colaborers in the work of religious reform. One of these in a recent address said: "Duties to man and duties to God is the common classification. But there are no duties to God, in that sense, . . . and the only duty there is to God is a duty to man." And another said on the same occasion: "God needs none of our devotion: he has all the honor and glory that he wants; but man needs to be uplifted. It has heretofore been, 'Everything for God, and nothing for man'; and now we wish to change that and say,

'All for man, and God will take care of himself.'"
I have great respect for the mental ability of both of these friends, and their earnest moral characters I reverence. I have entire sympathy, too, with the motive underlying these utterances, and understand their point of view. Their moral indignation is excited, and justly, against the formalistic worship, the merely ceremonial acts of piety, which have prevailed and still prevail so largely in the Church, while the pious devotees and the churches in which they dominate utterly forget the weightier matters of justice and mercy to man. In denouncing religion and worship of this sort, I go with these critics to the full. And there is ample Bible authority, if that be needed, for such denunciation in the scathing words with which Jesus and Isaiah rebuked these hypocritical worshippers of their respective times, who made many prayers, but forgot the moral law. Such denunciation comes, indeed, from the deepest places of religion.

Nevertheless, I believe that that old phrase, "duties to God," as something more than though always implying "duties to man," has still a distinct and valid meaning. At least, to my mind, to deny the truth of the phrase leads to a greater untruth than to affirm it. With all respect to these objectors, it seems to me that in these utterances their thought is still entangled in the meshes of the theological creeds which they have discarded, and hence their logic in this particular halts; and their radicalism, after all, though so sweeping, does not go down to the root of things. Both of them are sons of orthodox clergymen, and their early training was under the old creeds of Orthodoxy. It is difficult for those who up to mature life have been indoctrinated in that faith, and then change their belief for liberal views, not to continue to associate religion and religious institutions with the false conceptions which they have abjured. When I speak of religious services as a special expression of human obligations to Deity, and as still having in that sense a true and very vital meaning, I am not thinking, as these critics appear to be, of that theological image of a majestic being seated with sovereign power in the skies, whose ear is pleased with praises, and who hears and answers petitions, like a human monarch. Not at all. Nothing whatever of that Calvinistic Jehovah-conception of Deity is in my mind. I am thinking of the Infinite Energy which is, at every moment, the law and life of the universe, and of which on this planet man himself, with his moral sense, capacity, and aspirings, is the highest manifestation. I am thinking of a Power as Source and Sustainer of this universe, entirely compatible with the scientific doctrine of evolution. Take even Herbert Spencer's latest statement of his unknowable principle that is at the root of all the world-forces, transformations, and phenomena, "the Infinite and Eternal Energy whence all things proceed,"— take even that for a definition of Deity, there would be very ample and solid ground for the idea of obligation to this Power. Man is indebted to it for all that he is, and for all that he is capable of knowing and doing and enjoying. From it come his very ideas of justice and kindness and of all other duties to his fellowman. That which so nobly serves him he is bound in turn to serve. He is not only gifted to see the ideal right which is the aim of the universe, but he is equipped with faculties to help the aim onward to realization. It is evident, therefore, that our free-thought friend must have been thinking of his father's idea of God when he said that God needs no devotion and help from us, but will take care of himself. The Calvinistic God did, indeed, take care of his own interests, and elected man to grace or doomed him to reprobation solely by his own almighty decree, let man do or pray as he would. But the God of the evolution philosophy, the Deity of reason and science, does need man's thought, man's devotion and help, in carrying forward the plan of the universe; for man has been admitted as a co-worker with the Eternal Power toward the realizations of the highest beneficence and happiness, and is under obligations, which he cannot ignore, to render his best service. It is, thus, from our duty to serve the highest Law and Life of the universe that our duties to man are derived. And one of the friends to whom I have referred recognizes this thought in the same address. He says: "It is at no man's option whether justice and honor bind him. Man no more creates the moral world of obligation than he does the physical one of fact: he has only to fit himself into it, and let its sublimity make him sublime. Man is not the summit of things. As the heavens bend over his body and the stars unalterably shine, so the moral law arches over the soul of man; and he is greatest as he bends in lowly worship to it."

Now, I do not say that this Spencerian conception of the Ultimate Power contains all that can be rationally included in the idea of God. I have quoted this because it is pretty generally accepted by rationalistic and radical thinkers to-day. But, even if this were all that can be affirmed, it leaves ample room not only for a religious philosophy but for religious institutions. It declares man to be every moment in the presence of an Infinite and Eternal Power which has given him creation, sustenance, life, and not only physical life, but mental and moral life; and in his mental and moral life has given also the law and the possible self-direction by which his life may ascend to larger capacities and richer realizations.

What a realm of high themes is open for human thought by such a relationship as this! What heroisms of endeavor does it make possible! This Infinite Energy is a living power: it is the inspiration of the life of the universe and of the soul of man. More literally from such a philosophy than from the old theology even may man exclaim, "My heart and my flesh cry out for the living God,"— for more and more of that vital creative power within, that perception of and obedience to the law of life which shall be health to body and mind, inspiring purer purposes and lifting to saner thoughts and joys. Among all the institutions of man shall there not remain one which shall attempt to express this august and mysterious, but most vital and real and fundamental of all his relationships,— that relationship from which he cannot possibly escape? and not only attempt to express this relationship, but to incite people more fittingly and worthily to feel the high obligations it involves and to inspire them with stronger purpose to perform well their part in this high partnership wherein divine law is executed through human action? So long as the human heart is capable of being stirred to loftier and more heroic impulses by earnest speech on the highest themes, or by music and poetry and art, or by the silent sympathy that leaps from heart to heart when numbers come together with a common purpose, so long, I think, will some form of outward temple stand,— stand as a symbol of living union between man and the Most High, and serve as a vestibule through which the worshippers may pass to that inner worship which is in spirit and in truth and in living character.

THE WORLD'S PARLIAMENT OF RELIGIONS: ITS SIGNIFICANCE AND POSSIBLE RESULTS.

It would seem as if great eras in the progress of mankind should be marked outwardly by great events. Yet this is not always so. At least the date historically accepted as the beginning of a new era may have been distinguished by no incidents which at the time were noted as extraordinary. In such cases posthumous legend, generations afterward, is apt to weave fitting dramatic draperies of circumstance for signalizing the new historical departure. But, again, great epochs in history are not infrequently marked by correspondingly conspicuous events, by incidents which at the time were seen and felt to be great and epoch-making. Particular battles have changed the political maps of continents and the destinies of nations. There have been eminent ecclesiastical councils whose decrees have fixed the religious beliefs of men and women for centuries. The adoption of the Declaration of Independence by the Colonial Congress was a most meet and noble birthmark of this American republic of sixty-five millions of free people. In the nineteenth century, and especially in this latter half of the century, the progress of mankind has been so marvellously rapid all along the lines of human activity, and more particularly in the development of material civilization and in the advancement of learning, philanthropy, and all branches of science, that we appear to be in the midst of a new era without being able to point to any one conspicuous event to herald its beginning. As a part of this general progress, a most remarkable evolution in religious beliefs and activities has been taking place. I am, indeed, one of those who believe that the forces that have produced the various religions among men have not exhausted their creative capacity, but that the intellect and heart of mankind to-day, in vital touch with these forces, are in the birth-struggles of a new religion. That coming religion which the sagacious Count Cavour predicted thirty years ago, that new Church which our own prophet-eyed Emerson foresaw and foretold, is actually dawning before the eyes of this generation, whether we all consciously behold it or not. Though evolving gradually from the old, it may rightly be called a new religion, because all the tendencies prognosticate an essentially new basis of faith, new articles of belief, new objects and methods of organized activity.

And of this coming religion the World's Parliament of Religions, in connection with the International Columbian Exposition in Chicago, is pre-eminently the most significant general sign that has yet appeared. It is an event known now in all parts of the world and to be memorable in history, and will worthily mark, in the annals of mankind, the opening of the new religious era, whose dawn we may discern on the horizon of the future. More than twenty years back a fond vision appeared to me of some such gathering of the world's faiths; but little did I dream that my modest prophecy was so soon to be realized,— realized in somewhat different purpose and shape, but even more grandly than I had dared to hope, and under auspices such as then I could not imagine as possibly uniting in a religious conception and enterprise so world-wide and nobly inclusive. It is from this point of view, and with this sense of the greatness of the topic, however inadequately I shall treat it, that I have invited you here to consider with me the theological significance and the possible practical results of that unique representative assembly,— the World's Parliament of Religions.

Even the great Exposition at Chicago — which, taken all in all, is the grandest representation of the achievements of human art and industry the world has ever seen — paled its glories last month before the august assemblage of the world's faiths. The eager crowds of people that filled Columbus Hall for seventeen days, and thronged in the passage-ways leading thereto, bore unconscious testimony to the fact, well stated by the presiding chairman, that "there is a spiritual root to all human progress." I shall ever count it among the inestimable high enjoyments of my life that it was my good fortune to be present at the opening of the Parliament, and to witness the procession of the World's Religions, as their representatives, walking arm in arm, entered the hall, and marched to the broad platform together, their faces all beaming with one harmonious and gladdening light. At the head of the procession walked the president of the Parliament and its auxiliary congresses, a Swedenborgian layman, and at his side scarlet-robed Cardinal Gibbons, the highest official of the Roman Catholic Church in this country. There followed Jew and Greek, Christian and Buddhist, Brahman and Mohammedan, Parsee and Confucian, Indian monk and Methodist missionary. All races and colors and nationalities, and both sexes, and all the great religions of the globe, and their various sects, Christian and non-Christian, there mingled together in one triumphal march of human brotherhood. And, when the platform was reached and the delegates were seated, the spectacle was as picturesque as it was august. The Japanese High Priest of Shintoism out-cardinalled the Cardinal in the gorgeousness of his apparel. The white-robed Buddhist from Calcutta won all eyes by the purity of his dress, as afterward he won ears by the purity of his English speech, and hearts by the purity of his sentiments. The high-caste Brahmanical monk from India made some of us stiffly dressed Americans envy his loosely flowing and graceful silken garments. The dignified Chinese Confucian was at ease in the richly colored garb of his native land. The venerable archbishop of Zante, at the head of a marked group of representatives of the Greek Church, was not behind his Catholic brothers in the decorative insignia of his high office. Even the women of India were represented by a young woman in native dress from Bombay, educated and eloquent. The whole scene presented the materials of a picture, which some great painter ought to have been there to sketch,—a picture of the coming peace among the faiths of the world. No one could have been present without feeling that he was a participant in an event which is to become one of the great epochs in the history of mankind.

That first day was devoted entirely to addresses of welcome, and of responses from the distinguished representatives of the various churches and religions there assembled. Though several of the speakers referred, with perfect courtesy and propriety, to their loyalty to their own faith and church, yet there was not a word throughout the day which jarred the harmony of sentiment that was felt and spiritually breathed as an atmosphere binding the speakers and the great assemblage together. As if by a common instinct, the speakers found their points of agreement, with surprise and joy that they were so many, and forgot for the time their differences. The key-note of the Parliament was struck by the chairman of the Committee of

Arrangements, Rev. Dr. Barrows, in his welcoming address, when he said, "We are here as members of a Parliament of Religions over which flies no sectarian flag, which is to be stampeded by no sectarian war-cries, but where, for the first time in a large world-council, is lifted up the banner of love, fellowship, and brotherhood." And that note was not lost nor slurred through the whole day; but from the varied voices and manifold tongues, together with one accord in one place from all round the globe, rose a grand symphony of common aspiration, faith, and hope. It was worth going several thousand miles to hear the same Presbyterian doctor of divinity from whom I have just quoted utter in his address of greeting such sentences as these: "Welcome to the men and women of Israel, the standing miracle of nations and religions! Welcome to the disciples of Prince Siddartha, the many millions who cherish in their hearts Lord Buddha as the Light of Asia! Welcome to the high priest of the national religion of Japan! Welcome to the men of India, and all faiths!" It was worth going thousands of miles to hear a Cardinal of the Church of Rome say, "As man is one people, one family, we recognize God as our common Father and Christ as our brother"; or to hear on the same platform a negro bishop from Africa exclaim, in his joy of congratulations for his people, "This is the first gathering of all the races of men as brothers since Noah with his sons landed on Mount Ararat." And it was worth a lifetime of sixty years to have lived to hear, in a city near the heart of this great country, educated and refined men whom Christendom has been wont to stigmatize as heathen giving not only equally cordial answer to this cordial welcome, but, out of their own Oriental faiths and their own scriptures, responding with utterance of the same humane and celestial sentiments of love, benevolence, toleration, brotherhood, and peace, and evincing the same aspirations after truth, purity, and holy living.

That opening day alone seemed suddenly to have advanced liberal faith in the world a hundred years. To none who was there and imbibed the spirit of that meeting could it seem possible that the fences between the faiths should ever again appear so high, the partition walls so thick, as heretofore they have been. The brotherhood of the faiths and the races was there actually felt and tasted. Henceforth this was to be no abstraction of theological thinking, no visionary goal of religious ethics, but must take its place as a vital, practical purpose, which religion and social ethics are to join forces to achieve. For the five or six thousand people who at different hours made that pentecostal assembly, it was demonstrated to the eye and the ear, to the head and the heart, that the faiths of the earth are of one root and may have by right culture one fruitage, that all the religions and races of men are realms of one Power, eternal, omnipresent, working in and through all things and all men for right and for truth. And these thousands of men and women, it was felt, could not scatter to their distant homes around the globe without a broader, truer vision, and a more brotherly purpose in their hearts to work henceforth, in their neighborhoods, communities, nations, and churches, somewhat less for sect and creed, and a great deal more for the new old gospel of the Golden Rule, which has found expression in so many of the faiths, and for peace on earth and good will among men.

By that first day's exercises the great company was lifted to this lofty ecstasy of a new and large religious enthusiasm, consecration, and hope. It was the expressions which were most pronounced and pointed in the direction of the widest religious tolerance, liberty, and charity, and of a growing unity, fraternity, and peace among the faiths of mankind, that were received by the assembled multitude with the most marked demonstrations of favor. More than once that day the hearers could not content themselves with the usual methods of applause, but rose spontaneously to their feet with waving of handkerchiefs and cries of enthusiasm. For that day, at least, the races, colors, and religions were lifted above all their differences and antagonisms, and their inmost aims and hopes flashed out and blended together in one glowing spiritual vision of a coming practical human brotherhood.

But could this pentecostal flood of fraternal love, this high altitude of spiritual enthusiasm, be sustained for seventeen days? When the Parliament should settle down to its more solid tasks, to the reading and hearing of elaborate papers, and the analytical presentation of the beliefs, aims, and work of the various churches and religions, would not the interest subside, the old differences and conflicts appear again, and the spiritual unity be broken and lost? There were those present on that first day who almost felt sorry that anything more was to be attempted. They were apprehensive lest this high tide of enthusiasm for religious and racial brotherhood should ebb, only leaving more painfully evident than before the artificial dykes and mud-banks which were still to separate those who for one long day had been lifted to the high places of spiritual vision, where they had discerned together the dawning era of fraternal amity and co-operation. But these apprehensions were not fulfilled. Popular interest in the meetings increased rather than diminished, and was sustained to the end. A crowd was ever waiting outside for admission to the crowded hall, to take the places of those who might come out, when the doors were opened between the readings of the papers; and there was hardly a single session when some unexpected incident did not occur or some specially fine sentiment was not uttered, arousing the large assembly to the same enthusiastic demonstrations that marked the first day. The key-note of the opening ceremonial day was not lost, indeed, in the work-days that followed. If twice or thrice a jarring note was heard, the discordant twang of some individual dogmatist's conceit, like Mr. Joseph Cook's, it was soon lost to sound, if not forgotten, in the overwhelming unity of spirit which carried the Parliament along, amidst all differences of belief and statements, in the line of its declared purpose. And, memorable as was the opening day, the Parliament must yet be considered in its entirety, before we can comprehend its full significance and the possible results which may flow from it.

On this question of the significance and possible results of the Parliament much needed light may be thrown by keeping in mind the specified objects for which this unique gathering was called and the rules which were to govern it. Let me, therefore, quote the most important of these from the printed statement of the general Committee of Arrangements early in 1892:—

OBJECTS OF THE WORLD'S PARLIAMENT OF RELIGIONS.

1. To bring together in conference, for the first time in history, the leading representatives of the great Historic Religions of the world.

2. To show to men, in the most impressive way, what and how many important truths the various Religions hold and teach in common.

3. To promote and deepen the spirit of true brotherhood among the Religions of the world, through friendly conference and mutual good

understanding, while not seeking to foster the temper of indifferentism, and not striving to achieve any formal and outward unity.

4. To set forth, by those most competent to speak, what are deemed the important distinctive truths held and taught by each Religion, and by the various chief branches of Christendom.

5. To indicate the impregnable foundations of Theism, and the reasons for man's faith in Immortality, and thus to unite and strengthen the forces which are adverse to a materialistic philosophy of the universe.

6. To secure from leading scholars representing Brahman, Buddhist, Confucian, Parsee, Mohammedan, Jewish, and other Faiths, and from representatives of the various churches of Christendom, full and accurate statements of the spiritual and other effects of the Religions which they hold upon the Literature, Art, Commerce, Government, Domestic and Social Life of the peoples among whom these Faiths have prevailed.

7. To inquire what light each Religion has afforded, or may afford, to the other Religions of the world.

. . . .

9. To discover from competent men, what light Religion has to throw upon the great problems of the present age, especially the important questions connected with Temperance, Labor, Education, Wealth, and Poverty.

10. To bring the nations of the earth into a more friendly fellowship, in the hope of securing permanent international peace.

CONDITIONS AND SPECIFICATIONS.

1. Those taking part in the Parliament . . . are carefully to observe the spirit and principles set forth in the Preliminary Address of this Committee.

2. The speakers accepting the invitation of the General Committee will state their own beliefs and the reasons for them with the greatest frankness, without, however, employing unfriendly criticism of other Faiths.

3. The Parliament is to be made a grand international assembly for mutual conference, fellowship, and information, and not for controversy, for worship, for the counting of votes, or for the passing of resolutions.

This statement of objects and regulations makes it clear that the intent of the Parliament was educational and fraternal, and not propagandist. It was to be a mutual school of religion, wherein the teachers were of all faiths and the pupils of all faiths,—a school of religion, with picturesque object-lessons in the study of comparative religions. And the prearranged programme of the school, both in its general tenor and spirit and in its specific provisions, made all the teachers, whether they were Jews, Christians, Parsees, Buddhists, Brahmans, Mohammedans, Confucians, or of any other faith, the peers of one another. Whatever might be their ecclesiastical positions or relations elsewhere, on that platform they stood as equals, each entitled to receive the same consideration and courtesy as every other. And there was no tribunal of appeal except the common reason and conscience of mankind. Whatever mental reservations there may have been in the minds of any of the speakers (and of course there were such) as to their own faith having a special divine origin miraculously attested, they agreed to meet in that Parliament, for the time being at least, other faiths as peers, and to obtrude no pre-emptive claims to an exclusive divine revelation and authority for their own. And in this fact lies the special theological significance of the Parliament. Whether logically comprehended as such or not, it was a practical change of base in the attitude of the Christian Church (excepting a few small liberal sects) toward the pagan world and other religions of the globe.

For, if it be true, as Christendom has been commonly taught, that the Hebrews had only a partial revelation of saving truth from God, and that that had been dimmed and lost by their disobedience, and that, when Christ came, the whole world was sunk in trespasses and sins and utter moral darkness, and that, without the acceptance of his atoning sacrifice, all mankind was doomed to eternal perdition,— if this familiar system of theology be true, then it logically follows that Jew and Mohammedan and pagan must be converted to faith in Christ's blood to save them or be lost. And, in accordance with this logic, the attitude of orthodox

Christianity toward the other religions of the world has hitherto been that their devotees were needy subjects for conversion to the one true and saving faith,— namely, the Christian,— but that they had no saving truth in their own faith. On such a basis of theology, since the non-Christian faiths were not regarded as holding any truths promotive of spiritual progress or efficacious to salvation, how could those faiths, with any logical consistency, be invited into a Parliament one of whose objects was declared to be "to show what and how many important truths the various Religions hold and teach in common"? Or if, as Christendom for centuries has been systematically taught, the world outside of Christianity is lying under dense spiritual darkness, then what utter unreason to invite representatives of non-Christian faiths into this great Parliament of Religions to tell us "what light each Religion has afforded, or may afford, to the other Religions of the world"! How can any "light" come out of "utter darkness"? Or if, out of Christ, the whole world be sunk and lost in trespasses and sins, as all orthodox pulpits used to teach, then what can Brahman, Buddhist, Confucian, Parsee, or Mohammedan have to tell us of the spiritual effect of their faiths on personal and social life, as the Parliament of Religions invited them to do? Or, if one religion only be true and all others false, how can there be any "true brotherhood" among them, which it was one of the expressed objects of this Parliament "to promote and deepen"? Can there be any "spirit of brotherhood" between truth and falsehood? If the old theological claim be sound that Christianity is the one and only absolutely true religion, and essential to salvation, then the only possible religious unity must be effected, not as the World's Parliament prospectus proposes, "through friendly conference and mutual good understanding among the Religions," but by the old way of absolute conversion of all the rest to the one that is true. Hence I affirm that the World's Parliament of Religions, by its recognition, in its statement of objects and in its programme, of the facts that the various great religions of the world hold certain important truths in common, that each of them, even the so-called pagan, may shed some light and impart some useful information for the others, and that among them may be fostered friendly conference and the spirit of true brotherhood, has given expressed and dramatic denial of the fundamental principles of that orthodox scheme of theology which has for centuries dominated Christendom.

Similarly, it may be said that other faiths that have in times past been regarded by their adherents as containing an infallible revelation of truth unknown to other religions have now, by their representation in this Parliament, made an implied, if not open, confession of a change of attitude toward the rest of the religious world.

And this change of attitude among the faiths of mankind toward each other, to which the Parliament of Religions has given so dramatic an expression, can be no passing accidental occurrence. It is the meeting of converging tendencies which have for a quarter-century been noted in religious sentiment and thought, and been growing more and more marked every year. It is one of the results of the application of a more scientific method of study to the history of religions. It is a popular triumph of spiritual liberalism, due in part to such scholarly work as Professor Max Müller has been doing in England, and to the Hibbert Lectures, and the great scholars in France and Germany and Holland, who have been making of comparative religion a science. It is due in no small degree to many of the Christian missionaries themselves, who, going out to the Orient to convert the so-called heathen to the one true faith, have discovered that they were not merely teachers, but had much of value to learn from the heathen faiths. One such missionary said in the Parliament the other day that he had found in the religion of the Hindus, behind the idolatries of the masses and the manifold names of deities, a very clear and pure conception of one Supreme Being; and it is a common thing now for missionaries, especially for the more observant and thoughtful among them, to acknowledge not only this, but the high value of the native moral codes of the people they are to convert. The Parliament of Religions has come as the natural effect of these various causes, as the picturesque climax of these converging intellectual and ethical tendencies. And let me say, further, that the Parliament not only significantly marks a change of mutual attitude among the religions of the world, and a special change both in attitude and method on the part of orthodox Christianity toward non-Christian faiths, but this changed relation carries with it by logical implication a radical change of base from that scheme of Christian theology which has hitherto given motive and nerve to Christian churches for the work of their foreign missions. If the basis of the Parliament of Religions were to be stated with logical consistency, it would be in effect an affirmation similar to that which has become familiar in late years to liberal religious faith; namely, that all religions are more or less divine, and all of them more or less human; or, as stated with more scientific accuracy by one of the prominent speakers in the Parliament, a representative of the "Broad" Church of England, "All religions are fundamentally more or less true, and all religions are superficially more or less false." And if methods of missionary work were to be shaped in logical accord with this basal affirmation, and upon the model of this Religious Parliament's own method, missions would hereafter be conducted not on the principle of aggressive propagandism and absolute conversion from one faith to another, but on the principle of mutual education.

In strict accord with its declared intention, the Parliament passed no resolutions; and there is not the slightest probability that it could have adopted any statement embodying what I am about to say. None the less it was in itself one of the most eminent of the increasing signs of the times that religion is preparing to abandon its ancient basis of authority attested by miracle for that infinitely surer authority which it finds inherent in the constitution of human nature itself and in the vital relations of human nature to the universe. The ancient type of miracle is really dwarfed to-day before the stupendous wonders which science discloses as facts of nature. And if religion is to keep its place and power in the modern world, it will not longer appeal to the thaumaturgist's art nor beseech an unwilling god to declare himself by breaking the august and splendid order of his daily works, but will search and toil rather to find the ways of harmonious human adjustment with that order itself. Leaving the region of miracle and the multitude of fanciful speculations and conflicting theologies which have sprung therefrom, religion is beginning to plant itself on the more solid ground of a few simple and fundamental principles which must commend themselves to the cultivated reason and conscience of mankind the world over. Many years ago Ram Mohun Roy, the originator of the Brahmo Somaj movement in India, published a book entitled "The Precepts of Jesus." It was a most excellent collection of the ethical and spiritual sayings of Jesus skilfully separated from their New Testament setting in miracle and myth. When called to account for this book by some of his Christian friends in London, who charged that it robbed Christianity of its supreme credentials of authority, Ram Mohun Roy replied that these sublime precepts would commend themselves by their own worth to the minds and hearts of his countrymen; but, if the appeal for their authority was not to their own intrinsic truth but to miracle, they would secure no standing in India, for the ancient religion of India had miracles far more wonderful than any in the New Testament. Now the Parliament of Religions, whatever might be the views of its individual members, and though they joined in no written statement, stood practically in the same position with Ram Mohun Roy. Its harmony of spirit and its very existence were possible because its members were for the time being united on a few fundamental principles which commended themselves as true to the common reason and conscience of all. And they were joyously content with their simple platform of "Truth for authority, and not authority for truth."

There have been opponents of the Parliament of Religions in Christendom and in other faiths,— some of them powerful opponents ecclesiastically considered, notably the Archbishop of Canterbury and the Sultan of Turkey. Most likely these opponents have perceived the actual logical incongruity between the Parliament and their professed creeds, have seen how the missionary religions especially among which Christianity and Mohammedanism have taken the lead, were giving away their own case by consenting to meet the other faiths on terms of equality and fraternity. But, powerful by position as these opponents are, there appeared no gaps in Columbus Hall because of their absence. Their faiths were represented by subordinates and subjects who had not the fear of authority before their eyes. From a logical point of view the position of these opponents may be worthy of greater admiration for its soundness than was the attitude of some of the Parliament's speakers, which was that of naked emotion with no shred of logic to cover it. Yet the advance movements of mankind are not generally made in the strict grooves of logic. The impelling forces of progress are found rather in ethical motives and sympathies of the heart, which may be only dimly conscious, or not at all conscious, of their relation to any system of thought. So it is safe to take our position with the progressive sympathies and the heart-instincts that are carrying mankind forward to larger, truer, and more loving life, even though they may be able to give a very poor logical account of themselves. As Emerson said of prayer, "In your metaphysics you have denied personality to the Deity; yet, when the devout motions of the soul come, yield to them heart and life, though they should clothe God with shape and color. Leave your theory and flee,"— so would I say of the World's Parliament of Religions. Though the Roman Catholic and the

Greek and the Presbyterian and the Mohammedan, and representatives of other creeds, may perchance have found it somewhat difficult logically to square their presence there with their theological beliefs, yet it was cause for devout congratulation that they fled their theory and followed their sympathies; that, though logic might forbid, they came and shook hands together, and talked together of the truths they held in common, and looked withal so radiantly happy in their fraternal action that I for one was very happy to be there, too, to help cheer on the whole illogical proceeding. I prefer to go forward with followers of the heart, though their movement may have no logical coherence with the theology of the head, rather than to do mental homage to the stanchest logicians, who are held fast and stagnant in the morass of false theological premises. To paraphrase Emerson's sentence, "When the fraternal motions of the soul come, yield to them heart and life, though they should lead Jew, Presbyterian, Mohammedan, Greek, and Catholic to join hands as cobrothers in faith. Leave your logic to take care of itself, and flee to the strongholds of the heart." And the logic will take care of itself. By and by it will catch up with the larger action and make a new statement to cover it.

Hence I look for great good to come to mankind as a result of the fraternal mingling of faiths in this Religious Parliament. For one thing, I believe it will help toward these larger statements of faith and a revision of old creeds. Among those who have come under its influence — and they are by no means limited to the people who were in person at the meetings — the sectarian spirit must be less narrow, the dogmatic temper less dominant. The new creeds may contain fewer articles and much less of the metaphysics of theological speculation, but a good deal more of brotherly love.

But here, lest I should be charged with making a plea for mere emotional sentiment in religion as against logical thought, let me say that, after all, the conflict of which I have been speaking is not so much between logic and sentiment as between two different lines of logic in our mental activities. The logic of your creed is one thing: the syllogism may be technically all right, but the premises of it all wrong, and very antique. And that is what is the matter with the creeds of the English Archbishop of Canterbury and the Turkish Sultan, which those high ecclesiastics have brought forward in condemnation of the World's Parliament of Religions. But, on the other hand, there is another course of logic at work, perhaps, in your mind (at work, it may be, unconsciously) toward a new creed from different premises. Beneath the fraternal religious sympathies and the heart's ethical instincts there is a logic of thought. They are not mere baseless flights of feeling. What says Science of men's relation to the Eternal Power, to which all the great religions apply some name to signify Deity? That all men, of whatever race or faith or color or nation, live therefrom and therein; that all men, therefore, are its offspring: hence that all men are brothers. There, or in similar terms, is the logic which is beneath your fraternal sympathies. There is the rational thought supporting the demand of your conscience to treat your fellow-men as equals with you in origin and entitled to like opportunities with you for life's achievements. There is the philosophy of your heart's instincts when you hasten to the aid of a fellow-man in distress; though, if your heart's instincts are healthy and sound, they do not wait to be prodded to the Good Samaritan's duty by philosophy. Yet the philosophy, the reason, the logic is there, to be called into service if need be, to convict dull consciences of neglected duty, and to stir laggard hearts to brotherly kindness. Now I believe that this kind of reason, of logical thought, of scientific knowledge concerning the common origin and the social relations of men, has been in late years working, burrowing, more or less clearly or dimly, in the minds of great numbers of thoughtful people all round the globe; and from this wide-spread thought have largely come the fraternal impulses which have produced the World's Parliament of Religions, in itself a most practical and vivid illustration of the thought. And, the Parliament having been such a brilliant success,— a triumph beyond even the ardent expectations of its promoters,— its influence will now react to strengthen and multiply the thought which was its root, and to keep alive those active sympathies of practical fraternity which are the very life-breath of the thought. If the thought be not exercised in the vital air of a large liberty, it will dwindle and perish.

But I look not for its death, but rather for its growth and increase,— the green blade to-day, but the ear will follow, and then the full corn in the ear. This idea of human fraternity, of a fraternity of faiths as well as races, is to be a potent factor, I believe, in writing the creeds of the future and moulding the work of all the faiths and churches. There will be much less in those new creeds than in the old ones of attempts to define God, but there will be a great deal more about the needs and duties of man. The extensive work of foreign missions sustained by Christendom will gradually develop new methods consonant with this idea. There will be less talk of conversion, more of education and elevation. There has been of late a dreadful fear in the orthodox world that to cease urging on the heathen that their ancestors who never heard of Christ are in the bottomless pit of helpless perdition is going to cut the nerve of missionary effort; but this dread, it may be hoped, will not much longer trouble the minds of devout Christians. Even the venerable American Board of Commissioners for Foreign Missions, in its late sessions at Worcester, seems to have felt a whiff from the new religious breeze blowing from the Chicago Parliament, and has begun to adjust its sails, though cautiously, for a change of course. Who knows but that that aged corporation, relic of a by-gone time and theology, rejuvenated by a hundred new members and a new secretary, may yet come up abreast with the age, and at the next Parliament of Religions gather its missionaries and their expected heathen converts, still declining conversion, into one happy company under the bond of human fraternity?

But we must not expect, outwardly, any immediate great results. The progress will be slow: at first it may seem imperceptible. Yet it is coming. The great and powerful churches of Christendom are not going to drop their sectarian sceptres in the life-time of many, if any, of us. The benevolent Cardinal Gibbons, who, on the opening day of the Parliament, spoke with such entire sympathy with the larger breadth and brotherhood of the platform and seemed so fully at home upon it, when subsequently he gave his discourse on the service of his own church to the world, fell as if by habit and traditional beliefs, not corrected by scholarly research, into the extravagant claims that there was only the faintest glimmer of moral light on earth before Christianity was born, and that since that era Catholicism has led the world in advancing the interests of civilization and humanity. Thus many of the participants in the Parliament will drop naturally again into the routine work and phrases of the sects. Sectarianism and dogmatism have had such a vigorous life and held kingly sway so long that they will die hard. Their sceptres are beginning to waver, but few of us shall ever see them entirely prostrated in the dust. Yet we shall — nay, do already — see them floating the white flags of truce and amity and co-operation.

And when, too, we consider the differences among the religions of the earth, differences of ceremony and custom, and even of belief, which are based on differences of environment and the traditions of centuries, it is evident that it would be irrational to expect great transformations in any brief period of time. Some of these differences, it is likely, will remain in perpetual existence. Truth and sincerity do not require that all religions shall be pared and fitted to one pattern, more than that all individual persons shall be fashioned after one model of temperament. Such uniformity is neither to be expected nor desired. But, with the differences, there may yet be unity in spirit and aim and work,— unity, also, in the fundamental principles of belief and purpose. And this kind of unity among the world's faiths is already dawning. This is the fraternity of religions which the World's Parliament has made evident as a possibility, and has done not a little to further toward realization. More frequently than any other this idea kept pressing into utterance in the addresses of the seventeen days. "This Parliament," said the Catholic Archbishop of New Zealand, "begins a new era for mankind of true brotherly love." The eloquent and inspired Mozoomdar, apostle of the Brahmo-Somaj of India, that modern theistic church growing from the roots of ancient Brahmanism, said that he represented a religious society "whose only creed is the harmony of religions, and whose only denomination is the unity of all denominations." It was the white-robed Dharmapala who pleaded for "mutual benevolence, tolerance, gentleness, love, brotherhood, compassion," in the name of the gentle Buddha. And Prince Wolkonsky, of Russia, and of the Russian Greek Church, asked, "Why should it not be that all these religions which have so much in common should sink their differences and find a common ground of action in the interest of mankind?" Principal Grant, from Canada, exclaimed that it was cause for profound humiliation and shame that Christianity, with the example and teaching of its founder before it for nineteen centuries, had only just found the right way to religious unity and fraternity. The Brahman monk from India, Vivekananda, in orange-colored robes and turban, "fervently believed that the new liberty bell which rang that morning on the assembling of the Parliament was to ring out the death-knell to all fanaticism, to all persecution with the sword or the pen, and to all uncharitable feeling between brethren, wending their way through different paths to the same goal." Hon. Pung Kwang Yu, imperial delegate from China, found the famous word of his great teacher Confucius, "reciprocity," as expressing the sum of human duty, illustrated with new meaning and glory in the Parliament, which he called a noble school of comparative religion, where "each may discover what is excellent in other religions than his own." The high priest of Japanese Shintoism believed that "all the various religions of the world are based on the fundamental truth of religion, and that, since it is now impracticable to combine them into one religion, the special religionists ought at least to conquer hostile feelings, to try to find out the common truth hidden under different forms of religious thought, and to combine their strength in working for the common objects of the religions," and especially against wars and disputes between nations, and for international justice and peace, and for a supreme court of the world to take international disputes from the tribunal of war to the tribunal of equity and reason. Dr. Momerie, the Broad Churchman from England, said: "To each religion have been attached creeds and dogmas which the founders never anticipated. This conference will enable us to see more clearly the fundamental truths. It will show how unimportant are the differences of creed, and how important are the things on which we are agreed." The venerable editor of the New York *Evangelist*, Dr. Field, spoke of his training under the straitest sect of the Puritans, but of his own observations in personal travel among the different religions in the East as teaching him that they are "all sharers of the one Infinite Light and Love." A young Mchammedan delegate from Constantinople, with an unpronounceable name, said that "the young men of the Orient, from the waters of Japan to the Ægean, have the keenest interest in the outcome of this Parliament as a basis for the brotherhood of man."

And so the words of amity and brotherhood among the faiths kept pressing to the lips, and, white-winged, flew out into the free air. From Japan and Australasia, from China and Canada, from Greek Church and Quaker preacher, from English Churchman and American Presbyterian, from ancient Armenia and the newest State of the New World, the sentiments of brotherhood were heard, as they went their way, to echo and re-echo around the globe. It may almost be said, indeed, that this Parliament of Religions has given the creed of the coming universal Church, if such a Church shall ever grow out of the growing fraternity of feeling among the different faiths, and shall ever have occasion to state its beliefs. Though the Parliament stated nothing by resolutions, yet by general assent it seemed to be assumed, and individually was again and again declared, that the common foundation on which the various faiths stood there together was the recognition of Supreme Being, without any anxiety to make or require a definition of the supreme existence and attributes, a recognition of human brotherhood, and an expressed purpose to search for all truth and to toil unceasingly for human welfare. A church need not have a written creed, but it must have convictions and purposes if it is to be a vital power in the world. And for a statement of convictions and purposes, large, free, inclusive, and rational, I doubt if any religious organization can find anything much broader, stronger, or better than these four fundamental principles, corner-stones of the platform on which the Parliament of the world's faiths found its basis of agreements.

The possible results to which I have here referred as growing out of the Parliament are of the nature of changes to be effected in existing religious institutions and methods through the slow processes of evolution and under the transforming touch of scientific truth and of a clearer conception and intenser feeling of human brotherhood. But let me suggest, in conclusion, two ways in which a more immediate effect may be produced. First, why may not a Parliament of the World's Faiths be continued and perpetuated, its sessions to be held every five years in different cities and countries of the globe? Such meetings would serve to keep alive and further to cultivate the spirit of fraternity among the faiths, to which so strong an impulse has now been given, and would hasten the forces of evolution in their transforming, educating, and unifying work. An ecumenical council every five years, to consist of representatives from all the great religions and churches of the world, selected for their learning, devoutness, character, and practical ability, would serve as a valuable international exchange for religious ideas and methods, and might become a mighty power in advancing the interests of humanity and establishing the principles of justice and peace in the conduct of nations toward each other. Second, and finally, why should not those who are finding sectarian traditions and methods of any kind to be fetters, those who have already come out to this large place of liberty, hospitality, and fraternity in religion, and care not for any of the denominational names and conflicts except as they may represent heroic history, those who stand now essentially on the fundamental principles which the great historic faiths of the world are shown to hold in common,— why should not these draw together and join their forces in churches of the new dispensation, in churches of the new covenant of man with man and of the new thought of the Eternal,— that new thought of the Eternal which science teaches carries in its bosom a closer, surer covenant between the Eternal Power and man than ever the Hebrews conceived to have been made between their nation and Jehovah? The name of this coming religion awaits. Its organization awaits. But its spirit, its thought, its aspiration, are here. They are in the atmosphere of this new age. They call for apostles to voice the new faith, and to organize its service around the earth. And of whatever name these churches may be, and whether they be new churches or old ones transformed by new ideas, may they be linked together by this common bond,

— in that, to use the quaint New Testament phrase, they shall all be "lively stones" in the structure of the coming universal, catholic Church of humanity.

> "Tread, kingly gospel, through the nations tread!
>   With all the noblest virtues in thy train;
> Be all to thy blest freedom captive led,
>   And Truth, the great Emancipator, reign."

SEALED ORDERS.

In time of war vessels are often despatched from port by governments under sealed orders. Not even do their commanders know their ultimate destination or the special mission which they are to discharge. They only know at the start the general direction which they are to take. They sail out on the expanse of the ocean with no particular port in view, but directed only to steer for a certain position of latitude and longitude on the open sea; and, not until that position is reached, are the sealed orders which they carry in their pockets to be opened. Then for the first time they learn whither they are to voyage and for what task they have been sent.

And this very aptly illustrates the course of human life in general. We all begin the voyage of life under sealed orders. Not a child is born whose future is not wrapped in mystery. There in embryo is the man or woman; but what will be the career of the man or woman nothing in the child fully foretells, nor can the parents prophesy it. What talents it may develop, what vocations will be chosen or necessitated, what tasks and responsibilities may be assumed, what trials and tragedies or what successes and happinesses may come in the unfolding story, — all these are a sealed book in infancy. We start in life on an open sea. We know the harbor from which we depart, and we linger near its familiar shores; but we know not the harbor to which we sail nor the duties which await us there. Yet Time is a master that outranks all other authorities, and bids us depart. We can only have, at first, general directions, which are to be given in parental training and education, and which are to take us, as it were, to a certain moral and mental latitude and longitude, where the orders which contain our calling in life may be opened to reveal the mission on which we are sent.

Yet these general directions are of supreme importance for the time. There is a certain mental and moral equipment which is necessary to any kind of success in life, whatever the vocation or career is to be. And this equipment is what the home and school training should give to youth. As these general directions at the beginning of life's voyage are all the guidance that we can possibly have, so it is a matter of the gravest moment that they be faithfully followed. The whole difference between success and failure in the special calling afterward may depend on such obedience. The commander who sails from port under sealed orders knows well that his first duty is to steer for the spot where his orders are to be opened. If he sail over the ocean according to his own free fancy before going to the spot indicated, or if he go in another direction, assuming that a certain lapse of time is all that need be considered before he opens his orders, he may open them too late, or too far from the place of service, to accomplish the task assigned him. If the English government despatches a naval vessel down the Thames to-day with orders to be opened when she reaches the middle of the North Sea, her officer does not go down to the Strait of Gibraltar to open them, assuming that his service is to be in the Mediterranean, nor does he go to the North Sea by way of the Atlantic Ocean. He knows that not only must he open the orders in order to obey them, but that space and time are important elements in respect to his being in a position to obey them when opened. He must therefore first obey implicitly the general directions he has received. In like manner, though we all begin the journey of life under sealed orders, unless, when the time for breaking the seals has arrived, we have reached through educational training a certain moral and mental position, we may not be able to accomplish the service to which our natural faculties call us.

But, even after the period of opening manhood and womanhood arrives, when vocations begin to be chosen, and the special allotments in life begin to disclose themselves, and careers to open, there is still a very large element of uncertainty mingling in human affairs. Man may be sure of his endeavors, but not always of the result of his endeavors. We may know our desires, our choices, our aspirations, but not whether this or that is to be the fulfilment. We may steer our course to a particular object; but what may develop from that object, what may be hidden behind it, we are unable to say. There are too many personal wills acting besides our own, too many forces in operation besides human forces, too many moral hazards on all sides which may touch our lives, too much of undeveloped and unknown possibility in our own natures, for any person to be able to say at the beginning of life's activities just what and how much he will have accomplished at the end. Thus we embark even on the sea of our special careers under sealed orders. Young persons prepare themselves for some particular work or profession,— for law, medicine, art, the ministry, teaching, trade, manufacturing, or mechanical industry; but they little know the special chances, associations, experiences, which their occupation may bring, and which may profoundly affect their characters and their happiness. Marriage is entered under sealed orders. Love is proverbially blind. It knows its present satisfaction. But it little foresees, and it is best it should not, either the possible heights of happiness which may be in store for it if it be genuine and remain true, or the possible disappointments and sorrows which may come even to the truest hearts and into the truest homes. Much less does it picture the depths of misery which may be the fruit of its own falsity; for of that falsity it cannot beforehand dream as even among the possibilities. The wife, entering the sacred ways of motherhood, goes down into the valley of shadows for the consummation of the hope of her heart and the hope of the race, but knows not whether she shall emerge on the side of time or the side of eternity. Or, safe from all perils brought, she stands amid the flock of her growing little ones, their mother, their responsible home educator, but still under sealed orders. She sees an opening faculty here, she watches an unfolding temperament there, tries to bring out the good and check the evil, under a keen sense of momentous duty, yet with an ever-growing consciousness that she is working amid mysteries. Could she only see what the future is to bring to these young minds,— these buds of mental and moral promise,— how the faculties are finally to turn, for what spheres the temperaments are to adapt themselves, by what means passion might best be trained to self-control, how much more easily could her great obligations be discharged! But she cannot see. The seal of the future remains unbroken. She can only do the best she can on present knowledge, and wait in faith for the time when the hidden orders can be opened.

This element of uncertainty clings to our careers through life. We are never quite rid of it, even though we reach life's goals and may be rich with its successes. The morrow is always hidden. Some sealed order that we little suspect may be opened with the dawn of another day. We may be called suddenly to face some sorrow, to grapple with some calamity. No life is exempt from a change of fortune. Sooner or later the harrow goes over us, the burden comes upon our shoulders, the messenger of death knocks at our door, the summons comes for us to meet quickly some unexpected emergency. And the way in which these orders are met which summon us precipitately to untried duties tests the secret core of character as cannot the ordinary responsibilities of life. For the latter one may be on his guard and make a special preparation. For the sudden emergency he must draw on general resources of strength, which may or may not be adequate for all duties. They are the elect souls who are in the best condition to meet and obey the hidden orders of life, at whatever spot or moment these may be opened.

And there are sealed orders that not any emergency in life, but only death, can open. As we came into this life under sealed orders, so under sealed orders do we make our final exit. We sail out upon the great sea of the hereafter, knowing not what awaits us. Even though there be a firm faith, an unshaken confidence, that the future, as the present, must bring life, there is yet no sure revelation, only conjecture how, where, what, that life is to be. The most ardent Christian believer does not profess to define the where or the how of his heaven. Though Spiritualism, with all its claims, were to be admitted, it really answers satisfyingly no questions that go to the depths of things save the fact of continued existence; and to many minds its petty details of professed revelation mar its evidence of even that fact. We go out of life, as we came into it, therefore, enshrouded in mystery. We leave life's familiar harbor and sail out upon the vast unknown, with only one unsealed order,— to set sail. All other directions are hidden till the voyage is begun. We know not whether the country to which that journey leads is beyond the verge of this planet or still connected with it, though invisible to any mortal eyes. Will the stars still be above us as pilots, or will they, too, be hidden? Question as we may, no answer comes. The orders are closely sealed. We only know that we cannot go beyond the limits of an infinite universe, that we cannot be dropped off into empty space, that, even "if our bark sinks, 'tis to a deeper sea."

Let us look at some illustrations of our theme of a public nature. When, four hundred years ago, Columbus set sail westward across the Atlantic, he, too, was under sealed orders. He thought he was his own master, thought he knew his destination,— the East Indies,— and that he had only to follow the chart in his own brain to obtain his expected results. But his ship carried other commands than any he knew, carried a higher master than himself; and, when these sealed orders, held in the hand of historic fate, were opened, it was not a new way to Asia that he was sent to discover, but the New World of America. Our

Puritan forefathers,— how little knew they of the results of their voyage, or even of the destiny in store for themselves, when they put to sea from Plymouth, England, for the New World! The one order open to them was to find a place where they would be free to follow their religious convictions according to their own consciences. But in the sealed orders which they brought from a Higher Power were the schools, the churches, the civilization, the character, the popular government of New England and a cordon of free States across the American continent, wherein soul liberty should be guaranteed to all. Our fathers of the Revolution, again, entered that contest with sealed orders in their pockets. They thought to obtain their rights as colonists under Great Britain. To resist unjust taxation, to escape the imposition of a foreign military police, to have the rights of Englishmen,— this was their aim. Separation from the mother country was not at first dreamed of. Even when Washington drew his sword in Cambridge as commander-in-chief of all the colonial armies, independence of Great Britain was a sealed book, of whose secret scarcely a whisper was heard. The same lesson is enforced in the remarkable career of that silent man of destiny, General Grant. In the modest beginning of his service in the war of the Rebellion who could have read his great ending? Though he was a graduate of West Point, and had somewhat distinguished himself as a young officer in the Mexican War, he was so modest, so little known, that his letter to the Secretary of War offering his services in any capacity was not deemed important enough to notice; and, on going to Cincinnati with the thought that he might find a place on General McClellan's staff, he went home again without even gaining admission to that officer's presence. He went back to the work of drilling the volunteer companies of Illinois, which he had taken up from pure patriotism immediately on the issue of President Lincoln's first call for troops, serving for several weeks without even a commission from the governor of his State. But all the time the sealed orders were waiting for him. The worth of the man for the work needed was disclosed whenever there came any kind of test. He was always equal to the task assigned, always ready for the emergency. And so the sealed orders, that contained his destiny and the nation's destiny enwrapped together, were opened one after another, as he went on from success to success, from command to command, until the final seal was broken, and the Rebellion went down before his legions at Appomattox. Or take a career the very antipodes of that of military success, — a career of commanding moral success. Garrison little dreamed of the contest on which he was entering when he began, a mere boy in years, to think and to write on the iniquities of holding human beings in bondage. The Eternal Power that makes for righteousness was testing the moral mettle of the man. It rang true, and little by little the sealed orders of his career were opened. Each duty, faithfully and courageously discharged, led to the opening of a larger duty. In the first number of the *Liberator*, in words that rang through the land like the shot of the embattled farmers at Concord and Lexington, he took command of the moral forces of the nation in the gigantic conflict against the domestic, commercial, and national power of the institution of slavery. He little thought that he was to live to see that power demolished. The drama proceeded, one act opening after another; and the moral commander was alert and prepared for every opportunity, equipped for every emergency in the long and bitter conflict. He counselled not with prudence, with policy, with wealth, nor with fame, — not even with the expediency of saving the union as the prior duty. His sole query was, What does justice command to-day? That order opened and obeyed, the next followed in due season, and the next, until the final seal in that contest, too, was broken, and there came the decree of emancipation, and the slave rose up a citizen and a voter.

All the great moral and religious teachers of the world confirm the same lesson, — Buddha, Confucius, Socrates, Jesus. None of them foresaw at the beginning of their careers what they were to pass through, what weight of duties they were to meet. They began their great missions under sealed orders. They went down to their graves without seeing all that they had done. They wrought in faith, and were ready to seal their testimony with their blood, yet were not permitted to see the full fruit of their works. Within their deeds lay greater deeds concealed. When Jesus went to be baptized of John, he knew not that he carried in his bosom an order to found a new religion, which was to abrogate the dispensation of John's baptism. Confucius began his pre-eminent career of public service in China when a youth of twenty years in being appointed to the humble, though responsible, position of keeper of the public stores of grain. As keeper of the stores he said, "My calculations must all be right; that is all I have to care about." And making his calculations right, putting his virtue into this simple office, the next year witnessed his promotion to the charge of the public fields and lands. Another order was unsealed. And then he said: "The land must be well tilled. The oxen and sheep must be fat and strong and superior. That is all I have to care about." And thus he went on, putting his whole moral faithfulness into whatsoever work he was called to do, until, passing from one office to another, he rose to the position of prime minister, and became the trusted adviser of kings, the moral censor of his country, the collector and transmitter of its ancient wisdom, and the wise educator and example for thousands of generations to come.

And such examples also teach that, though much of the most important work of life, on account of the element of uncertainty running through all human affairs, must be done as it were under sealed orders, yet this need not and should not lead to any doctrine of fatalism. These persons were able to do the duties assigned them when the time for the revelation of those duties came, because of their docility and their faithfulness in all the minor duties that went before. They had the ready heart, the equipped mind, the prepared spirit. By obedience to each day's command, as it had come to them, however small and however incomplete it might seem, they had placed themselves in the moral latitude and longitude where the larger order, when it was unsealed, could be promptly and effectively obeyed. Their own moral faithfulness to whatsoever light had been given had indeed led the way to the larger and clearer revelation, and made it possible.

Nor, again, is any important order that concerns present duty hidden. The sealed order is for the future. The bridge is not to be crossed until it is reached. But it will not be reached by waiting for it by the roadside. The duty for to-day is always an open one. It may be a humble one, the lot where it is cast may be narrow; yet it is none the less needful, and faithfulness to it none the less important. It is a necessary and artistic part of the great drama of life, without which the larger and succeeding duties will miss their needed preparation and support.

Further, there are certain moral qualities that are the essential equipment for the right performance of all life's genuine commands, whenever and wherever the seals shall be broken. These are the single eye, the pure heart, the incorruptible conscience, the humane sympathy, the unquailing courage and strength that can hold the helm to the line of reason and right, let storm and tempest rage, or sunshine allure. Whoever is thus piloted journeys as calmly and safely in night and storm as when he voyages by light and day under clear skies. These qualities make all duties performable, however suddenly revealed, all trials passable, all sorrows bearable. These furnish the constant woof for all substantial character as it is woven day by day, year by year, in the loom of time.

We are all spinners at Time's wheel. We must all contribute our part, great or small, good or ill, to the great world-life. Often we may not be able to see how our work is to fit in with the completed web of the whole, or to be of any avail. Often, indeed, we are blind spinners (as Helen Hunt Jackson pictures), working by feeling and not by sight. Yet feeling may become as sure a guidance as sight; and, if we are but faithful to the appointed task of the hour, we may do our work in faith and confidence and joyous hope. All good work finds its fitting place. It makes its own stability, its own qualities of endurance. Perhaps

> "Like a blind spinner in the sun,
> I tread my days,
> Yet know that all the threads will run
> Appointed ways;

I know each day will bring its task,
And, being blind, no more I ask.

. . . . .

"Sometimes the threads so rough and fast
    And tangled fly,
I know wild storms are sweeping past,
    And fear that I
Shall fall: but dare not try to find
A safer place, since I am blind.

"I know not why, but I am sure
    That tint and place,
In some great fabric to endure
    Past time and race,
My threads will have."

Such qualities as these keep the identity of character amid all time's changes, and through all duties and circumstances. One who is permeated with the spirit and power of such moral principles can never be at a loss how to act in any strait of life, can never be lost — can never be otherwise than at home — in any moral realm of the universe; and, when the final seal of all earthly orders is broken, and the summons is sounded to depart on that journey whence no traveller returns, such a soul cannot go to a strange country, but to a land with which it is already familiar. Moral realms are not separated by space nor time nor outward condition. Whoever lives a life of righteousness on whatever planet, in however lowly sphere, dwells now in heaven and inhabiteth eternity.

WHEAT AND TARES.

"Let both grow together till the harvest."— MATT. xiii. 30.

JESUS' parable of the tares, which were to be allowed to grow with the wheat until the time of harvest, suggests one aspect of the moral condition of human society that may profitably engage our attention this morning. Note that I take only the point of the growing together, and not the conclusion of the parable. Within the questions of the existence of evil and of the continuance of evil is involved the subsidiary question, Why should evil be allowed in such close association with good as to imperil the existence of the latter? And this question touches human life at so many practical points that it probably perplexes and worries more people than does the more metaphysical question, Why should evil exist at all? Evil and good are so intricately blended — in the relations of social life, in the home, in marriage, in problems of education, in affairs of politics, in questions of recreation and amusement, in matters of trade and business, aye, in the individual heart — that somewhere to almost every person the query must daily arise, How can I here, at this point of experience, secure the good and escape the evil that lies close beside it? In the midst of the commonest duties required of us there lurk temptations that might work our ruin. Accompanying our richest blessings come seeds of evil that may fructify in curses. Within our best hopes are possibilities that may overshadow them with despair. While we lift our heads into a clear atmosphere of joy, a deep chasm of disappointment and sorrow may be ready to yawn at our feet. We thrust forth our hands with courage and enthusiasm to the culture of certain virtues; we draw them back pricked with the thorns of vices that are growing on the same field. Thus, everywhere we find the wheat and the tares together, the good and the evil side by side, in the same soil, growing, of course, from different yet from intermingled roots.

Now, however much we might be disposed to complain of this state of things and to impeach the wisdom of the Power that has so arranged it, the complaint and the impeachment are alike useless. Wiser is it to accept the facts of existence as we find them, observe carefully the natural moral suggestions which lie in them, and then bring out of the facts the best result possible. It is very evident, from the experience of mankind, that good and evil are in such close neighborhood for a purpose, — at least, that the mightiest results pertaining to the world's progress have depended upon this proximity. On the mutual relation between good and evil on account of their necessitated existence side by side turns the drama of the life of mankind. This is the fulcrum of all historical movement,— the point whence we may trace the development and education of the human race.

Various attempts have been made from time to time, under the auspices of different religions and nationalities, to make an unnatural separation of good and evil,— to withdraw, for instance, good and pure persons into a society by themselves, to shut them off from contact with the motley world, in the hope that they in their protected enclosure would not only be safer themselves from the world's evil, but might send out into the world an influence for redeeming it. But no such experiments appear to have been successful in attaining either object. Such protected enclosures have not, on the one hand, kept out the power of evil. Corruption has somehow found entrance into these consecrated places. And, on the other hand, the devout persons thus set apart from the world, if they have preserved their own integrity, have too often become too ignorant of the world's condition and needs and ways to be efficient workers against its vices. So, in spite of all such attempts arbitrarily to separate them, the wheat and the tares have continued to grow together side by side.

We may say, indeed, reasoning from the history of the past, that the world has been built on the plan of self-improvement. Whatever Supreme Power may have initiated and vitalized the process of advancement, that process has been carried on through the action of finite agencies. Within the finite world itself have been stored the forces for overcoming and casting out its own evils. Though the agencies are necessarily imperfect, they have been gifted with the power to advance the world toward perfection. The good elements, by struggling against the evil, have increased their own strength, and have thus gradually brought the evil under their dominion. This is the law of the world's development and progress. It has been in a certain sense the law of the material world, and it is especially the law of the human world. Man has not been lifted out of evil toward good by any power extraneous to him and acting independently of his own exertions. The necessary regenerating power has been placed in man himself. He is himself the field of the struggle between the opposing forces on which his fate depends. His own education, enlightenment, moral advancement, are the result of the struggle. He secures the good, creates it, in fact, by conquest of the evil. To put the good and the evil, therefore, at once by an unnatural division into separate fields would be, if such a division were possible, a reversal of the plan of the universe.

First, the theory that in morals the wheat and the tares ought to be separated loses sight of the primary fact of all, — the moral improvement and salvation of the evil. It might be a very comfortable thing, if good people could be permitted to dwell together in a country by themselves, where they could have exclusive management of affairs. But what of the bad people who would thus be left together in a country by themselves? Are they to be left to go to perdition? left alone to their own folly and wickedness and wretchedness? left to prey upon and torment and outrage and still further to debase and dehumanize each other? Have the good no responsibility, no duty, no pity toward the bad? Such a plan would be as inhuman as it is unnatural. We can hardly suppose it possible that such a community of utterly bad people would be capable of regenerating themselves. And, even on the theories of supernatural regeneration, it has always been allowed that the supernatural power must have natural agencies for its communication. Hence the alleged need of the preacher, the missionary, the exhorter, the tract, the revival meeting, the hymn and prayer, and all the machinery and power of the visible Church for the sake of converting and saving people. The source of the regenerating power might be supernatural; but it is admitted that it made use of these natural instrumentalities to accomplish its objects, — that is, made use of persons already redeemed, already supposed to be good, to redeem and convert the bad. But the hypothesis that the bad are separated in a community by themselves and the good by themselves forbids any such intercommunication even for the sake of saving the bad. The gulf prophesied in that terrific parable of Abraham and Lazarus is already fixed, so that none can pass from one side to the other. The wicked are left to their doom. And hence the question comes, by way of corollary, whether that could be a genuine human goodness which could thus, for the sake of peace and quiet and its own unhindered development, separate itself from all contact with wicked people in some exclusive community? Are not sympathy, compassion, and helpful charity toward the wicked necessary elements of goodness? Can he be a good man himself who can let his brother fall into a pit at his side without an effort to save him? Love to one's brother man, shown in active endeavors for his welfare, is certainly the highest test of human goodness; and how can any manifest this quality who strive to get away from their unfortunate brothers when they most need their help? The very hypothesis of a separation of the good from the evil in the affairs of the world is shown to be logically untenable by the argument, *reductio ad absurdum;* since, if any persons should have a disposition to depart into some secluded retreat to care for their own interests and to leave the wicked to their fate, they would, by that very fact, prove themselves to be wanting in that benevolence which is the most essential quality of goodness, and hence would themselves have to be excluded from that select abode as not good enough. They would exhibit a moral selfishness, an ambition to secure the highest seats in spiritual places, an appetite for the first chance to the good things of personal enjoyment, which would certainly soon breed the dire results of evil in their new home if they were to be admitted to it.

And this suggests the further question whether any such division of the good and the bad as individuals, even if it were natural and desirable, could be possible. Who are to go with the bad? Or, harder question, Who will go with the good? Will you? Will I? Judged by our aspirations, our prayers, our endeavors perhaps, we would. But shall we be so self-righteous as to assume that our conduct would take us that way? Who is to draw the line, and where is it to be drawn? Do you say, Let it be drawn by the public judgment of the courts of law, by the line of prison walls? But how ineffective a separation would thereby be accomplished! You know that there are vastly more of wicked and morally dangerous people outside of prisons than in them. Would you draw the line at the openly degraded and socially outcast classes of population? But, again, you know that there are many persons who are morally degraded, and who, except for the accident of birth or wealth or sex, might be socially outcast, who yet move in reputable circles of society. And you know that, even in the classes called degraded and outcast, there are not a few individuals who have honest and true aspirations, and who, in spite of their surroundings, maintain a virtuous character. Will you draw the line, then, between actual virtue and actual vice wherever found, letting the line run wherever it will, separating families, passing through communities and neighborhoods without any reference to the lines of social distinction, drawing the bad out of good circles and the good out of bad, and thus dividing people according to their real moral worth, as it might be viewed by an Omniscient Eye? But what power less than Omniscience could survey that line? Nay, would not even Omniscience have to run such a line through individual characters as well as between individuals? Where is the person who, at least to his own eye, is wholly good? Even Jesus refused to be called good when the young man addressed him as "Good Master." And what man is there whom any one but himself would dare to pronounce wholly bad? The good and the bad, the virtue and the vice, intermingle in individual hearts and characters. The struggle goes on there, in the secret places of personal temptation and action, as well as in the broad fields of the world outside; and unless we are to have a mutilation of personal character, a division of our very personality, there can be no arbitrary separation of the good and evil elements in our earthly life.

I said above that the theory that in morals the wheat and the tares ought to be separated loses sight of the primary fact of all in the social education of the human race; namely, the moral improvement and salvation of the evil. But the questions just started, as well as the common experience of mankind, show us that the theory loses sight hardly less of the welfare of the good,—

misses, indeed, some of the principal means by which the good qualities of character are nurtured and maintained. There can be no question that many of the most substantial virtues of mankind are acquired by struggle with and conquest over evil. The finite moral consciousness itself appears to have been wrought out under the stern discipline of experience, to which the primitive human and ante-human races were subjected in the struggle for existence. And the education of this moral faculty, from its first rude manifestations to its present height of culture, has been by no smooth road, by no course of easy lessons, but by the severest conflict and battle with hindering conditions,— in short, by constant struggle with opposing evils. Whatever theories and fancies we may like to entertain of a possibly better world than our own, in which men should have been gifted from the outset with only virtuous desires and capacities, that certainly is not the plan of the world we live in. Virtue, according to the plan of our world, is a possession which man is to achieve by his career, not an endowment with which he sets out. There may be certain graces of character, certain excellences of spiritual temperament and moral disposition, with which, especially at this stage of hereditary moral accumulation, individual human beings may be born. But virtue is a quality of character that is not born, that does not appear in cradles, but has to be earned by the solid moral labor of life; and whoever starts with hereditary advantages at birth is only put under obligation to earn more, to reach a higher standard of virtue, than he who comes into existence weighted with an inheritance of moral evil. But, however we begin, it is the plan of the world we inhabit that a large measure of the discipline by which our moral education is secured comes through our necessary contact with evil. This is the school where the sinews of our virtue grow, and moral character is strengthened and established. So long as the moral ideal keeps its supremacy and enlightened conscience holds sway within, evil, whether it present itself in the form of moral transgression or of outward calamity, is only a challenge to more heroic self-command and to braver deeds of mental or moral conquest. In that conflict between the moral law that presses upon the conscience and the pressing, tempting thing which that law condemns, virtue is hammered and shaped into personal character. Out of this struggle in some one of its forms, with inward temptations or with outward evil conditions and wrongs, have appeared the heroes whom we honor, the saints whom we reverence and love, the philanthropists and prophets of all ages who still teach us to-day by their word and example. Upon man himself, indeed, has been placed the dignity and responsibility of detecting and overcoming the evil that besets his race, and thereby creating moral character and establishing society on a moral basis.

Many souls, it is true, in their earthly career appear to have succumbed in the struggle to the strong power of evil. With many more it has apparently been a drawn battle. But, with the world at large, and considering the whole history of the race, though the expression may seem a paradox, it is true that mankind has grown and thriven in virtue on the moral evils it has had to encounter. Think of the true and holy men, the noble women, whose lives are held in grateful remembrance for what they became and did, because the presence of human woe about them drew them out of selfishness into careers of disinterested beneficence! This fact of the transformation of moral evil into moral benefit, through some remedial spiritual process of counter-irritancy, may not, metaphysically speaking, give us a satisfactory reason for the existence of the evil. But, practically, it is certainly cause for congratulation, if evil must exist, that man has learned to turn it to so good account,— that, by the very effort to overcome its resistance, he has increased his vigor and capacity for virtue; and it is a strong argument for a divine element in his own nature, as also for a divine plan and purpose in the universe, that he has so learned.

And in human experience we have abundant illustration of the wisdom of the arrangement by which good and evil are allowed to exist together instead of being arbitrarily separated, both in respect to the effect upon the good and the effect upon the evil. We naturally shrink from sending out the young from the seclusion of well-guarded and virtuous homes into places where they must come into association with those who have not had their moral protection and who have probably learned not a little of the roughness and viciousness of the world. Yet experience does not show that those whose entire educational period has been kept carefully guarded under pure home influences from contact with the possible evil of the world make the strongest or most virtuous characters. They are quite likely to break down, when the emergencies of life throw them upon their own resources and the great temptations come in their careers. What is needed is that the young should take out from their virtuous homes such a loyalty to moral principle that they can effectively resist the evil influences that may come from any ordinary contact with rough or vicious associates. The home that can send out with its young this stanch fidelity to virtue, this inward loyalty to truth, to honesty, to purity, to manliness, not only saves them "unspotted" from the evil of the world, but through them wields a gracious, healthful influence that can but do something to redeem the manners and the morals of those less fortunately born and educated.

So in the single home. It is certainly fortunate, when we consider the whole problem of human advancement, that the virtues do not all appear in one household, the vices in another.

The strong and the weak, the virtuously disposed and the viciously inclined, are born into the same family, and are to be reared together. If only a wisely directing hand hold the helm, this may be no detriment to any, but a great good to all. The different individualities, the opposing and even clashing temperaments, may help to educate each other. The strong may give of their strength to the weak, and yet lose none in the giving. The virtuous disposition may check the vicious into bounds of self-control, and yet train itself to needed patience and charity in the process.

And, even in the marriage relation, it is, on the whole, fortunate for human society that the good are not always mated together and the bad together, but that here, too, the wheat and the tares, if tares there must be, are united; fortunate that love to a certain extent is morally blind, so that even saint and sinner may be drawn together in the marriage bond. There are, indeed, certain grossnesses of sin (more on the part of men than women) which should forever debar from the sacred relation of marriage, because not only the rights of the living, but the rights of the unborn, are involved; and there are certain gross excesses of evil which, on either side, and equally on both sides, may be deemed an adequate ground for breaking the relation when once formed. But, these exceptions aside, Nature knows her aim; and it is a beneficent one, when she makes love overlook faults, and see only merit and beauty, and so draws together characters of very different moral quality and temperament. And what is the aim? Not, surely, to degrade the higher character; for that, though possible, is never necessary. No: it is the lifting up of the lower, and the broader education of both, and, in the course of coming generations, the neutralization and elimination of the bad moral quality in the human stock. And husband and wife are faithless to these high educational obligations of the marriage relation when at any time, love being off guard, cold reason lifts the veil of illusion and bids either see in the other faults incompatible with love. Far better, excepting the extreme cases I have noted, is the sacred relation observed and honored by those who learn to bear and forbear, and forgive much evil, and who finally triumph over it and win the crown of a love purified as if by fire. And such instances are not infrequent,— instances where, though the grievance has been great, yet by persistent faithfulness to the marriage vow, remembering that each took the other in the fresh morn of love for better or worse, the saintliness of the one has at last conquered the sin of the other, and both have been blessed by the fidelity that won the victory. So again in society at large. It is wisely ordered by the very conditions of the existence of human society that the different moral classes and grades of mankind cannot live wholly apart from and independent of each other. They must come into contact, they must affect each other for weal or woe, whether they will or not. And here the responsibility rests chiefly upon the moral and cultivated classes. They are the leaders. They cannot live to themselves alone. They can only save and strengthen their own virtue by helping the ignorant and the vicious. Society is, indeed, imperilled from these degraded sources. There is moral poison in the contact, there is taint in the very atmosphere. But upon mental and moral culture is devolved the obligation and privilege to disinfect the atmosphere, to extract the poison. In thus redeeming others from the sloughs of moral degradation, the virtuous and educated members of society redeem themselves from the dangers of a refined selfishness. There are many social questions pressing upon our time with alarming urgency. They are not to be escaped. To try to get away from them into some quiet corner where we may be permitted to pursue our own vocations and follow our own tastes in peace and prosperity is cowardly. It is also in vain. The peace and prosperity cannot be secured; at best they will be but temporary, so long as vice and ignorance are left rampant to their own devices in any grade of society. These foes must be met by the culture and virtue of society, wisely and humanely, but firmly and persistently,— met at the ballot box, by the press, in legislation, in business, in the home, the school, the pulpit, the street, met everywhere where knowledge can be imparted and virtue get a foothold and philanthropy obtain a place for her lever, met not despairingly, not half-heartedly, but courageously, heroically, with fulness of faith and of hope, else will the kingdom of heaven not gain much ascendency on the earth.

I have spoken only of the application of the theme to our present earthly life; and this certainly is for us the most important application. Yet, though we may not dogmatize on a question where we have no real knowledge, I know not why it is not reasonable to suppose that the same principles will extend into any life that may be in store for humanity in the future. If we are to preserve our identity in that coming life for which we hope, it would seem that the life must consist of essentially the same elements and go on upon essentially the same basis as our present life. The things that make goodness here must make it there. The law of moral fidelity must be as binding there as here. Compassion, fraternal sympathy, loving-kindness, helpful charity, must be the same benignant active qualities in the heavenly as in the earthly life, only lifted up to purer intensity and freer scope. So I cannot conceive that in that other world evil is to be removed beyond the reach of goodness. I believe that the two must exist together there as here, so long as one needs the help which the other has to give. Why should death fix at once an impassable gulf between the good and the evil, so that mercy cannot pass from the one to the other? That good and evil characters are different in nature, and crave different satisfactions, and must needs enjoy different pleasures, is true; but they need not for that reason go to different and forever divided worlds then more than now. I believe rather that the change of relation between the good and the evil which death is most likely to effect is the lifting of them both into more favorable conditions for bringing the evil under the redeeming influence of the good; that, so far from being implacably separated from the evil, the good will have a better chance then than now to throw around them the healing sympathies of their love; and that this larger, better opportunity for such saving service will be one of the joys of heaven. Why, we believe, do we not, that this better opportunity and its attendant joy will surely come with the improvement of society even here on earth; and I can conceive nothing less than this as making the felicity of heaven. Surely, for a being with a human heart there can be no felicity in any heaven below which opens an unapproachable and irredeemable gulf of perdition. There as here the good and the evil must grow together till the time of harvest.

The harvest may be long postponed; but even man, in his brief years on earth, by his intelligent skill can make wonderful transformations in the plants and flowers which he cultivates, as well as in personal character. When the final harvest of all comes, may not even the tares be found fertilized from the pollen of the wheat, and the Infinite Reaper have only pure grain for his garner?

COURAGE OF CONVICTIONS.

The persons who have moved the world are those who have had the courage of their convictions; that is, those who have not only clearly, thoroughly, and firmly believed in certain principles and truths, but have also had the disposition, will, and vigor to act upon their beliefs and to endeavor to get them adopted and acted upon by other people. There is a class of persons who, in quiet retirement, like to work at problems of thought or in scientific research, but whose interest in their work seems to be chiefly a theoretical one. They manifest little care whether the truths they discover are made known to the world and adopted by other people or not. They might stand by their convictions, if summoned to do so; but they feel no call to enter upon a voluntary struggle to propagate and maintain them. They enjoy the work of discovery; but the work of propagandism is not to their taste, and they decline it. These persons have a use in the world; for the thought-problems they solve or the discoveries they make are taken up by other people, and are thus thrown into the current of the world's activities and made available for human benefit. But they do not themselves aim at that benefit nor seek actively to promote it.

They do not stand with their hands upon the levers of the world's movements. Their brain employment is for private luxury rather than for public profit.

But, if we look along the line of the world's progress, we see that the great leaders in that progress have been men of action as well as thought,— not, by any means, the men who have been most boisterous in action, not, certainly, the men — and there are many such — who have rushed noisily into action without the thought, not the men who have the activity and the dash and the courage, but no convictions, but the men who have both the convictions and the courage, convictions of truth worthy to be contended for, and the courage to stand up against all obstacles, to contend for them.

And these qualities are needed in about equal measure to make strong characters. If either be greatly deficient, character is necessarily weak and ineffective. If both be possessed in very large measure, supporting each other, then appear the great leaders of human progress. And, where both are possessed in exceptionally large measure with specially favorable adjustment to each other, there are found the few exceptional leaders of humanity, — the persons of such rare and conspicuous mark on the field of history that not more than a score of them can be counted in all the annals of mankind. In this small class, "at the top," — where, indeed, in every classification of mankind "there is always plenty of room," — are the founders of religions, the organizers of states, the thinkers and discoverers who, by the rare profundity and courage of their mental action, have revolutionized entire systems of thought and practice among their fellowmen.

As a noted example of this class we readily recall Luther, who, though not the most eminent scholar and thinker, nor even the noblest character of the Protestant Reformation, yet became the leader of the Reformation because convictions and the courage to stand by them were welded in him to the white heat of the most vigorous action. Savonarola was a man of the same calibre, and in some respects of even finer mould, who a half-century earlier preached a dawning Protestantism in Italy, in the face of king and pope, demanding a purer faith and cleaner morals, and going finally to the stake to expiate the crime of his courage and the audacity of his faith. And in the very beginning of Christianity there was Paul, a Hebrew Luther and the real founder of ecclesiastical Christianity,— he, too, was a man who had both strong convictions and a corresponding strength of courage to stand by them. The result was seen in the primitive systematizing and propagandism of Christianity. But before him, though of very different temperament, was Jesus, who unconsciously laid the basis of Christianity, but built no structure thereon. Yet he was a genuine leader in that he changed the thoughts and dispositions of the people who saw and heard him. Less theological than either Paul or Luther, he towered above them both in catholicity of spirit and in purity of moral discernment. Savonarola, perhaps, of all the great disciples of Christ, came nearest to him in character. But Jesus, notwithstanding his catholicity of temper and gentleness of spirit, stood not a whit behind the most vigorous leaders that have ever appeared in Christendom, in respect to depth of convictions and the courage to maintain them. The heart side of his character, the tenderness he manifested toward the penitent erring, and his ever active sympathy for the poor and the distressed have sometimes blinded the eyes of his disciples to the masculine robustness of his nature. A disposition has even been manifest to soften down and explain away some of the more vigorous of his denunciations of the formal sanctity and hypocritical pretences of his time as inconsistent with the idea of his gentleness and forbearance. But I would not take one iota from this side of the story of his life, even though the expression of it may possibly sometimes shock our ideal of a perfect Christ. Possibly our ideal of the perfect Christ lacks this very element of vigor which comes into the story of the real Jesus. Certainly, it was not merely the heart side of Jesus, gentle and sympathetic as that was, which made him the dominant character he was. Behind his affections and sympathies he had deep convictions and the courage to abide by them. He drew men and women to him, and helped and healed many of their troubles by his mere tenderness. But this was not the part of his nature that specially caused his career to make a new epoch in the world's history, and has drawn the admiration of after ages. His mission was to bear witness to the truth, and for this cause came he into the world. He lived in sympathetic and helpful heart-relations with the men and women right around him; but he lived, also, from and for deep convictions of mind and soul. For these he wrought and suffered and died. Persecution could not deter him from proclaiming them, danger could not daunt him. Though church and state marshalled all their powers against him, his courage did not blanch nor falter, until he sealed his testimony with his blood.

Others of the world's great teachers, in Christendom and out of Christendom, have had in pre-eminent degree this same trait of character. It was the courage of his convictions that gave Confucius power to remodel both the religion and the government of large portions of China. It was the courage of his convictions whereby Buddha and his followers, five hundred years before Christ, swept India with a religious reform which, in its relation to the more ancient Brahmanism, was not unlike the Protestant Reformation in Christendom. It was the courage of his convictions which made Socrates the father of a new standard of ethics as well as of a new philosophy in Greece. Though he wrote not a word, but, like Jesus, only talked, yet he so impressed his words on the minds of his disciples and the people of his city that the world has never lost them, and we have probably to-day almost as true a picture of his thoughts and character as had his contemporaries in Athens. His thoughts, too, were printed on the heart of the world in his martyr blood; and that is a printer's ink that never fades.

So, too, in the world of science, of discovery and invention, of statesmanship, of social and political reform, and on the lower field of generalship, the prime leaders are always those who not only have strong convictions, but a strong power to impress them upon others and to carry them into effect. The scientific man who, like Copernicus or Darwin, should find himself in possession of discoveries that must meet with obloquy and persecution before the world will accept them, would be no true devotee of science, and could be no leader in his vocation, unless he is ready to face the fiercest opposition without quailing and still hold by his opinions. Science in its progress has always had to join swords with theology and the Church; and hence its apostles have always had need of the martyr's courage, as not infrequently they have met the martyr's fate. What a power was Garrison in the anti-slavery struggle, peace-man and non-resistant though he was, because he possessed not only those clear moral convictions that were a candle to his own conscience, but had also the nerve to hold up those convictions as a burning candle before the guilty consciences of Southern slaveholders and their Northern abettors, though he had to face mobs and death to do it! Sometimes the courage is even a more important element than the convictions; that is, it is not necessary that the convictions should be very original or striking in order to insure a great and beneficent career, though it is necessary that they should be clear and strong. We cannot claim for Washington that he had a profoundly original mind. There were intellects in the Revolutionary era superior to his in the origination of ideas, as Adams, Jefferson, Franklin, Hamilton. Yet, take him all in all, in generalship and in statesmanship, Washington was the master character and leader of the American colonies in their perilous passage from colonial to national existence. Not brilliant in the power of intellectual conception, yet the intellectual principles from which he acted were clearly grasped by his mind and tenaciously held; but, what was more important, he had that kind of courage in carrying his ideas into effect which does not consist so much in a dashing assault as in judicious persistence. There were two generals in our late war who illustrated our theme in opposite ways. General Sherman was brilliant and inventive in plan; but, if anything, he was still more daring in execution. The danger with him was that his courage might hurry him into action without the support of a well-conceived and well-organized plan behind it. General McClellan, on the other hand, gave his whole mind to the problem of planning a campaign and organizing his army for it. His plans may have been excellent; but, when the hour for action came, he seemed to lose faith in their success, and delayed for some minor amendment of them until the golden moment passed when success was possible. He lacked the courage even of his military convictions. And his own memoirs show that he had a personal ambition and conceit that fatally sapped his moral strength.

And in the smaller and obscurer fields of service, where each of us may be stationed in the work and struggle of life, both of these qualities are also needed for the successful discharge of the task assigned to us. A life without convictions, without principles, is like a vessel sailing aimlessly over the seas without a cargo. A character with convictions, but without the courage to maintain them, is like a vessel lying at wharf after its cargo has been put on board, but having no wind nor steam nor other power to take her across the seas to her intended port.

Of course, convictions and principles may be bad as well as good; and the man who has the courage of thoroughly bad convictions is the scourge of his race. The cruel despots in church and state, whose personal malignant ambition or hot zeal in the service of a false piety has left a trail of blood across many a page of human history, have been men who had, unhappily, the courage of bad convictions. Better, indeed, would it have been for the world if they had had no convictions at all than to have been dominated by such false ones. The first duty, therefore, is to store the mind with honest and true beliefs, to seek just and beneficent principles, to strive to attain correct views of one's relation to the world in which he lives. This question of what our convictions or principles may be is not a matter merely of chance or fate or inheritance: it is a matter of mental and moral culture. Convictions may be reformed by broadening the mental vision, by enlightening the conscience, by increasing the acquisitions of knowledge, by clarifying the moral perceptions through more active exercise of them, and by cultivating the benevolent dispositions of the heart. What are called convictions, in the sense in which the word is here used, are not intellectual perceptions alone, but they are the product of intellectual perceptions and moral sentiment, or they are intellectual principles suffused with moral feeling. They are warmer and more glowing than are the pure abstractions of mental truth. One may accept without question the demonstrated propositions of geometry, but it is not these mathematical beliefs that are ordinarily called convictions. But, when one gets a perception of the relations of justice and veracity and brotherhood in which man should live with his fellow-man, or when one perceives by what subtle and inviolable laws man is related to the life of the invisible Power in nature that has fathered and mothered him, then he is in the region of convictions; and the beliefs that he will attain will depend on the breadth and accuracy of his intellectual view, and will also be vitalized by moral emotion. The conditions, then, for attaining convictions that are true and good may be cultivated. Mankind are under obligations to have good convictions instead of bad or indifferent ones. Civilized man may train himself and may train those whose instruction is confided to him to look at their relation to other men and to the world in which they live with broad and enlightened vision and with moral susceptibility. The result of such educational training will, in all probability, be mental and moral convictions that are altogether worthy of being carried into action.

And then comes the need of the courage. And at this point many otherwise quite good people — at least, well-intentioned people — practically fail, and lead in consequence weak and inefficient lives. They have good principles enough, but they are weak in execution. Their convictions are all right, yet they fail to impress them upon others. They see clearly enough, for instance, the course which truth and right demand, yet perhaps it is an unpopular course: the fashionable or the majority do not go that way. And so they are tempted either to keep their opinions to themselves and remain inactive or else to go with the multitude. In either case they lack the courage of their convictions. Or, perhaps, it is some enterprise of philanthropy which they are convinced would be of great benefit to the community. They feel moved to enter upon it. They have the time and the means to devote to it. But they see, on closer acquaintance, that there are many obstacles in the way, that hard labor will be required, that misunderstandings will have to be met and popular odium encountered; and so they withdraw, in cowardly timidity, from the field, retreat to the enjoyment of cultured retirement instead of pressing on to the higher joy of well-won repose after a conquered wrong. They lack the courage of their convictions. Or, perhaps, it is some false and injurious social standard of behavior that troubles them. Mentally and morally they inwardly protest against it. But social conventionalities and traditions are strong: to combat them causes fret and annoyance, and is liable to put one outside of the charmed circle. And so they yield their better judgment to the force of custom. Again, they lack the courage of their convictions. Or, perhaps, — a more critical peril, — reason and conscience pronounce clearly for a certain moral decision in personal conduct: a certain vice is to be abjured, a certain well-understood ruinous temptation is to be resisted. The habits and popular opinion among companions are on the side of the vice. The fear of ridicule, of a laugh, of being thought Puritanic and prudish, helps the temptation. The hour for action comes, and there is no strength to say No, though reason, conscience, heart, all plead for it. The victim lacks the courage of his convictions.

No great work can be done unless the worker throws himself into it with the full ardor of enthusiastic belief. But marvellous achievements have been wrought even by one man or one woman, single-handed, who was equipped with the enthusiastic courage of a good conviction and with the needed practical energy to support it. Such workers are wanted to-day. There are neglected and ostracized truths that need them. Educational reform is waiting for them. The manifold problem of the curse of intemperance cries out for their solution. Wronged and struggling women plead for their aid. Oppressed and discontented labor calls for their leadership. The tenement-houses of the poor, reeking in filth and misery and vice, pray for their knowledge and humanity. Corruption in politics demands their most invulnerable conscience in the herculean task of cleansing its stables. The field is vast, the laborers are few. Yet there are large numbers of men and women, sitting in their parlors and in their libraries, with excellent ideas and sentiments concerning the work that needs to be done. But they do not do it; and they will probably go down to their graves dissatisfied with their success in life, because they have lacked the courage and energy to carry their best convictions into execution.

The opportunities are waiting, not only for the clear sight, but the ready hand. Nay, the faith that is alive to humanity's wants makes its opportunities. It does not wait to find them. It does not stay at home expecting them to come to it. Human beings not only help the world, but perfect themselves, by throwing themselves with generous enthusiasm into the world's work. "Blessed," says Carlyle, "is he who has found his work: let him ask no other blessedness."

HEROISMS IN DAILY LIFE.

My subject this morning is the heroic element in daily life. It is a common impression that heroism must have a rare and conspicuous field for its display. The heroes, it is thought, belonged to the old days of knight-errantry; or they are gallant soldiers, or valiant philanthropists, or, at least, doers of some work by which their names are emblazoned around the world. The General Sheridans, the John Browns, the John Howards, the Garrisons, the Captain John Smiths, the Joan of Arcs, the Grace Darlings, the Ida Lewises,— it is characters like these that are generally thought of as representing the quality of heroism. And these, of course, do represent the quality. But they are by no means its sole representatives. There may be men and women every whit as heroic in the quiet walks of daily duty, whose names will never be known to history or even beyond the boundaries of their own neighborhood. For what is the essence of heroism? It is valorous action, against great odds, for a noble object. And this is a definition that does not cover public and conspicuous deeds alone. The deed may be in secret, it may be curtained in domestic privacy, it may perchance be known only to one's own breast; and yet it may have all the elements of true heroism. It is the silent heroisms of virtue, never blazoned abroad, known perhaps only to the home or the neighbor or the secret heart, which keep the moral health of mankind.

According to our definition there are three conditions essential to heroic action. First, the action must be valorous, it must manifest courage. You cannot imagine a craven spirit as heroic. Valor is the root-meaning of the word from which our word "heroism" is derived. At first it meant physical valor. But, as human life has developed, valor has come to have a mental and moral, as well as physical, significance. It means the courage of one's convictions, the bravery that can face and do the right without fear or favor. And there may be mental and moral heroism that will stand up fearlessly to do the true and the right, though there may have been little training in acts of physical valor. Second, heroic action is conditioned by great odds opposed to it. It implies hardship, antagonism, a struggle, and battle. It means that there are strong forces to be wrestled with and conquered. They may be physical forces, or they may be mental and moral forces. For Grace Darling and Ida Lewis it was the mighty forces of the winds and the waves that were to be met, as they launched their boats to go out to the rescue of shipwrecked fellow-beings. For John Howard it was depraved moral forces, so hopeless of cure to the thoughtless majority, that he set himself to overcome. For Garrison it was the combined powers of state, church, and society that he, a physical non-resistant, challenged to combat on a practical question of justice. The resistance to be overcome may thus differ in kind; but all heroic deeds imply a hostile power to be fought down, and a hostile force, too, that appears to have the advantage greatly on its side. You would not call any action heroic which was done by spontaneous desire, with no opposition. Such an action may be good, moral; but it is not of the kind called heroic. It is a necessary condition of the heroic act that it should encounter great obstacles. Third, heroic action must have a noble object. Here, perhaps, some persons might at first thought demur. They might object that very valorous deeds have been displayed on the wrong side of great public causes, or even for bad personal ends. But this objection loses sight of the distinction between mere physical valor and the valor that has a moral impulsion,— a distinction that has been growing clearer to mankind as they have advanced in civilization, until now it is precisely this moral quality attached to the valorous deed that entitles it to the praise of being heroic. Of course, a bad cause, as history finally gives judgment, may be espoused by good men, acting from conscientious devotion to principle. And such men may manifest heroism because acting for what to them are good objects. And so, too, in the strifes of a bad cause there may be many incidental occasions for genuinely noble deeds of the heroic cast. What is meant by the statement that heroic action must have a noble object is that it must be a disinterested, self-forgetful, self-denying action; not a deed, however bravely facing danger, undertaken for mere personal pleasure or selfish profit or for any selfish satisfaction whatever: it cannot be a deed of mere passion, or of cruelty, or of brute force, or of intellectual cunning, however high daring may be displayed in accomplishing the end. Heroism, wherever shown, commands admiration, it excites our moral homage; and, in order to do that, it must have a moral quality, it must be an action impelled by an unselfish sympathy or benevolence, or one that the doer believes to be commanded by his convictions of truth and right. In a word, it must be action for a noble, and not an ignoble, object.

Our definition of heroism, then, I believe, is justified in its three particulars: it is valorous action, against great odds, for a noble object.

Now, is there no opportunity for this kind of action in the common walks of life? Is it only the soldier, the explorer, the public philanthropist, the people who live on the frontiers of civilization and in places conspicuously exposed to sudden emergencies of action,—is it only classes of persons such as these that have any occasion to act valorously against great odds for a noble end? Indeed, thus to put the question is almost to answer it. When we say "hero," the imagination conjures up some distant, dazzling personage, of whom we have read in some history or fiction, — the actor in a tale that is seldom repeated, the rare beings who in ancient days were even declared after death to be demigods and gods for their great deeds. But, when we examine the attributes of these beings, and say that the hero is one who acts valorously against great odds, for a noble object, we have brought the quality of heroism home to our own doors. If this be heroism, who of us is not called to act the part? To whom of us does not come the opportunity to act it? and the opportunity, not at rare intervals, once or thrice in a life-time, but constantly in our daily effort practically to solve the problem of life?

There is no one of us, surely, who does not have, or may not have, a noble object for which to live. The object may, in fact, be far above our achievements. We may be daily denying it in practice. We may seldom strive for it as we might. And yet we are conscious of a law which imposes upon us an obligation to live for noble purposes and pursuits. To every man and woman is given the task to form a character, according to the demands of truth and rectitude, for the expression of divine righteousness in the human world. To do the utmost possible toward this end out of the materials given is the duty. The materials may not always be of the best. Sometimes they may be amended, and then that is the first duty. But, when they cannot be, when our lot and circumstances and relations in life are fixed for us, then the duty, keeping ever the rules of rectitude and truth as guides, is to mould character to the highest form possible from the given conditions. This law never relaxes the tension of its obligation upon us for a single moment. We are bound to live for the right and the true. Intuition, experience, the motive of highest usefulness, the desire for the greatest happiness, the instinct of moral sympathy, all enforce upon us the sanctity of this obligation. It is an obligation that we cannot violate with impunity. It is an obligation that we cannot violate and feel entirely at ease, unless we have suffered our moral perceptions to have become dulled by abuse. There is before us, therefore, the highest and noblest of all objects,—the formation of true, upright, beneficent character, an object that is constant, that is not for rare days and infrequent opportunities, but for all days; and there is no act that we do that does not have some bearing upon this object either as helping or hindering its achievement. None of us, then, can say that we have no opportunity for at least this one among the essential conditions of heroism,—a noble object.

But do we find it easy to keep this object steadily in view, and to keep our acts steadily bent to the task of achieving it? By no means, we answer. We imagine it might be much easier if the circumstances were different; and we sometimes picture to ourselves how much more truly we might live, how much better might be our characters and more satisfactory our achievements, if we had only been thrown amidst other circumstances, if we could change places with some of our neighbors, if we had lived in some more favorable locality, if we had had more money, or perhaps less, or if a different kind of fortune had attended us through the years. But all these imaginings are but excuses for present delinquencies. If we could only get rid of the special difficulties of our lot, of the common-place duties that so absorb our faculties and time, of the drudgeries to which we are compelled, but which so stand in the way of our achieving those things that we most want to do, we profess to believe that we should be much better men and women, that then we should have more energy and enthusiasm and opportunity for the culture and pursuit of those higher objects which we recognize as demanding our allegiance, that then we should be able to present a higher type of character and conduct. But here, then, in these antagonistic conditions and circumstances of which we complain, are the very obstacles and hardships for calling forth that heroic quality of character which appears to us so admirable. Did our lot in life make it entirely easy to attain the lofty type of character which our consciences most approve, there would be, as we have seen, no room for heroism in the pursuit. By the resistance to be overcome is that quality measured. Heroism is gauged not by favoring circumstances, not by the wheel of fortune bringing an aspirant's wishes to the top, but by that moral pluck and determination and will-power which push their way against unfavoring circumstances and compel success from adverse fortune itself. The success, be it remembered, of which we now speak, is the noble life, the true character, the honorable moral career. It may have or it may not have outward wealth. It may attain or it may not attain the external position and conditions that once seemed desirable. But the very hardness of an unfavorable lot has been met by moral pluck and vigorous determination in such a way as to develop the inner fibre of a strong moral character, and this is human life's highest success. Heroism looks for no other. And here, in the conditions of the common lot, the drudging daily labors that have so little of romance, the unpalatable ever-recurring duties, the plodding necessities that appear to allow so little room for the culture that is craved, the homely struggles with common, unexciting temptations, which have no epic flow and never rise to the interest of a tragic crisis,— here is a field where heroism may find ample opportunity to test its mettle. We have our moral ideals of life. They are of celestial heights of attainment. But here are the petty conditions of the day, of the hour, the selfish anxieties and passions, the home care and trial, the pressing earthy work, the distracting errands hither and thither, which drag upon our feet and threaten to prevent our ever reaching that goal of our hopes. The odds are perilously against us unless the heroic quality of character come to the rescue; and that the odds are against us is an appeal for aid which heroism by its very nature, if it be present, must recognize.

We find, then, in the common paths of daily life two of the essential conditions of heroic action,—a noble object of pursuit and obstacles in the way which throw the odds greatly against the chance of attainment. Why, then, do we not oftener meet this quality of heroism in the common paths of life? It is true we often do meet it there; and still oftener perhaps we know that it exists there, although it may be concealed from all eyes until we see it in its results. But why do we not very generally see it? Why do we not meet it everywhere where we meet these two of its essential conditions? The reason must be because the third condition is wanting. Heroism we defined as valorous action, against great odds, for a noble object. We have found the common paths of daily life affording ample opportunity for the noble object, and also, in the obstacles to that object, supplying the resistances which challenge heroism to its tasks. If, therefore, the heroism does not appear, it must be because the valor is not there to respond to the challenge. There is a deficiency of moral courage, a lack of brave, robust vigor in attacking the evils that beset character, a too willowy weakness in bending before them, a want of moral muscle to resist and conquer them. And this, our logical conclusion, would doubtless correspond with the practical diagnosis of the trouble in such cases. We should discover a deficiency of that healthy moral sentiment which has such an instinctive aversion to evil that it is inwardly compelled to assail and destroy it. This sentiment being defective and diseased, moral atrophy and paralysis ensue. A character of flabby moral fibre cannot be heroic. A vigorous moral sympathy, pushing by inherent compulsion to action against all distress and wrong, is the first condition of heroism. That supplies the valor, without which all the opportunities for heroic deeds, whether in common life or in extraordinary emergencies, would be offered in vain. But, having the valor, then there is no need to go beyond the limits of that daily common life in which we are all sharers to find a field for the truest heroism.

Let us now bring these generalities down to some special application. What is it that we individually first and most need to do, beginning now just where we are, in solving the problem of life? It is not to dream or even to inquire how we might act, were we differently situated; but it is to make a vital junction here and now between the actual conditions given to our hands and that better, higher life we hope to attain. And probably most of us will think at once of certain temptations which severally beset us, and which we know must be resisted and overcome; of certain evil habits which stand in the way of our progress, and which we know must be put off before that progress can be assured; of a certain routine of unprofitable activity or of sloth that is to be exchanged for useful service; of certain trials and sufferings that may be borne with more equanimity and courage; of certain obstacles that stand in the way of our better ideals. Whatever may be the nature of these moral reforms which we see to be needed in our lives, there is no other way to accomplish the work but by definitely and faithfully taking it in hand, piece by piece and day by day, keeping to the task till it is finished. It is vain to expect that a reform will come by mere general regrets over present failures and a general wish and hope for better things; and it is perilous to wait for a change of circumstances to effect the desired result. The temptations, the bad habits, the trying circumstances, are to be met each on its own field. If it is a too easily angered temper, if it is a slanderous or untruthful tongue, if it is an indolent, dilatory disposition, if it is a complaining spirit, if it is a rebellious physical appetite, if it is moroseness or avarice or covetousness or unjust greed, if it is persistent neglect of well-recognized duties, if it is inclination to selfish ease or pleasure, each one of these faults calls for a special vigilance and effort to overcome it. Having learned what are the faults which we need each in our own case to conquer,— and those of us who have come to years of discretion know pretty well what is the moral matter with us,— there is no longer time nor occasion for parleying with our errors or excusing them; but the demand is for action. Each morning should witness a resolute purpose to do battle against these foes of our moral nature, these obstacles which stand in the way of that ideal of character which has our highest homage; and every evening should have, if possible, the satisfaction of noting some progress achieved. Nowhere in the whole wide range of human activity is there more call for the heroic spirit and the heroic deed than in this struggle of our moral natures to put down their own evil tendencies, and to shape character by the highest patterns of rectitude, purity, truthfulness, and kindness. Here are the fields, and they are open to us all, where the highest prizes of heroism may be won. Here is the noble object,— the very noblest to which we can apply our powers; here the obstacles, which valiant souls pride themselves on conquering; here the valor, as great as that which fights in armies a nation's battles for the right,— nay, the need often is for greater, since that contends amidst the plaudits of an on-looking world, while this may have to struggle all in secret, with no applause save that responsive echo in one's own breast which is God's whisper of satisfaction.

And, if we are complaining that our lives are monotonous, that they are void of incident and interest, day following day on one arid level, then I know not how we could better break the monotony and give ourselves the high delight of a fruitful activity than by engaging, one by one, the faults and vices and evil habits which now may enslave us, throwing off their domination, and making ourselves their master, making the soul the master of the flesh and of circumstance. It is these contests and conquests that make the interest of the biographies and the stories which we read; and we have, therefore, the materials of a real romance in our hands every day. What prouder thought can I have than to know that this day, in this very part of life's drama I am acting, the good within me has got the better of the evil? To have made that conquest is the hero's title to the proudest claim on his escutcheon. Changing a single word in Tennyson's lines, they strike the key-note of this moral battle which we wage for high ideals against our own lower inclinations and habits:—

> "Ah, my God,
> What might I not have made of thy fair world,
> Had I but loved thy highest [pleasures] here?
> It was my duty to have loved the highest:
> It surely was my profit had I known:
> It would have been my pleasure had I seen.
> We needs must love the highest when we see it."

And in the battle of life, friends, we do see this Highest Law, which asks for our fealty.

THE SAVING POWER OF TRUTH.

THE new President of Columbia College, in his inaugural address a few days ago, speaking of the beneficence of such a seat of learning in the midst of the metropolitan whirl of business activities in the city of New York, said: "The work of the college would be valueless to-morrow if even the wealth of New York could bribe her instructors to teach as true what they know to be false. Truthfulness is the one essential fundamental quality of a teacher. Without it he may not be a teacher. Yet it is not the only quality. The teacher, like the scholar, must himself be teachable. An ever-heightening sky for human thought, an ever-widening horizon for human knowledge, an absolute truthfulness in the expression of the light within, — these are the distinguishing marks of a great university."

If President Low had been describing the objects of a religious society, he could hardly have chosen more fitting words. Add to his description the inculcation of the sacredness of duty, — which may yet be implied in his large and noble generalization, — and we could not ask for better terms in which to express the chief uses of a church in the midst of the prevalent passions and ambitions that are such dominant, every-day factors in the affairs of mankind. At least, the words suggest that learning and religion are natural coworkers for the highest welfare of humanity. Learning, thus nobly defined, and religion, rationally interpreted, come into the same road and lead finally toward the same end, — the supreme devotion of man to truth, truth in its largest, highest, and ever deepening and increasing sense. If absolute truthfulness in the expression, through word and conduct, of the light within, be the object of learning, it is no less the object of religion. Truth itself, since it is but the reality of things to which man stands in constant, vital relationship, should have that saving efficacy and power which religion has always promised as its gift to man. Hence my subject this morning, "The Saving Power of Truth."

But a curious anomaly of human history presents itself to us at the outset. The moral and religious leaders of all nations have always asserted that truth is all-powerful, that it is the essence of Almighty Being, that it will make men free, and guide them safely; and the mental and moral sense of mankind in general has given assent to these propositions. Yet everywhere, from the times immemorial when Adam of the ancient legend attempted concealment in the Garden of Eden, and from the later times when Peter denied and Judas betrayed their Master, men have tried to live by a falsehood. The attempt has always in the end proved to be vain; yet the lesson of its uselessness has been a hard one to learn, and has not yet been mastered. Even in the old legend of Genesis, the penetrative eye of Jehovah detected the hiding-place of the disobedient pair and brought them to the light. Peter's falsehood only confounded him with tears of shame; and the lie of Judas was too great for mortal man to bear, and, like the fraud of many a man since, confessed itself in the coward's act of suicide. Still, everywhere, the old attempt goes on as if some time or other it could succeed. Still people are afraid or ashamed of the naked simplicity of truth if it threatens to lead them to espouse an unpopular cause; and they try to cover themselves with some petty contrivance of deceit for eluding their own consciences. Still, there are people who betray truth with a kiss, and sell her for gold. Still there are the cowardly whose minds see the truth, but whose hearts are too timid to follow when danger to position or popularity appears. Thus the effort continues to live by a lie. The effort is of manifold grades and kinds, from the minor deceits of trade and social life, which try to protect themselves under the guise of special moral codes for business and society, to the deeds of men who rob a bank of its securities, and then profess amazement that the world does not recognize their operations as in accordance with approved methods of Wall Street finance. It appears again in the sharp manœuvring of partisan politicians to outwit each other in parliamentary law and legislation and in election campaigns. It rises in religious robes in the Assembly of Presbyterians to plead that the creed and the catechism remain unrevised, because the very words have become reverend and sacred with age, and can now be repeated with new meanings and mental reservations by those who cannot accept them in their original significance. In the Episcopal General Convention, for similar reasons, it deprecates, against many conscience appeals, a revision of the Prayer Book, which has guided the worship of so many generations. It lobbies in the National Unitarian Conference, of which a large body of the membership now says, in respect to the theological phrases of its constitution: "They don't mean anything to us: they are a dead letter. But to a few among us they mean something, and to the world outside they seem to mean a good deal. So don't touch them, but, in the interests of harmony and quiet and peace, let them stand there, though on the frontals of our temple; we don't or need not see them as we go under." And if, among men who have risen to such conspicuous positions in the world as religious and political leaders, there occur these evidences of carelessness, timidity, and betrayal in the presence of truth's commands, is it any wonder that young people, young men especially, should deem it easier and safer to evade the law of moral truth as it affects personal character, and, when tempted into crooked paths for sudden riches or into courses of pleasurable and vicious self-indulgence, should think it may be possible somehow successfully to escape the retribution?

But perhaps I shall be asked, How, among the many statements and standards of truth that are offered, are we to know what to accept as the genuine truth which saves? Let us, then, divest ourselves at once of the ecclesiastical and theological definitions of truth which the various sects have set forth. Let us not suppose the saving truth to be all contained in the limits of any creed or between the covers of any book. Let us not presume it to be identical with any particular scheme of belief which any church of mankind, however venerable or learned, has taught. These, at best, are but partial and temporary expressions, finite apprehensions and interpretations, of that which in its nature is universal and absolute. The truth we want, the truth which is to be sought through "an ever-heightening sky and an ever-widening horizon," is the absolute and total Reality of things in the universe, whether pertaining to the earth or the heavens, or to matter or thought or spirit, or to any other possibilities of life and existence. Truth, in this absolute sense, is synonymous with Infinite and Eternal Being. To use the words of an old writer, it is "the breath of the power of God; . . . and, being but one, she can do all things, . . . and in all ages, entering into holy souls, she maketh them friends of God and prophets."

To illustrate the beneficent power of truth in this large universal sense, we may begin on the lowest plane of truth; that is, with that kind of material and practical knowledge which is gained through observation of the facts and laws of nature. What independence and power the human race has attained simply through increasing knowledge of those natural forces and laws which have been applied to the arts of life! The difference between the savage man and the brute animal is scarcely greater than the difference between the most civilized nation of the earth to-day and the nation that stood highest in civilization a thousand years ago. Within that time the methods of domestic, industrial, and social life have been revolutionized and built up anew by the practical application of that kind of knowledge which the physical sciences have brought. In the acquisition of this sort of truth we may largely trace the history of modern civilization. To civilize a people, in the modern sense, is to educate them to the use of the forces and laws of the natural world, to teach them how to build dwellings so as at the same time to shelter from the cold and the storm and to let in the air and the light; how to get warmth in winter from fire, instead of burrowing in the ground like the brute to find it; how to tame wild beasts from savage ferocity into submissive helpers; how to make the cold zones inhabitable by converting natural growths from plants and animals into clothing; how to cultivate the earth and to extract the riches of its soil and its mines; how to transform its products into wholesome food; how to convert wood and metals into countless utensils and tools for better utilizing and multiplying the power of human hands; how to use nature's powers so as to enable one man to do the work of a thousand; and, finally, how through the printing-press, to preserve all this knowledge and the thoughts of the wisest men so that the child thereafter may know them without the tedious experience of discovery, and they may never again be lost out of the world.

Who can estimate the power which this knowledge of nature has given, and will yet give, to mankind? And, literally, it has been a saving, uplifting, educating power. That one fact — the discovery of fire — lifted man from the grovelling condition of the brute into the erect posture of the human being. Before he burrowed: afterward he built. Before he crouched: afterward he stood. Before he was of the earth, confined by its tether: afterward he walked earth's surface free, and all zones and climates became accessible to him. The savage is the slave of Nature: he lives in subjection to her conditions and in terror of her forces. To the civilized man Nature is the willing servant: he has learned her secrets and mastered her forces. In defiance of ancient Scripture, he has "measured the breadth of the earth," "entered into the springs of the sea," and "into the treasures of the snow." He has dared even to lift his head toward the heavens to compute the paths and the times of the stars. The sea is his highway. Fire and water he has yoked together for his strongest steed. He has hooped the earth with his iron roads, converted miles of space into moments of time, and chained the lightnings so that they say to him, "Here we are," and obediently do his errands.

Thus it is that the knowledge of truth as it is in nature has lifted men out of the limiting and degrading conditions of savage life, made them masters of natural forces, and given them dominion over the earth, with a measure of the freedom and power which we conceive to be the attributes of Infinite Being. It has been estimated that, through the application of nature's help in the various mechanical arts, the effective power of every person's hands in the State of Massachusetts has been increased more than a thousand-fold, so that even a child of ten years could now do work that would require, if not thus aided, the strength of a thousand able-bodied men.

But all this is only one kind of truth and one form of its application, and these the lowest. This domain of physical truth, vast and momentous as it is, needs to be included in and balanced by that larger realm of truth which is both intellectual and moral. It needs this balance and enlargement of relationship in order to insure its full and permanent beneficence for man. Mere knowledge alone is power, but it is not always nor necessarily beneficent power. The human mind may be educated to great ingenuity and skill in certain directions, and yet the intellectual life as a whole remain narrow, shallow, and unfruitful, and the moral nature lie dormant, or even be perverted and enslaved to evil. What, indeed, is most of all wanted, in order to make available for the highest uses that human power which results from conquest of the truths of nature, is secure establishment in some truth that is deeper and higher. No advancement in the physical sciences and arts, no accumulation of material power and riches, can promote man's highest good without a corresponding increase of moral perception and accumulation of moral power. All material civilization, however splendid, is but a gaudy, empty show if it does not ascend to moral and spiritual ends. Boast of our modern civilization as we will, and, though we claim that it is bulwarked against peril by the printing-press and the public school, yet we can never be sure that it will not lapse into another dark era of barbarism, or a social condition of things as bad as that, unless it be penetrated through and through with moral ideas and consecrated by an ideal, moral enthusiasm. This wonderful progress of mankind through the discovery and application of the truths of material nature must be guided by the constant and higher application of the truths of the spirit. Popular liberty will find no stable throne nor lasting crown until the realm of material forces is subordinated to the power of ethical laws.

And it must be admitted that there is much in our modern civilization that is unsatisfactory and unsound. Its dominant activities spring from and appeal to motives that are selfish and sordid. While it has lifted us out of the depths of traditional ignorance and gross degradation, it has nourished vices peculiar to itself. It has fostered an unwholesome love of gain, irrespective of the rights of fellow-men or the calls of human sympathy. It has whetted certain appetites of the flesh to a keener edge. The Chinese government has in vain besought Great Britain to keep the deadly opium drug of her civilization at home. Missionaries in the new Congo State in Africa, which was to civilize the negroes through commerce, find their work paralyzed because of the rum flowing in there from civilized — aye, from Christian — England, Holland, and our own Boston. If our civilization has brought us immense power and freedom over nature, it has also brought a new bondage. Millions are enslaved to its mad lust of gain. The quiet, domestic virtues go down before the rushing train of material enterprise. Homely honesty is often eclipsed by the blinding dust and smoke. Justice and humanity may get on board, if they can; but the train bound express for the terminus Plutocracy cannot stop for them. Commerce rules, the manufacturing interest rules, gold rules. Trade sets up a moral standard of its own quite different from the Golden Rule of Jesus and Zoroaster and Confucius. This great country of ours tried to live for nearly a century with a dreadful lie in its bosom,— proclaiming equal rights for all men, but legalizing the enslavement of black men because cotton was king. "The higher law,"— that was all transcendental talk, and touched not the earth. For practical life there was no higher law than expediency.

This, I believe, is no exaggeration of what modern civilization has been on its evil side. I acknowledge that it has another side, and have tried to sketch it. I recognize the vast power the human race has acquired through use of the forces of nature, and the magnificent foundation thus laid for future achievements. But, in order that these achievements may be secured and the evils of our present one-sided civilization neutralized, there should be the same fearless pursuit in the discovery and establishing of intellectual and moral truth. We are now applying to life, for the most part, only one fragmentary part of truth. We want the whole truth, full rounded in all its constituent elements, to make individual life worth the living, and worthily to complete the unfolding drama of human history. Our material civilization is only a basis on which mind and heart and soul are to rear their structures. What high art should come, what literature, what poetry, what philosophies and humanities, what equity of law and administration, what social fraternity, what strength and graces of personal character should appear, as the legitimate sequence of this conquest of nature by the powers of mind! The true, the just, the beautiful,—not till these shall rule in private, in public, and in national life, will our present era of material civilization be worthily crowned.

But there are many who aver that these higher truths of the human soul are impracticable; that they must remain as ideals in the sky, while practice must come down to a lower level, more nearly in accordance with the methods in vogue around us. Here is one of the strangest delusions that the world has known, yet it is a delusion that has assiduously been kept up from age to age,— that truth is not so practicable as error; that a half-truth is stronger than the whole truth; that wrong and falsehood may be perfectly practicable, but their opposing truth, though clearly known, is impracticable. If this were so, it would be the strongest argument that could be offered against there being any valid basis of truth or any moral purpose in the universe. The delusion is born of a scepticism that is thoroughly atheistic. Believe me, the highest moral truth known to man is practicable. If it is not practised, the fault is in human character, and does not spring from any cause in the nature of things. And what better evidence can be had that any truth, whether of religion or of science or of ethics, is meant for human use than that it has come within the scope of human intelligence? Or what better intimation of the time it should be put to use than the date of its discovery? That, at least, is the time when all who understand and acknowledge it should begin eagerly to labor for its supremacy, content no longer that any error or half-truth should occupy its place. And yet people parley, defer, compromise, evade. They say, in effect: "Excuse us, O Lord, but this truth of thine comes altogether too soon for safety. Next year, or next century, the world may be ready for it. But now it is utterly impossible to get it established. To attempt to disseminate it will produce only a vain agitation and bitterness. Pray take it back to thyself again. Keep it hidden till a more auspicious season, and leave us for the present harmonious and happy in our error." But to such timid parleying the answer always comes back from the Source of truth, "Now is the acceptable time, now is the day of salvation." And, if we try to pass this reply unheeded and still put aside the truth that is knocking at our doors for admission, then, sooner or later, the inevitable stern voice of retribution will ring through the chambers of conscience, proclaiming "the day of vengeance of our God." That ancient Scripture still has a meaning for mankind. It means the dread retribution that by natural law follows the fracture of righteousness. Truth cannot be safely tampered with nor violated. This is the lesson of all history, the lesson of individual life and of every nation's annals.

Nothing can be more fallacious than the idea that individual character ever derives any greater efficiency from lowering the standard of truth or virtue to make them more practicable, or that any half-way rule of honesty will work better than the perfect rule. You will see men enough, it is true,— there are, alas! too many of them,— who have attained a certain outward success, a certain measure of influence and power perhaps, through methods of concealment and trickery. We may sometimes see fortunes accumulated through extortionate and fraudulent practices in trade; vulgar demagogism, cunning, and hypocrisy mounting to places of high trust and authority in the community; selfish ambition riding rough-shod over the unostentatious merits of solid wisdom and moral sincerity. All this we see; and a hasty inference might be that, in this world, hypocrisy succeeds and truthfulness fails, that fraud is rewarded and honesty punished quite as generally as the reverse. But it would most certainly be a hasty inference. Look through a lifetime, look at people in the mass and in the long run, and the rule is that men find that level to which their characters respectively fit them, and stand in the community for what they really are. There are some exceptions to this rule; but they are exceptions, and do not make the standard. They are enough to suggest that this life may not complete the moral course, that there is somewhere a beyond for rectifying the judgments of the earthly life. Yet even here, in general, it is reality, genuine worth, that reaches the highest places of respect and achieves the truest success. You may say that here is a man who lives respected in the community, though on ill-gotten gains. But he does not have your respect. He does not have the respect of any one in the community who knows with you of his dishonest ways. It is to be put to the credit of human nature that no compromise of personal integrity, no evasion of personal truthfulness, ever wins regard from others or retains power over them. Sooner or later the fraudulent disguises are exposed. The flimsy veil of outward respectability is blown away, and power vanishes with it. It is only truth, reality, that ultimately commands.

And what is true of individual character is true, also, of communities, of nations. No community nor nation was ever made strong by a compromise of justice. Personal and sectional interests, merely outward and material matters, may be compromised for the general welfare; but the right and the true never. The majority may not support nor even comprehend the highest political truth. Let them, then, put into act the ideas that belong to their level and keep the responsibility therefor; but let not those who do see the truth that is needed yield one jot or tittle of it because it cannot be enacted to-day. If they cannot be legislators, let them be prophets. Stronger was Jesus hanging upon the cross than Pilate, at the command of the political voices of the day, signing his death-warrant. Stronger is the man or the party that stands for the truth, though in a minority and having no official power, than the man or the party that may possess all the insignia and patronage of office, but denying the truth. Better wait a whole century than help to enact a lie or even a half-truth, if the half-truth can only be obtained by a compromise against the other half. The proverb sometimes preached in such cases, that a half-loaf is better than no bread, does not apply to any question where the point yielded is a point of morals. For then the half loaf is not bread, but a stone; not food, but poison. Every national compromise of justice legalizing an injustice brings the inevitable retribution of corruption and disease in the body politic, which only the bitter discipline of suffering can expiate and cure.

But, having spoken with somewhat of severity of certain tendencies of the age, I forbear to close without a word of encouragement and hope. For back of all and through all there is one "stream of tendency," which is never to be forgotten, and which is always the world's strength and the sure hope of mankind. It is the pressure, from the hidden Source of all sources, Cause of all causes, of the Absolute Truth itself toward the realization of its own ideals in human character and society. Steadily, firmly, under this Divine pressure there come solid gains for man. The millennium is still far away. The Elysian fields are not yet in sight. But, even in our own time, the burdens have been somewhat lifted from overburdened shoulders. The chains of oppression have been loosened, and some of them broken forever. Miseries have been somewhat assuaged. Hope and honorable aspiration have been stirred in hearts that never knew them before. Knowledge, culture, and refinement have increased. Justice and good will and brotherhood are rising to higher thrones in the sovereignty of nations. Thus slowly, but surely, do the great moral ideas and purposes, which crown the universe with a fitting noble aim, work their way into the heart and life of humanity. The Power in the world that makes for truth and righteousness is patient, but it wins at last. All history substantiates the truth that there is a Power in the world, not simply above it or outside of it, but in it, that is reconciling the world unto itself, bringing it into harmony with its own ideal aims, shaping and fashioning it to the service of Truth, Goodness, and Beauty. Let us call that Power our God, God with us, — God working in man, and through him, and for him.

> "One God, one law, one element,
> And one far-off divine event,
> To which the whole creation moves."

THE VOICE OF THE DRAFT.

"Make full proof of thy ministry."— 2 Tim. iv. 5.

The subject intended for to-day's discourse, my friends, must be put aside. I can speak to you only of what is uppermost in my thoughts, especially as, according to our annual custom, this is the last opportunity I shall have to address you for several weeks. You must allow me, too, to speak to you familiarly, very much as I would talk to you individually in my study. I have no carefully arranged discourse, neither the time nor my tastes have permitted it. But the thoughts that are passing through my mind, and in just the shape they pass, since they may ultimately concern you in the result to which they may lead, I have felt that you have a right to know.

From the beginning of this rebellion, which for more than two years has shaken and devastated our land, I have been preaching to you, friends, of national themes, with greater frequency than some of you, perhaps, have thought expedient, and not always what all of you would have best liked to hear, yet always, both as to time and matter, according to my own solemn convictions of duty; and from the bottom of my heart I most devoutly thank you to-day for the very general welcome you have given to these efforts, and still more, if possible, for the generous liberty you have accorded me to speak my thought, even though you might not always agree with it when spoken. As I now look back upon my utterances here on these themes, I have no misgivings, save that I have done so little, and done so poorly. I have tried, so far as possible in the small range of my ability, to bring the support of this pulpit to the cause of our country. I have endeavored so to speak as to excite among you and in this community a patriotic sentiment that would prepare our homes for sacrifices, that would help fill our armies in the field, that would inspire men and women with a desire in some way to serve their country, and that would aid in bringing the moral and religious strength of the whole community to the side of the national government in this struggle. I would fain have filled the breast of every man with a wish to give himself to this holy cause; and I have sought so to speak as to induce the young and healthy and capacitated, not only to have the wish, but honorably to gratify it by going to the field. I have spoken of the sublimity of self-sacrifice, of the nobleness of doing and dying for one's country, of the immortal glory which our hero-soldiers, living or dead, are achieving for themselves and for the nation which they redeem. I have thus tried to make it easier for parents to give up their sons, wives their husbands, sisters their brothers, and all of us those whom we may love better than ourselves; and I have striven to keep up among us at home a spirit and a habit of charity that should help relieve the sufferings of our soldiers in the hospital, or add to their strength and comfort in the camp and on the field. I have endeavored, moreover, to excite not merely a patriotic sentiment, but a patriotic sentiment founded on a sense of justice and a reverent regard for human rights. Never for a moment have I lost sight of the fact that, to make the cause of the nation a holy cause, and one which can properly receive the support of any Christian pulpit, it must be the cause of truth, of liberty, of humanity. I have sought, therefore, to go below the fact of civil war to its causes: I have endeavored to keep the thought clear that, by this rebellion, truth and liberty and humanity were assailed,— the very fundamental principles of our government,— and that it is only as we go to the defence of these, and make them victorious throughout the land, that any real triumph or lasting peace can be secured for our country.

I speak not of what I have done,— oh, how little is that! — but of what I have endeavored to do. And even that is not much, nothing exceptional. It is only what almost every pulpit in the loyal States has been doing, and what hundreds of men in my place would have done as well or better; and I have spoken of my endeavors now, not for any merit there is in them, but simply for their bearing on what follows. I have merely uttered here from time to time what was in my heart, and so uttered it, I trust, that the voice of your pulpit has given no "uncertain sound." I have meant only to bring the whole strength of this desk and of this church, so far as my position and poor abilities would allow, to the support of the cause of our country and humanity.

A call now comes to me, my friends, to make other proof of this my ministry among you. I have spoken to you heretofore by words: I am now called to speak to you by an act. I am bidden to make that full proof of the sincerity of my utterances which only deeds can give. I have held up before you the beauty and the sublimity of sacrifice: I am now asked to bring my sacrifice to the altar.

This call does not come to me unexpectedly; nor do I answer it hastily, or in any narrow enthusiasm of the moment which shuts out a view of the many collateral questions and consequences it involves. I see all, and on all sides, just, I think, as you see, and more than any of you can see. Long foreseeing the probability of the call, my mind has been silently, and with full deliberation, preparing its answer; and, so seeing and so judging, there is but one course that conscience opens to me. My friends, this call is imperative: I must obey.

I would not make the matter too serious. There may be little service or sacrifice required,— perhaps the showing a readiness to obey will be all; and I am glad to see that the result of the military draft is accepted in this community with such cheerfulness. Still, I wish there were a deeper feeling of seriousness beneath this good, but almost too jocose, cheer. Probably there is more than there seems. But I wish that our obligation to our country was more sacredly considered and revered, and that the whole question was decided more in the light of solemn duty. I wish that those whose names have been drawn were asking rather if they cannot go than seeking reasons for staying at home. There ought to be such a sentiment of patriotism in the community that the presumption would be that every drafted man would go, whereas the presumption now seems to be that he will stay at home if he can, and go only if he is obliged to. I should count it a much higher testimony to my own character and the value of my past preaching, if I were met with the remark, "Of course, you will go, if you are allowed," than to be addressed, as I more frequently have been, "Of course, you will not think of going."

I assure you, my friends, I can think of nothing else. My words to you with regard to our duties to our country have expressed my sincere convictions. I have preached what I believed, and I still believe as I have preached, and what I have preached to others I have meant also for myself; and I could never come into this pulpit and utter again such words as I have spoken here — for they would then seem to me mere empty breath — unless I obey, so far as I have the capacity, this call.

I do not know as I shall be pronounced physically worthy for the service into which the lot would take me, though I am aware of no defect that would legally exempt me, and sincerely hope that none may be found. I only wish this matter were beyond doubt. I have wanted since last Thursday, as never before, strength of body, and shall regard it with profound mortification if I shall be declared physically disabled for meeting this demand which my country makes upon me. I cannot at all understand the feeling which prompts so many men to search their bodies for some weakness or disease whereby they can escape this service to their country. I know very well that one physically incapacitated should not go as a soldier, and that patriotism sometimes may require that one abstain from going rather than to go and become a burden to the service. But how any one can exult if such incapacity be discovered in himself is what I cannot comprehend. Aside from the mean and craven nature of such a sentiment, a proper pride in the possession of a sound body should keep one from grovelling so low. How much nobler is the spirit of the drafted sailor, who, already in the sea service of the government, came before the examining board the other day with a certificate from some local physician, trumped up for him, probably, by his home friends, stating that he had an internal organic disease, but who, when the board found no disease, but, on the contrary, pronounced him a sound and perfectly healthy man, exclaimed with exultation: "Good! But I shall go back to the service in which I now am, for I can serve better there; so here are my three hundred dollars, which I willingly pay for the sake of going back knowing that I am a sound man!" Young men, if your mothers should be assailed, would you exult because you were feeble-bodied, and could not go to their defence? Our country is our mother; and shall we not pray for strong arms, in this her hour of peril, to defend her? I decide not for others; but for one I do so pray continually, and I shall use all possible means, between this day and the day of examination a month hence, to make myself physically worthy to answer her call. And, if accepted, I must go,— go wherever and in whatever capacity the legally constituted authorities may place me, seeking for myself nothing that is not equally open to all, only trusting that, if there be any kind of service in which I may be more useful than another, it will in providential ways come to me.

And, if not accepted, if I shall be doomed to the mortification of physical unworthiness, I shall still feel that this call is a new voice of duty which I must in some way try to obey. In what shape I can respond to the demand I know not now; but I have for some time felt that I must get nearer to the heart of this national struggle, that I must enter more interiorly into the life of this hour of our national history, that I have done what I could by word, and must now make some fuller and more personal proof of my ministry in this regard. And this call from the conscription wheel I accept as an intimation that another field of duty may be somewhere opening for me.

You say it is all accident, that the turn of a hair's breadth more might have drawn the next name instead of mine. True; and yet no accident happens to us which does not bring for us, if we listen, a divine message. And this is the message that this so-called accident brings to me: "Make full proof of thy ministry." I have spoken to you so much by words that I feel that my words have lost their power,— at least that my absence, in some service to which the nation calls, would now speak more forcibly than my presence for the truths which I have endeavored to uphold.

I know what may be rising in your hearts to be uttered, and what many have already said to me,— that there is a certain fitness of abilities to be considered, and that I can do better service here than in any other position, particularly in a military position. I accept gratefully this evidence of your favor and regard, and readily acknowledge that considerations of this kind are to receive attention. But we must be careful not to allow them too much weight. So long as the question was concerning the raising of a volunteer army, I have not felt called to any kind of military service. Neither by temperament, education, nor tastes, have I any special qualifications for it. I could consistently encourage those who had the qualifications to go, while at the same time I felt that I could remain with greater usefulness at my present post. But the question is now changed. The conscription law has put an end, in great measure, to these considerations of fitness, as also to those of convenience. It is to be presumed that two years' opportunity for volunteering has taken all those into military service who have any special liking or adaptedness for it, or who could leave home and business with ease. Whatever the fact may be, the presumption on which we must act is that it is now an even matter who shall go to make up this new army; and for this reason we have drawn lots to decide the question.

I say we have drawn lots, — we, the people, have done it. It has not been done for us or over us by any despotic authority, but it is our act done at our demand. And this leads me to say the word which I wish to say on the Conscription Act.

The conscription law is our law, the people's law. It was passed by the legal representatives of the people, and at the demand of the people. The people said to the government: "All have volunteered who have any special fitness for war or who can go with convenience to themselves or to their families or to society. It is now as difficult for one man to go as another: we will draw lots to determine who shall go." And the government has accordingly put our names into the wheel, and the fates, at our command, are turning it: shall we not abide by the lot?

If any think that I have put the point too strongly, that the draft is the act of the people, let them call to mind the fact that a little more than a year ago there was a general call through the newspapers of all parties in the loyal States, and through the popular voice as expressed in private and in public, for taxation and a draft, — a fact which will ever be remembered to the honor of republican institutions and of the American people. And, if any, having in mind the troubles incident to the draft, now think that another army might have been raised by volunteers, let them remember the troubles and disgust which a year ago attended the volunteering system.

But, whether an army of volunteers could have been raised or not, is a question that can no longer be discussed. We have decided for conscription, the people asked for it: the government through the people's representatives have given it, and given it in the form of a law of which humaneness is the characteristic picture. The exemptions which the law makes are none of them on the ground of class, or profession, or wealth, but all on the ground of humanity. I venture to say that, except, perhaps, in some points of practical detail (and these are receiving a liberal interpretation), a conscription law could not be framed, wiser or more compassionate. Imagine what hardships and opposition there would have been, had the law given no alternative but going to the field. Even the three hundred dollars commutation money, which has been the chief cause of complaint, was put in from regard, not to the rich, but to laboring men and men of moderate means, in order to keep the price of substitutes within the reach of most men of honest industry. There will doubtless be cases of hardship under the law, but so there have been under the system of volunteering: the hardships do not grow out of the fact of conscription, but out of the fact of war. The law could not attend to such cases; but private charity can and should, and doubtless will. The law, I believe, in its main features, is as good a one as could be drawn; and, had it not been for a few political demagogues with hearts so bad that they would ruin their country for the sake of party, there would have been no outbreak of hostility to it.

Regarding, then, the draft as the act of the people drawing lots among themselves, the people of course will honorably abide by it. Still to those who are drawn a choice is left, and how shall this choice be made? It is not, most certainly, to be taken for granted that all whose names are drawn should enter the service. The feeble-bodied — wretched men they should consider themselves — are exempted by the law itself. Only those who are pronounced physically fit will have the question to decide what they are to do. And this question we cannot decide for one another. We may present motives that will help to a decision; but, in the end, each must decide for himself,— decide solemnly, and under a full sense of his obligation to his country and to God. Yet there is one question which all whose names have been drawn must alike ask, if they mean to abide honorably by the lot; and this question is, How — that is, by accepting which of the three alternatives presented — can I best serve my country? not, How can I best serve myself, my family, my business? but, How can I best serve my country? I can conceive, indeed, that there may be cases where men who have no special fitness for military service, but do have a very special usefulness in other work, can best serve their country, even in this crisis, by paying their commutation money or sending substitutes, and remaining themselves in their business to keep that in operation. So, too, there are doubtless strong exceptional cases of domestic obligation, where, fully in accordance with the spirit of the law, one would be released from the choice of personal service. Let every one, however, if he would keep his honor, be on his guard against the specious forms which this exceptive pleading may assume. He must decide unselfishly, patriotically, conscientiously, putting foremost, not the grounds for staying at home, but the grounds for going.

It is quite commonly said, I know (and such a report I now see is in the newspapers), that the commutation fee, by which a veteran volunteer may be procured, is more acceptable to the government than a raw recruit. If the government should make an authoritative statement to this effect, it would decide the question for many of us. But no such statement has yet been made; and, until it is made on official authority, the presumption is that, since the law was made for raising an army, the men are wanted more than the money.

Again, it is urged that one of no special fitness by nature or education for military duty can best serve the country by sending a substitute who is fit; and thereby he may actually show a higher patriotism than if he should go himself. There is truth in this argument as a theoretical proposition, and at one time I gave it great weight in my own case. But practically there is a very dangerous fallacy in it, and the fallacy lies in our not considering sufficiently the qualities that must make fitness in the substitute; for fitness consists by no means solely in the possession of muscle or in belligerent training. I might send many men in my stead who have stronger bodies and are better fighters; but no man could be my substitute who does not believe in the justice of our cause as thoroughly as I do. No man could be my substitute who does not, by birth or adoption or principle, feel a personal interest in the triumph of our cause and the salvation of the country. No man could be my substitute who would fight merely for pay, or who would fight on the other side at any price. For one to be my substitute in this struggle he must have some other allegiance to our cause than an allegiance that is bought: he must believe in it. He cannot be a good and true soldier without belief. But the substitutes that are procurable and that are being accepted are most of a very different sort from this. They are Canadians, or aliens just from the other side of the Atlantic. They have no intelligent appreciation of our struggle or our institutions. They come only for money. They would serve just as readily, many of them more readily, on the side of the rebels; and they will desert at the first opportunity, or, guarded against that, are, at least, very likely to prove faithless in battle.

[Since the above words were spoken, we have had a practical proof in this city of their truth. I ask you, young men, and brother-conscripts, — you who mean to be true sons of your country and do your whole duty to her and answer honorably her call for help, — Is it such creatures as fled the other night from Pierian Hall that you are willing to send in your stead to the defence of your mother, the country? Can you, without a blush of honest shame, call such men — swindlers, perjurers, runaways — your substitutes? Are you ready to have your patriotism measured by their character, and to own that men who can only be kept for the service by being guarded in jail can do your work in this holy cause?]

There are some reasons of feeling, which, with many persons, are conclusive against a substitute in their own case; but these, since they are reasons of feeling, and therefore not of general application, I do not here consider. But this point which I have considered — the danger there is of putting into our armies, through the practice of procuring substitutes, a large class of men who have no zeal nor faith in our cause — presents to every drafted man, and to the whole community, an argument that should receive the most weighty and serious attention. Besides, leaving out of view the danger of bad faith on the part of the substitutes that are generally procurable, there ought, I think, to be some patriotic pride in this matter. Is it possible that, with the large population there is in the loyal States of the requisite age, still untouched, the country cannot raise another army of its own citizens to go to its defence? Are we so degenerate that we cannot close this war, and save our country and its cherished principles without calling in to our aid an army of foreign mercenaries?

But let me conclude by giving briefly the three positive considerations which, in addition to the more personal reasons I have expressed, have outweighed all objections in my own case, and brought me to the decision that I have made; and they are considerations which, in my opinion, should have general regard. First, the value of the moral element in an army is to be considered, and alongside of this the moral effect of men leaving positions of usefulness and comfort and honor to enter the army. If our cause is the just and sacred cause that most of us believe it to be, then no man among us is too good or stands in too high a position to give himself to it, or for it, in whatever way the country may call for his services. And the better and more enlightened the men are who go to make up the army, the purer and higher becomes the cause, and the more it becomes linked with the truest and holiest interests of the country, and the more elevated and earnest becomes the patriotism of the country. Moreover, this war has proved, if it was not proved before, that it is not bad men, or rough men, or always men of the stoutest bodies, that make the best soldiers, but that character, earnestess, faith, serve in an army as everywhere else. Not the low population of our cities, brought up to fighting, but youths delicately nurtured in wealthy and refined homes, and polished with the culture of colleges, have done some of the best service as soldiers in this war. Other things being equal, the truer a man is in character, the better soldier will he make. And, when other things are not equal, solidity of character and a heart in the cause will often more than make up for deficiency of bodily strength.

Secondly, men who might choose the alternative of staying at home ought to consider their duties toward those who, on account of their circumstances, must accept the alternative of going. The great complaint against the draft has been that the rich and cultivated — those who can easily command three hundred dollars — would remain at home, while the poorer class would be obliged to go. Now every one, if possible, ought to act so that there shall be left no show of justice in this complaint. Every drafted man who is not kept at home by very important considerations, every one who might stay at home, but can go, ought to go for this reason, if no other, — the encouragement and support of those who must go. Let it be seen that this draft is a fair thing, and that we mean to abide by it fairly, and that it is a democratic thing, — the rich and the poor, the educated and the uneducated, the man who labors with his hands and the man who labors with his brains, as they all have an equal interest in the country's preservation, so all standing side by side and shoulder to shoulder in its defence.

Thirdly and finally, — and in some respects the most important consideration of all, — what is most needed now for putting an effectual end to this rebellion, with all its causes and consequences, is a general uprising of the people to the support of the government, to the support of it against not only rebellion in the South, but against secret treason and open violence at home. Let the people of all classes not merely show submission, but respond with cheerful alacrity to this draft, each one going to his place in the army as to a post of solemn duty, and not only would the war soon come to an end, but the stability of republican institutions would be insured forever. The spectacle of a great people, including all classes, thus rising cheerfully and harmoniously together to meet the demands of a draft, saying to one another, "Our sons and brothers who could volunteer in this holy cause have gone, and we have now cast lots to see who shall go to stand by their sides or to defend their graves; and we, to whom the lots have fallen, now come ready in hand and heart for the service to which our country calls us,"— such a spectacle would be a grander exhibition than was that first uprising of the people at the outset of the war; and an army so formed would be nobler in its invincible determination than even an army of volunteers. God grant that I may be one in such an army! God grant, and the patriotic hearts of this community grant, that there may be many to stand with me! Could such an army spring up, I doubt if it would even have to march out of the loyal States, for it would be recognized as the army of the invincible fates, as the hosts of Heaven's retributive justice; and rebellion, violence, treason, oppression, lawless rage, and every foul wrong of war that now devastates our land, would shrink from before it into the darkness of annihilation, and law, liberty, and peace would be established in triumph and forever over a reunited country.

THE DRAMATIC ELEMENT IN THE CAREER OF ABRAHAM LINCOLN.

"For where a testament is, there must also of necessity be the death of the testator; for a testament is of force after men are dead."—HEB. ix. 16, 17.

It is sweet to linger in the fragrance of a good man's memory. The part that Abraham Lincoln has acted in our history can never become old or worn. It is a career upon which historians will ever love to dwell, and which will never lose its charm for the people. And, after all that has been spoken and written concerning him, there is yet one phase of his wonderful life and tragic destiny which has great attractiveness, and which I have hinted at once or twice in previous discourses, but which, so far as I have seen, has not anywhere been fully developed or much noticed. Mr. Sumner, in his eulogy just spoken, touches more closely upon what I refer to than any other writer or speaker whose words have come to my eye; but the object he had proposed to himself did not allow him to more than skirt the border of this phase of the great theme.

The point of view that I have in mind is the perfect dramatic unity and progress of Abraham Lincoln's life,—the wonderful line of destiny, or of providence, by which his career, from his birth to his death, was unfolded, in all its parts and acts and through all its shiftings of place and scene and time, on the thread of a single vital truth and to a single moral end. This life moves across the stage of history with the dramatic march of one of Homer's heroes. The stern demands of ancient Grecian tragedy were not more observed by its great artists in their greatest works than they have been observed in the actual life of this American President. Here must be no side issues, no confounding of moral lessons, no division and distraction of one prevailing moral purpose and force, no departure, amid whatever private or professional or domestic episodes or whatever change and variety of action, from the one truth which this individual career from its outset was chosen to embody and to teach for humanity. From its entrance on the stage of earthly being to its exit, this life must be moved by one inexorable purpose and will, and march to one inevitable fate, in order to print upon the heart of the world one of the grandest truths of human civilization and government and progress.

This is our theme. But why bring it here, and make it a subject of religious meditation? It may belong to the dramatist and the poet, it may serve the uses of the lecture-room and the magazine, but why bring it to the church? Because, first, there is a providence behind the scenes, the hidden infinite manager of the great drama. The ancients called it fate, destiny: we call it Providence, God, the Infinite Spirit. Abraham Lincoln, though self-possessed to an extraordinary degree, though having great independence and originality of being and native resources and capacities very largely at his command, was yet impelled, as few men have been, by a power beyond his own, possessed, used, chosen for a special work by a spirit above himself. And, secondly, I bring the theme here because of the grand moral importance to humanity of the truth which his life was selected thus dramatically to unfold and teach.

And what is this truth? It is the truth of republican freedom, simplicity, and equality,— in one word, the truth of democracy, as theoretically stated by Jefferson in the opening sentences of the Declaration of Independence. By the strict line of this truth, the life of Abraham Lincoln, act by act and scene by scene, was developed, from the day his eyes first saw the light in a log cabin on the Western frontier of civilization to the day when, as President of the United States, standing at the very topmost height of official position and honor, he was slain by the hand of an assassin, and those eyes closed forever to mortal things. To this truth he was born; to it he was apprenticed by the necessary conditions of his lot, during all the years of his boyhood and youth. At manhood it became his property purchased by conviction; it stamped henceforward his whole character, and all his personal, social, and professional habits.

When he was called into political life, this was at once his creed and the central principle of all his measures and acts; and, when this truth was challenged and defied by rebellion to the government founded upon it, then he, seemingly by accident, yet inevitably, became the leader of the loyal hosts in the fierce struggle with despotism and slavery, led them to triumph, and, in the hour of triumph, fell,— fell that he might have the greater triumph, as the Greek tragedians made their heroes fall in order that they might ascend to Olympus and to the society of the gods, fell that he might seal his testament to this truth of republican freedom, simplicity, and equality, with his blood, and sanctify it henceforth as the solemnly established polity of the nation. Is not here a life-drama such as is seldom enacted on this earth?

But let us bring out some of its features in fuller relief. Let us see how, in every part of its course, this career is vitalized, and its direction and progress determined by the truth I have stated,— see how close the hidden, inimitable Artist ever holds it to the one purposed aim, how statelily and solemnly it advances, by steps that seem almost to know whither they tend, to the inevitable tragic end.

The drama opens in the rudest and humblest condition of democratic life, the farthest possible removed from wealth and culture, and from any influences that may have been transmitted across the seas from the forms and refinements of monarchical civilization. Not amid the schools and cities and growing luxuries of the East, but in the far West, where nothing is yet established but the pure democratic idea, must the hero be born who is to testify for that idea through life and by death. He must be born of nothing but pure democracy. The world must see that this future republican ruler owed nothing by birth save to republican freedom, simplicity, and equality. Therefore he is born in a hut without floor, with but one room, with no articles of luxury, with very few even of comfort or necessity, born to toil and poverty, born of parents having no lineage, no learning, no library, having nothing but a little spot of soil and a rough shelter over their heads and honest hearts and hard-working hands. Yet, according to the theory of the country written in the Declaration of Independence, and partially established by the Revolution, those parents are a part of the sovereignty of the land; and from their loins must be born the strong man who is to be leader and ruler of the nation through the severest contest that democracy has ever known, and who is to testify to all history and throughout all time for the truth of the democratic idea.

But the contest against democracy has already begun. There is an institution in the land that flagrantly denies its most fundamental principles, — an institution of caste, inequality, oppression, and despotism. This institution has spread out to the frontier settlements. It is closing around that democratic hut, menacing its prosperity, its virtue, and the precious promise it holds. Slavery joins issue with the democratic idea in Kentucky, and threatens utterly to overwhelm it. But the times are not yet ripe for the great struggle: the hero is still a boy; the strength and integrity that his honest parentage and home have given him must be saved from contamination. The drama is just beginning. Not prematurely must the crisis be developed. The parents, indeed, do not thus reason with conscious reference to the future; but the genius of the republic is jealously guarding its hero. The prophetic Spirit of Truth, sitting calm behind the scenes, will not permit the whole future to be changed and robbed at this dangerous point. The little spot of land, which slavery was already beginning to envelop and impoverish, is sold, the rude home is abandoned; the parents escape from the snares and dangers of slaveholding Kentucky, and seek across the Ohio, still farther in the wilderness, a new home, but on free soil.

And now still further is our hero trained for the stern tasks of democratic sovereignty before him. It seems as if he must understand every atom of that sovereignty by going through the condition of every individual constituent of it, before he can be ready to assume it in his own person for the great ends designed. Hence he must exhaust every democratic occupation from the most menial to the most honored. He is a pioneer, and day after day, with sturdy blows, cuts a way through the forest to his home and to the land that is to feed him. He is a farmer, and by the sweat of his brow gathers his daily bread from the soil. He is a mechanic, and helps build the family house and its furniture. He is a famous rail-splitter, and fences the farm with his own hands. He is a flatboatman down the Mississippi. He is a clerk in a store. He is a militia captain, and has a little touch of war in the Indian troubles of the frontier. He sets up in business by himself as a country trader; he is postmaster, land surveyor, and finally lawyer and legislator.

And all this time, too, he is gathering knowledge,— not in schools and colleges and lyceums and public libraries, but out among the Western forests and prairies, gleaning from nature, from life, and from the few books to be found among his scattered neighbors or bought with hard-earned savings, laboring over his books in solitude by his democratic fireside, with his solitary democratic brain,— gathering knowledge, not to veneer over weakness and poverty of capacity, not enough even to cover and conceal the rugged fibre and homely solidity of the native stuff from which his being is made. All his knowledge is perfectly assimilated and used by his nature; for this man, born out of the loins of pure democracy, and destined to be the leader of American democracy in a deadly contest for national existence and to die its martyr, must be purely American and democratic through every nerve and fibre and pulse of his being.

But again the scene changes. The great struggle between democracy and despotism is approaching. The hosts are preparing on either side for the combat, and the destined leader of freedom must come forth into the public arena. Already in Congress he had voted steadily for freedom and equality in the national Territories, and even at that early day had tried to make the national capital free soil. But now the contest had thickened, and the smell of blood was already in the land. The virgin soil of Kansas was the prize. Should it be polluted and ruined by the demon of slavery, or given in pure wedlock to freedom? The plot against democracy begins to unfold its horrors: the "coming man" must now come. Unavoidably he is drawn from his retirement into the political field; and, although several years have yet to pass before he is hailed as leader, his powerful sword can never be sheathed again.

In the contest concerning Kansas, and in the famous Senatorial campaign with Stephen A. Douglas, which grew out of the Kansas conflict, it is remarkable how sharply the lines were drawn between freedom and slavery, how the debates constantly turned on this one point, and how radical and thorough Mr. Lincoln's utterances always were as the chosen champion of liberty. It is to be noticed, too, how he uniformly planted himself on the broad ground of the Declaration of Independence,—that is, of free and equal government for all classes and races; and he attacked slavery, because slavery attacked this invincibly true and fundamental principle of the republic.

And at this point in the development of this dramatic history we come to a very important and rarely noticed fact,— the key of the wonderful drama. Abraham Lincoln was the first politician or statesman who publicly proclaimed the doctrine of the "irrepressible conflict" of ideas between the South and the North. This he did on the 17th of June,— the anniversary of the battle of Bunker Hill,— 1858, in a speech to the State Convention of Illinois, which nominated him for Senator against Douglas. That speech opened almost with the words now become so famous and familiar: "A house divided against itself cannot stand. I believe this government cannot endure permanently half slave and half free. I do not expect the Union to be dissolved, I do not expect the house to fall; but I do expect it will cease to be divided. It will become all one thing or all the other." And this was the beginning of that noted Senatorial campaign which was but preliminary to the Presidential campaign. It was the striking of the key-note of this great American contest: it was the clarion voice of the true, destined leader, summoning the hosts of freedom to his standard. For, mark you again, this was the first political utterance of the doctrine of the irrepressible conflict between freedom and slavery, declaring that one of the antagonists, even in the domain of the States, must yield before the other. The moral reformers — the abolitionists — had declared it; but no statesman or leading politician proclaimed it before Abraham Lincoln. It was he that first took up and ingrafted upon the politics of the country the moral ideas of the abolition reformers. He made this remarkable speech several months before Mr. Seward took the same idea, clothed it in philosophic shape, and christened it by the name of "irrepressible conflict."

Can we longer wonder that Abraham Lincoln should be the chosen leader of the hosts of democracy and freedom, when this conflict comes to arms? that he, the first statesman who announced the divine necessity of the moral conflict, should be summoned to represent divine justice in the martial struggle, and to give thereto the costly testimony of his life? Not otherwise could the drama preserve its unity. Blind fate, destiny, could have made no other choice. Shall Providence be less wise than destiny? Shall the prophetic, preparing, managing Spirit be balked of its purpose? Shall a mighty national contest, involving national existence and the virtue and happiness of millions of human beings, be subject to accident? its sublime end postponed or thwarted by some political marplot? No! Providence is as grandly steady as destiny or fate; and not more inevitably, in the old Greek tragedy, did the fate-impelled hero, at the proper moment, come upon the stage than did Abraham Lincoln, in the dramatic ripeness of events, assume the political leadership of this nation. Consciously or unconsciously, when the clash of arms had come, the hosts of loyalty and liberty could only rally around the man whose voice had first uttered the true battle-cry. And therefore it was that, when that moment came, we found Abraham Lincoln, the leader that democratic freedom had been preparing in the West, in the President's chair at Washington, and Commander-in-chief of the army and navy of the United States.

And now events hasten more rapidly to the grand dénouement. Yet, like Hamlet, the hero hesitates. He dreads the awful conflict. He shrinks, as it were, from the very greatness of the task imposed upon him. Already, too, villany lurks in his path, assassination is dogging his steps; and he walks henceforth as if burdened with a mysterious, foreboding consciousness of his destiny. In his kindly, democratic nature there should be, and is, no taste for civil war and blood. He tries to conciliate,—puts forth his arm to avert the rushing fates: he holds the chalice of the Constitution to the white, maddened lips of the foe. But all in vain. With boastful, furious words, the cup is dashed to the ground: "We have a new Constitution, founded on the divine right of slavery: we fight for it, and take and give no quarter!" And so freedom's leader is held to his divinely purposed work,—defied by despotism, until forced in self-defence into the impregnable citadel of equal justice.

Yet the steps were all taken, not in passion, not in routed haste, but deliberately and with dignity, some of us thought too slowly and hesitatingly taken, and feared lest freedom would be betrayed. But the great Dramatist knew better than we,— knew the metal of the man, and knew he would not, could not, yield the principle to which his life had been, as it were by solemn vow, devoted.

Months before, in his contest with Douglas, with inspired earnestness and in the old Roman spirit of absolute self-consecration to the highest welfare of the republic, he had exclaimed:—

"Think nothing of me: take no thought for the political fate of any man whatsoever, but come back to the truths that are in the Declaration of Independence. You may do anything with me you choose, if you will but heed these sacred principles. You may not only defeat me for the Senate, but you may take me and put me to death. . . . I charge you to drop every paltry, insignificant thought for any man's success. It is nothing. I am nothing. Judge Douglas is nothing. But do not destroy that immortal emblem of humanity,— the Declaration of Independence."

And, again, on his way to Washington, in the old Independence Hall in Philadelphia, after inquiring what great sentiment it was in the Declaration there adopted which held the colonies so firmly together in the revolutionary struggle, he answered, "It was that sentiment which gave liberty, not alone to the people of this country, but, I hope, to the world, for all future time: it was that which gave promise that in due time the weight would be lifted from the shoulders of all men"; and then he added, "If this country cannot be saved without giving up that principle, I was about to say I would rather be assassinated on this spot than surrender it!" and closed the remarkable speech with the solemn words, "I have said nothing but what I am willing to live by, and, if it be the pleasure of Almighty God, die by." It was not in the nature of the man who had given himself to the whole truth of republican government with such vows as these, and whom the angel of the republic was guarding for her highest service and greatest glory, to betray the sacred office for which he had thus received Heaven's commission. He was cautious. He saw every difficulty in the way; for a time it seemed as if he reasoned with destiny, but he could not betray the cause so solemnly committed to his hands.

He was mortal, indeed; and, with all the care in preparing him for his high office, it was impossible that he should escape entirely all infection of the evil from which the whole nation suffered. He still had some respect for the local laws of slavery. And so the conflict must go on in him, as in the nation, until he should be purified by the fires of battle from all taint of the evil, and be lifted clear above all its entanglements, ready to strike the fatal blow with full moral strength. Observe, too, that, consistently with his past record and training, he came to the contest, not as an abolitionist *per se*, but on the broad ground of democracy. He was an emancipationist because a true democrat. He believed in freedom and equality for all, and therefore for the black man. He came to the conflict not avowedly to destroy slavery, but to save democratic government; and he destroyed slavery because incompatible with the continued existence of democratic government. The one is the broader position, and necessarily includes the other. Democracy necessitates abolitionism. This is the truth he is to proclaim to the world, and lead on to victory.

And now see the solemn steps of the grand march. We shall notice that there is no retrograde movement,— that there is really no delay, that every step comes in its place with the sublime constancy of fate, but also with the paternal, humane promise of a tender Providence, and that every step lifts the nation upward upon higher and broader ground, and nearer to the glory of its final triumph. Even in the first Inaugural Address, though conciliatory and seeking in some respects by compromise to avert the conflict, the key-note of democratic faith and assurance is sounded. "Why," said the President, "should there not be a patient confidence in the ultimate justice of the people? Is there any better or equal hope in the world? In our present differences is either party without faith of being in the right? If the Almighty Ruler of events, with his eternal truth and justice, be on your side of the North, or on yours of the South, that truth and that justice will surely prevail, by the judgment of this great tribunal of the American people." We passed these words by at the time with little notice; but, now that the drama is complete, they sound like the solemn utterances of the chorus in ancient tragedy, pronouncing upon the gathering combatants the warning and the judgment of the gods. It was the presiding, oracular genius of the republic that uttered them, giving judgment in advance.

Again, in the first message to Congress, dated July 4, 1861, though slavery is not directly attacked, there are brave sentences that strike at its root, and that must one day strike the fetters from all men's limbs. "This is essentially a people's contest. On the side of the Union it is a struggle for maintaining in the world that form and substance of government whose leading object is to elevate the condition of men, to lift artificial weights from all shoulders, to clear the paths of laudable pursuits for all, to afford all an unfettered start and a fair chance in the race of life." None but the Western pioneer, cradled in poverty, and, by his own sturdy hands and the "fair chance" that democratic institutions put into them, hewing his way into public position by a purely democratic path, could have uttered these words from the Presidential chair. Already we see in them the promise of a united and emancipated country. These are the same syllables that, by a little change of articulation, are to pronounce Richmond fallen, and the slave of South Carolina free.

In the message of December, 1861, there is an elaborate discussion, on principles of political economy, of the question of capital and labor, in which the pure democratic ground is taken that labor is superior to capital, and must be free and own capital, and not capital, labor. The discussion seemed to us abstract and ill-adapted to the pressing emergency of the hour; but we see now how fittingly it takes its place in the great struggle to complete the loyal argument. It is the bud of emancipation in the loyal border States. It is an appeal to prudent, thinking men, on grounds of industrial prosperity and self-interest. It brings the re-enforcement of material and social well-being to the cause of divine justice. Hear, too, how at the close, the grand choral strain comes in again, giving utterance to the sublimer principles that underlie the irrepressible conflict, and summoning the contestants again to the bar of future judgment.

"This [the free system of labor] is the just and generous and prosperous system, which opens the way to all, gives hope to all, and consequent energy and progress and improvement of condition to all. No men living are more worthy to be trusted than those who toil up from poverty, none less inclined to take or touch aught which they have not honestly earned. Let them beware of surrendering a political power which they already possess, and which, if surrendered, will surely be used to close the door of advancement against such as they, and to fix new disabilities and burdens upon them, till all of liberty shall be lost. . . . The struggle of to-day is not altogether for to-day: it is for a vast future also."

Closely following,— only three months later,— a special message is sent to Congress, recommending the passage of a resolution by which the federal government shall be authorized to co-operate by pecuniary aid with any State that will enact gradual abolition of slavery. Two months afterward, in a public proclamation, attention is called to this resolution, which was adopted by Congress; and the States most interested are earnestly appealed to, to avail themselves quickly of its privilege. Says the President:—

"You cannot, if you would, be blind to the signs of the times. I beg of you a calm and enlarged consideration of them, ranging, if it may be, far above partisan and personal politics. This proposal makes common cause for a common object, casting no reproaches upon any. It acts not the Pharisee. The change it contemplates would come gently as the dews of heaven, not rending or wrecking anything. Will you not embrace it? So much good has not been done by one effort in all past time as in the providence of God it is now your high privilege to do. May the vast future not have to lament that you have neglected it!"

And so the chorus echoes back with added intensity the divine plea of impartial justice that was the sublime burden of the previous message.

In the regular message of December, 1862, the same subject is taken up again, and discussed more elaborately and with greater scope. It is now proposed that Congress shall not wait for the States to accept, at their option, its offer of pecuniary aid toward emancipation, but shall initiate emancipation. An amendment to the Constitution is recommended, by which slavery shall be gradually, yet entirely, abolished in all the States and throughout the country. But the great import of the paper was not so much what it recommended, for its plan of emancipation was too heavily conditioned to be practically available, as the fact that the abolition of slavery was for the first time boldly and seriously discussed and made the most important topic in a regular Presidential message. More memorable still is the message for its closing words, in which the chorus of the drama again speaks, inspired by the genius of republican freedom, who thus urges her champions up to the true battle-ground, and holds the now fast developing action close to its divine intent. Hear the deep, stately, measured tones as they seem to come from the distant heavens:—

"The dogmas of the quiet past are inadequate to the stormy present. The occasion is piled high with difficulty, and we must rise with the occasion . . . We must disenthrall ourselves, and then we shall save our country. . . . No personal significance or insignificance can spare one or another of us. The fiery trial through which we pass will light us down in honor or dishonor to the latest generation. . . . We — even we here — hold the power and bear the responsibility. In giving freedom to the slave we assure freedom to the free, honorable alike in what we give and what we preserve. We shall nobly save or meanly lose the last, best hope of earth. Other means may succeed. This could not, cannot fail. The way is plain, peaceful, generous, just, — a way which, if followed, the world will forever applaud and God must forever bless."

But this paper coupled with its plan of gradual abolition the principles of compensation and voluntary colonization. Its proposed method of action was not so lofty as the spirit that inspired it. The noble goal aimed at condemned the halting effort. It was not for any such imperfect result that this mighty contest was proving the metal of the nation. The human instrument was not so far-sighted as the Providence which wrought through him, — the actor not so wise as the manager behind the scenes. Yet he is faithful and true, and submits himself with unwavering loyalty to the teaching of events and of God; and with ever-lengthening and bolder paces he goes forward. One after another all imposed conditions of emancipation drop away. Compensation, gradualism, colonization, vanish and become obsolete ideas; and the champion stands, clean from all alloy of the evil he is to annihilate, alone with God and justice.

In August, 1861, he had modified General Fremont's proclamation of emancipation in Missouri to conciliate Kentucky. In May, 1862, he had countermanded General Hunter's decree of abolition in the Department of the South only because he reserved the great right for himself and would not allow it to be frittered away powerlessly, and with little moral effect, by subordinates. It is evident in the very order of countermand that he begins to see clearly what the line of duty and destiny must be. He appeals to the insurgent States, in the words already quoted, to smooth the way to peaceful emancipation by voluntarily acceding to the logic of events and to the plain intent of divine Providence. Even as late as the 13th of September he had received a religious deputation from the city of Chicago, appointed to urge him to declare emancipation by military proclamation, and replied to their arguments with such a strong array of objections to the measure that the deputation had departed in great doubt as to his adopting it. But it is as clear as noonday now that the President had been debating the measure in his own mind for months, and marshalling the arguments for and against it, and that in this interview he summed up the difficulties in the way, as they had presented themselves to him, in order to draw forth, if possible, from the deputation new light upon the question. He also significantly added at the close of the conference: "I can assure you the subject is on my mind by day and night more than any other. Whatever shall appear to be God's will I will do." And now God's will is rapidly revealed to him, not through miraculous interposition,— for, as he says, "these are not the days of miracles,"— but through an earnest desire to "ascertain what is possible and learn what appears to be wise and right." Events are his instructors. The spirit of Almighty Justice, unfolding its high purpose more and more in the daily history of the struggle, is his teacher. He consults his cabinet for suggestion, not for advice. Upon him Heaven has put the responsibilty, and he will decide and bear the weight of the decision alone. And the decision being made, the duty clear, on the 22d of September he issues the preliminary declaration, and gives the final warning to the rebellious States; and on the 1st of January, 1863, appears the great Proclamation of immediate emancipation.

The critical blow has now been struck. The deed is done for which all before has been only preparation; and all that comes after — emancipation in the border States, the enlistment of negroes in the army, the Freedmen's Bureau, the anti-slavery amendment to the Constitution — is only the gathering up of the fruits of that victory and making it secure forever. The issuing of the Proclamation was the crisis in the drama; and so, when that blow was given, the embattled hosts rushed to the conflict with a more furious and deadlier onset. It was now life or death to the foe and slavery, life or death to the nation and freedom. But through all the deathly contests on the martial field and through all the struggles on the equally dangerous field of politics, threatened by foes and importuned by friends, the President never recedes from that decree. "The promise," he says, "being made, must be kept." "While I remain in my present position, I shall not attempt to retract or modify the Emancipation Proclamation, nor shall I return to slavery any person who is free by the terms of that Proclamation or by any of the acts of Congress." And again, "If the people," he says, "by whatever mode or means, should make it an executive duty" to reverse the action of that Proclamation, "another, and not I, must be their instrument to perform it." Here speaks the stern stuff from which strong men are made and martyrs come. But the people will stand by the Proclamation, nor will they choose any other hand than his that had written it to execute it. Not to another can the true champion's glory be given before the field is wholly won.

And now, with clearer vision and more entire surrender to the divine purpose of events, he consecrates himself to the remaining tasks before him. Henceforth union and freedom are synonymous. Two conditions are necessary to peace,— the abolition of all acts of secession, the acceptance of emancipation. But hear again the lofty strains of the chorus, pronouncing judgment on the new aspect of affairs: —

"Peace does not appear so distant as it did. I hope it will come soon and come to stay, and so come as to be worth the keeping in all future time. It will then have been proved that among freemen there can be no successful appeal from the ballot to the bullet, and that they who take such appeal are sure to lose their case and pay the cost. And there will be some black men who can remember that, with silent tongue and clinched teeth and steady eye and well-poised bayonet, they have helped mankind on to this great consummation; while I fear there will be some white ones unable to forget that, with malignant heart and deceitful speech, they have striven to hinder it. Still, let us not be over-sanguine of a speedy, final triumph. Let us be quite sober. Let us diligently apply the means, never doubting that a just God, in his own good time, will give us the rightful result."

And so, with ever broader comprehension of the divine meaning of the contest and deeper conviction of the divine hand controlling it, the President renews his vows, and leads on the loyal hosts of freedom to new achievements. Under God, and the providential choice of the nation, he is the instrument for establishing the government on the true democratic basis of liberty, justice, and equality, and so for fulfilling, at last, the prophecy of the Declaration of Independence to all the people of the land.

At Gettysburg, standing among the graves of the heroes who on that glorious field had given their bodies to death, but who, with their blood, had written their names in the book of immortal life, he opens his address with these memorable sentences: "Fourscore and seven years ago our fathers brought forth upon this continent a new nation, conceived in liberty, and dedicated to the proposition that all men are created equal. Now we are engaged in a great civil war, testing whether that nation, or any nation so conceived and so dedicated, can long endure." And then he solemnly consecrates himself and the nation to finish the work which the heroes there buried had so nobly died for, in order "that this nation, under God, shall have a new birth of freedom, and that government of the people, by the people, and for the people shall not perish from the earth."

What a perfect recognition of the eternal principles involved in the conflict, and of the Providence watching over and directing with far-reaching vision the struggle, does this reverent dedication disclose! Henceforth the nation's President is God's servant, and the war is a religious war,— a religious war more really than if it were to set up some idol of theology, or to enthrone some ecclesiastic power, or to rescue the tomb of Jesus from the hand of unbelieving Saracens; for it is a war to disenthrall and redeem humanity, to rescue a whole continent from being the grave of liberty to become its throne, to lift from the shoulders of a whole people, through the expiatory suffering of just retribution, the monstrous burden of a gigantic iniquity, and to bring, through the reconciliation of obedience to divine law, the grandest opportunity for national and individual development that was ever offered to the human race: it is a war, conducted by unseen powers in the heavens, for the divine right of mankind, without reference to race or class or color, to self-government and self-development. And the President acknowledges himself but a willing instrument in the hands of the mighty celestial forces directing the combat. Hear how the lips of the loyal leader give utterance to the sentiment of this advanced position: "Now, at the end of three years' struggle, the nation's condition is not what either party, or any man, devised or expected. God alone can claim it. Whither it is tending seems plain. If God now wills the removal of a great wrong, and wills also that we of the North, as well as you of the South, shall pay fairly for our complicity in that wrong, impartial history will find therein new causes to attest and revere the justice and goodness of God."

From this high position it is but a step to the final consummation of the moral progress of the drama. After a political struggle, filled with critical and perilous incidents and the most solemnly momentous of any that has occurred in our history, the people rechoose for their leader the man who now confesses himself to be not only the servant of the people, but the servant of God; and they choose him with the express purpose that he may finish the work for republican freedom which the retributive justice of Almighty God has given to his hands. And now the recognition of this truth of the expiatory nature of the war, and the divine instrumentality of his office, culminates in the majestic, almost awful solemnity of the second Inaugural Address, which rises clear above all earthly taint and human infirmity and reservation, to the prophetic and divine standpoint. The political orator is clothed with the mantle of the inspired prophet. The wise statesman utters his counsels as from the tribunal of heaven. The leader of the nation becomes the oracle of divine laws and judgments. From the mouth of what other human magistrate in all history shall we find such utterances as these?

"The Almighty has his own purposes. 'Woe came into the world because of offences, for it must needs be that offences come; but woe to that man by whom the offence cometh.' If we shall suppose that American slavery is one of these offences which in the providence of God must needs come, but which, having continued through his appointed time, he now wills to remove, and that he gives to both North and South this terrible war as the woe due to those by whom the offence came, shall we discern that there is any departure from those divine attributes which the believers in a living God always ascribe to him? Fondly do we hope, fervently do we pray, that this mighty scourge of war may speedily pass away. Yet, if God wills that it continue until all the wealth piled by the bondman's two hundred and fifty years of unrequited toil shall be sunk, and until every drop of blood drawn by the lash shall be paid by another drawn with the sword, as was said three thousand years ago, so still it must be said that the 'judgments of the Lord are true and righteous altogether.' With malice toward none, with charity for all, with firmness in the right, as God gives us to see the right, let us strive on to finish the work we are in, to bind up the nation's wounds, to care for him who shall have borne the battle, and for his widow and his orphans,— to do all which may achieve and cherish a just and lasting peace among ourselves and with all nations."

In these words the highest possible utterance of the struggle is reached, the moral triumph of the drama is here achieved, the eternal majesty of the divine laws is acknowledged and vindicated; and the hero stands perfectly submissive to the divine Purpose, docile to the slightest behest of Almighty Power, and his eye anointed with heavenly wisdom. These sentences read like a solemn choral response to the half-illuminated, oracularly uttered judgment of the first Inaugural: it is the genius of the republic, gathering up, as in the ancient chorus, the whole meaning and purpose of the drama, and echoing back, through all the vast, intervening events of the action, the august announcement that the mystery is unravelled, the struggle ended, the judgment finished and unalterably given. Battles, victories, capitulations, the surrender of armies and towns, the submission of the whole rebellion to the cause that is thus decided for by the celestial umpires, follow in rapid and natural course.

But is the hero to have no more visible triumph than this? Yes: he enters the fallen capital of rebellion and slavery. His entrance into Richmond, with no imperial pomp, with no military escort even, attended only by a few sailors from the navy,— emblem of republican Executive simplicity; walking up the long, desolate streets of the captured city, in plain citizen's dress, holding his little boy by the hand,— emblem of republican domestic simplicity; followed by a growing throng, as the news ran from street to street, of men, women, and children, from whose limbs his hands had broken the shackles of slavery, their skin black, but hearts white with joyous gratitude, as they crowded round to hail their deliverer, baring their heads in reverence before him, and he, with instinctive courtesy, standing with uncovered head in response,— emblem of democratic liberty and equality,— this journey is his triumphal procession, this throng of emancipated slaves his imperial escort, the benedictions of these new-made freemen are his crown, the crown of democratic sovereignty.

There is now but one remaining glory that can

be accorded. The strict laws of tragedy require that the hero shall die for the truth he has lived for, shall fall in the hour of triumph. And so the President must fall. Does Providence therefore direct the assassin's blow? By no means: only as the Providential laws surround, limit, and penetrate every contest between good and evil. But the deadly blow is aimed 'by the hand of the foe. It is the last, desperate, maddened effort of the struggling combatant. It is the crowning wickedness of the rebellion and slavery. The evil principle of the drama must culminate, as well as the good: it must develop all its inherent and hidden horrors of evil. It must leave no seed of crime that belongs to itself unfruitful; it must leave not the smallest vestige of honor attached to its name. And so, filled with revenge, mad with defeat, inspired with demoniac frenzy, it puts forth all the remaining energy of its mortal strength to slay the man whom it recognizes as the incarnation of all the principles that have contended against it, and the leader of the hosts that have defeated it in battle. It slays him, and thereby, according to the moral intent of the drama, brands itself with everlasting infamy, while it lifts him to an immortal glory, and saves forever the truth to which his life was devoted. The assassin's crime is the rebellion's infamy, and his and freedom's apotheosis. The President falls. But over his grave the nation has a new birth, a resurrection. He seals his testament with his blood, and sanctifies republican truth forever. The President falls. But over his grave his spirit rises into the renowned halls of the celestial heroes, welcomed amid the triumphant songs of a nation redeemed, a people emancipated, a country saved.

With the hero's triumphant departure from earth the drama is ended; but the Spirit of the drama lingers, and utters an epilogue for the awestruck, listening spectators, and this is the epilogue it speaks: —

The President falls, "for, where a testament is, there must also of necessity be the death of the testator." The President falls. But his testament remains with us, "for a testament is of force after men are dead." The testament remains. The nation, humanity, the world, are its legatees; but we, the people of this generation, are its executors, and we have given sacred bonds, written and attested on many a battlefield with our kindred's blood, that we will administer it,— administer it with exact and impartial justice to all classes and castes and races among us,— in order "that government of the people, by the people, and for the people shall not perish from the earth."

THE HIGHER PATRIOTISM.

THERE are certain familiar phrases on the lips and in the press to-day, such as "the higher education," "the higher criticism," "the higher culture." The meaning of these phrases may not be clearly grasped by all who hear or see them, nor even, possibly, by all who use them. Yet they all denote, in some way, a higher or more comprehensive standard of judgment, with regard to the subject-matter considered, than was in vogue even less than a half-century ago. "The higher education" means not merely an advanced course of instruction beyond the traditional "three R's" of the old-time common school, but it means an advancement of the whole realm of learning. It means that there is a higher school than the high school, and that the college course of studies has been widened immeasurably from the routine of a generation or two back, and that, even in the common school, glimpses are given of this larger realm of knowledge. It means, too, quite as much, a different educational method in every grade and kind of education, that education is no longer the mere hammering of facts into the brain, but the training of the brain into the perceptions and use of facts. So "the higher criticism" means the application of a new and more scientific method of research to the subject-matters of learning, and particularly to the study of the Bible and the general phenomena of religion.

But the phrases themselves, even more than their meaning, have suggested my topic this morning, in connection with the annual recurrence of our national birthday. The age which is talking so much of the higher education, the higher criticism, the higher culture, the higher civilization, should certainly recognize the need of a higher patriotism. And we of this country, at the present hour, are, in my opinion, in a condition of urgent need of a higher standard of patriotic sentiment than that which apparently animates the active majority of our country's population. If the country is to do its part worthily in behalf of these great interests of education, culture, civilization, and religion, if it is even to hold worthily the traditions of the past in these respects, it is of the utmost importance that the standard of patriotism among us should be lifted to a higher level, that the sentiment of patriotism — that is, our love for and our pride in our country — should be infused with a loftier and purer principle. These great interests, it is true, are not bounded by national frontiers. Humanity overleaps the distinctions of country and race. Religion is as wide as the world. Learning and civilization are not provincialized to any one land. The philanthropist may truthfully say, "My country is the world; my countrymen are mankind." Yet we cannot live in all countries at once. Our work must be done in some special part of the world, in connection with some special country and people. And the more and better work we do for the elevation of our own country and people, the more effectively will our power be manifest in promoting the interests of mankind the world over. The working end of our lever for lifting the human race forward is in our own land.

These statements, again, presuppose that our regard and service for our own country are based on ethical principles. The kind of patriotism whose motto is, "Our country, right or wrong," or even, "Our country, however bounded," is not to be commended. National selfishness is just as immoral as individual selfishness. The self-aggrandizement of one nation at the cost of another nation, especially if the latter be a weak nation at the mercy of a strong neighbor, is just as much a violation of the principles of honor and justice as would be a similar course of conduct by one man toward another. The building up of one country by defrauding another is just as much theft as it is when one individual land-owner adds to his estate by some fraudulent depredation on his neighbor's property rights. "Thou shalt not steal," "Thou shalt not covet anything that is thy neighbor's," "Thou shalt not bear false witness," are commandments which apply to nations as well as to individuals. Yet, on account of the difficulty of fixing the weight of moral responsibility so that it may be felt, where for the acts of nations there are so many who may properly share it, there is a too general acquiescence in the idea, though few would openly defend it, that there is a lower moral code for the conduct of nations than for individuals. Then, too, on account of sentimental associations which people have with the land of their birth and their homes, of their fathers and their kindred, a glamour is apt to creep over the conscience when it is a question of moral judgment concerning one's own country's deeds. It is a feeling akin to that which leads one to look blindly, if not forgivingly, toward the faults of one's own family. But, however excusable or even commendable such tenderness may be toward moral infirmity in the family circle, it is not a mood of mind that is morally wholesome for a citizen to entertain toward his country. The relation is, in fact, so different that no moral parallelism exists between the two cases. In the family the upright and the infirm are equally members of one body, and the relation is between one individual and another. But the citizen is a part of his country. The citizen is not one individual and his country another, but the citizens together are the country. Its acts are their acts. Its morality is their morality. Its infirmities are their infirmities. Hence, when the citizens are induced to look tenderly and forgivingly toward their country's faults, they are really excusing and petting their own faults; and this is a national mood of mind that is anything but wholesome and reformatory. We want no patriotism in this age which asserts that one's own country can do no wrong, more than we want the antiquated doctrine that "the king can do no wrong." One assertion is as false as the other. The higher patriotism must be interfused, through and through, with the ethical sentiment. It cannot be merely the love and defence of one's country because it chances to be one's birthplace and home and to hold the graves of one's forefathers, but it should be an aspiration and purpose to make a country which shall be morally worthy of the love and defence of noble-minded citizens. Not what our country is, but what it can and ought to be, is the central pivot of the higher patriotism.

As to our own country, there is so much in its history and in the basic principles of its government that is worthy of the utmost moral admiration that the danger is that any one generation is tempted to trust too much to that roll of honor and to boast of it as a shield against any arraignment of present delinquencies. And then, too, ours is a country so magnificent in its extent and resources, its growth and prosperity have been so unexampled, its natural scenery is so diversified in beauty and grandeur, and its people, rapidly multiplying by migrations from all parts of the earth, have shown, on the whole, in the little more than a century since they became an independent nation, such a marvel of success in the art of self-government, that our patriotic sentiment is quick to go out to all these outward marks of national greatness and wealth, and to overlook some of the weightier matters which make a nation morally great and powerful, wherein our record would not be so much to our credit. It is a pity that on the anniversary celebrations of our national birth so little is done to stimulate the higher phases of patriotism; that, with all the noisy fuss and furor, the parade and show and cost, there is rarely anything done to recall and heighten the moral significance of the birth of this people among the nations of the earth, nor to educate and strengthen the sense of moral obligation, on the part of the present responsible actors of the nation, worthily to develop a country whose moral greatness shall correspond with the proportions of its material prosperity and power. On the contrary, oftener than not, the methods of celebration have so little of appropriateness and dignity, and are accompanied with so much of positive annoyance and discomfort, that a large number of citizens are put into anything but a mood of congratulation over their country's birthday.

The need of a patriotism of a higher moral quality has been especially intensified by certain features in the recent history of our country. It is not pleasant nor usual to speak of national faults on the Fourth of July. Yet, I can but think it would be a good thing for this nation to-morrow, in the midst of its patriotic celebrations, to have some of its moral shortcomings and perils so presented to its conscience that that organ would be pricked into a wholesome conviction of sin. It certainly cannot be good nor safe to allow the political conscience of the people to be lulled to sleep under any such doctrine as that which has been promulgated by a person in high political position and authority, that the Ten Commandments and the Golden Rule have no place in politics. That, too generally, they do not find place in practical politics is cause not for declaration of the fact as a political principle (Heaven forbid!), but cause and urgent call for political reform. It is one of the wise features of the system of government in the United States, and a feature whose wisdom has been so corroborated by time that its consistent and thorough application is only made the more apparent, that state and Church shall be separated. But woe to the country if it shall ever accept the teaching that politics and morals shall be separated, or that practical politics shall be separated from even the high ethical sanctions of religion! Where, pray, do we want our religion and ethics? What are they for but to guide us in the practical duties of life? And what duties are more immediately practical than our political duties?

It may, I believe, be truthfully said that there is no political duty of any sort which does not involve some moral question. Duty itself is the primary word of morals. Even the political issues that to-day, and in the just entered great national campaign, are most conspicuously to agitate and divide public opinion in this country — that is, the tariff question and the silver, or money, question — involve at bottom ethical problems. The ethical bearing of such complicated political problems as these is not always visible to the disputants; yet, through free discussion and gradual enlightenment, these questions will ultimately work themselves down to their moral bases, and will never be permanently settled till settled according to the requirements of impartial justice between citizen and citizen, and between the whole body of citizens and the world. Politics means the science of government. And there is nothing which a political government has to do, even if it be but the building of a road or the chartering of a bridge, which does not at some point touch the question of right between man and man.

But, while on many matters that are at issue in politics equally good men may differ as to where the right lies, and a period of educating discussion is necessary for making clear the moral bearings, there are other matters on which momentous political issues and elections are made frequently to depend,— practices in vogue, motives appealed to, passions aroused, concerning which the moral aspect is already so evident that it would seem as if there could be no division among men of tolerably upright consciences as to their condemnation. And there would be no division on such matters, were it not for the hallucination that, at the mandate of party and in the alleged interest of partisan success, the moral law may be somehow temporarily abrogated for the individual conscience. Take, for instance, that class of politicians, of whatever party, who may be said to define politics, not as the science of government, but as the science of getting government office for themselves and friends,—the men who are in politics for what they can make out of the business. Tammany Hall, in New York, is the most conspicuous representative of this class of politicians in this country. But every State, and every city of any considerable size, has the same species of political aspirants with more or less of political power, though they may be kept under measurable control by the force of public opinion in many places. And everywhere we should say that all right-minded men would combine to condemn and put down such self-seeking aspirants, many of whom are not merely seekers for political favor, but miscreants bent on plunder of the people's property. But too often in such cases party attraction is stronger than the moral law; and we find even the otherwise good and right-minded men, instead of combining against this party of political plunderers, dividing their own forces and then each division rivalling the other in making bargains with the plunderers and the spoilsmen. It is commonly believed that Tammany Hall decided our last Presidential election; and it is now prophesied that, though it has not succeeded in nominating the Presidential candidate of its choice, it will yet decide the election this year between the two great parties. It should be cause for the utmost humiliation and shame that a society so thoroughly disreputable and immoral, so in league with metropolitan vice and crime, should be such a power in politics as to tempt either of the great parties of the country to make bargains with it. But more cause for humiliation is it that any of the managers of the great parties of the country should be ready to accept the tempter's price. The Tammany element, unfortunately, is in the parties themselves. Wherever found, it is after the spoils of office and the scalps of its enemies. It is an element that goes into politics with no moral principle whatever. It is always for self. It corrupts whatever it touches. And yet good men, enlightened men, divide on minor issues of political policy and succumb to its power.

Akin to the Tammany evil, and springing from the same root, is the increasing use of money as a power in political elections. Of course there is a legitimate use for money in political campaigns. Literature is to be printed and circulated, public meetings are to be held, the people are to be roused from apathy to action by intelligent and spirited discussion. But such needs for money as these would demand but a small portion of the vast sums of money that are raised and spent for campaign purposes. In many places it has become a rule to assess candidates for office at a fixed sum, according to the amount in salary and perquisites the office is considered worth. In New York even candidates for judgeships are thus assessed by political bosses to the figure of thousands of dollars; and some of the most eminent and worthy of the judges of that State have had to submit to this mulct, if they would reach the places for which they may have a proper ambition and for which their fellow-citizens deem them specially qualified. In this case the vicious custom which has assumed the force of law should certainly be forbidden by law. Of all official personages, a judge should be clear of even the suspicion of contributing money for his own election. And, generally, it would be more becoming, even if statute law cannot accomplish it, that the unwritten law of public opinion should prevent a candidate for any office paying money for a campaign in which his own election to office is in question. But now the expectation is just the reverse. A candidate for public office is not only looked to for such courtesies as dinners and railroad tickets to delegates on convention days,— all of which courtesies are of the nature of small bribes,— but he is expected to pay largely into the campaign fund, if he has the means to do it, and is quite likely to be chosen as a candidate because he has the means and the disposition to use them freely in behalf of his political ambition. And so we have, at election times, our political journals full of suggestions, which should make our cheeks tingle with shame, that the candidates with the largest "barrels"— as the political slang is — are winning the political race; and intimations are thick that rich men buy their way even into such high offices of dignity and power as that of a United States Senator or a Cabinet position. That campaign funds are used, in one way and another, for the bribing of voters, for the actual purchase of voters at so many dollars a head, has become an open secret: it is practised in cities and in country towns, and even our new ballot laws have not yet stopped this profanation of the freeman's duty of voting. To this shameful degradation has fallen the sacred right of self-government by the ballot which our fathers fought to establish. Oh, for the higher patriotism before whose indignant scorn both the briber and the bribed should be driven, at least, into outward respect for the Declaration of Independence and the decencies of free citizenship!

Then, again, the extravagant pension legislation of the country has opened another most fertile source of corruption. It is a kind of corruption that is infinitely subtle, working like a deadly disease at the very roots of patriotism. The United States Senate has just passed the "Annual Pension Appropriation Bill," aggregating nearly $145,000,000. The Commissioner of Pensions, however, estimates that this immense sum will fall short of the requirements, which he puts at $156,000,000; and in the course of the discussion it was stated that, even with no additional legislation increasing the list of pensioners or their pensions, the present laws would bring the necessary appropriation up to nearly $200,000,000 in the course of two or three years. When General Grant was President, he thought that a sum less than $30,000,000 annually should suffice to meet all just pension claims, even when they should reach the highest point. And up to 1879 his estimate was, on an average, correct. In that year Congress passed the "Arrears of Pensions Bill," which at once nearly doubled the annual amount required. And, what is worse, it disclosed to the ex-soldiers of the country the fatal facility of Congress for passing such bills. The legislation had not been called for by those whom it would benefit. The soldiers had, up to that time, been self-respecting. There was no argument of any weight to show their needs. It was simply a demagogue's measure to catch their votes. And from that time to this, as still more liberal legislation has been proposed and adopted, there has been no party in Congress that has dared to oppose it. A new business for pension claim agents and pension lawyers and lobbyists sprang up, the soldiers themselves were plied with circulars reminding them of the government's bounty, and setting them to work to look up their diseases and disabilities and establish their claims. The result was that thousands and scores of thousands of soldiers went on to the pension rolls because of some wound or contingent disability, though abundantly able to take care of themselves and their families, or possessing an ample fortune; and a multitude of others are there who may be disabled, but whose disability is in no wise the result of their wounds or exposures in the country's service. Moreover, nearly thirty per cent. of this enormous annual appropriation does not reach the soldiers at all. It goes to pension agents and to the expenditures of the Pension Bureau. Now, I am well aware that to raise any criticism of this enormous pension system of our country is to subject one to the charge of being disloyal to what was our Union soldiers' cause. Do you ungratefully forget the debt, it is asked, which the country owes its soldiers? To which I reply, No: I can never forget it, nor is it a debt which the nation can ever pay. It is a kind of debt which cannot be measured nor paid in dollars and cents. If the old soldiers were disabled by the war, and they or those dependent on them are in need, then let the help be prompt and generous. The nation should see to it that none such should suffer. But to provide that a soldier not of this class should be aided by the bounty of the public treasury is to transform the proud and honorable tie of patriotism into a mercenary relation. As to loyalty to the cause for which our soldiers fought, I claim that it was not the thought of pay, but the spirit of patriotism which was the impelling motive which led to enlistments in the army. It was enough if our State or the nation promised to care for those dependent on us, should the fortunes of war deprive them of our support. That was the only contract which the nation undertook,— that and the support of the army in the field. The rest of the compensation was to be found in the prizes of valor and self-sacrifice and in the honor of doing honorable service for the salvation of one's country when in peril and for human liberty. It was my privilege to be one of those who did some slight part in that great service. But, though I had been wounded and maimed in the conflict, so long as with brain or hand I can earn my bread, I trust I should have the grace to say to my country, "Keep your pensions for those who are disabled and in want: leave to me the sole but ample satisfaction of having served my country as I would have served my own mother in peril, from filial love and duty." The true loyalty can ask no other reward than that. Apply not your silver knife to cut the nerve of the higher patriotism, which places honor above silver or gold or comfort or life.

There are other evils of recent growth in this country which are a great strain on the patriotism of good citizens. But I can only briefly allude to them. There is the growing misgovernment of great cities, due largely to political entanglement with the vicious power of the liquor saloon. There is the utter failure of free government in some of our cities, owing to this and other causes, and a condition of practical anarchy,— as when, in New Orleans, if the courts fail to do justice, a mob of citizens breaks into a jail and deliberately murders a dozen imprisoned and defenceless men;

and this great nation of sixty-five millions of people is powerless by law and in fact to prevent the massacre or to bring the murderers to trial. There, again, are the outrages committed against the liberties and rights of the colored people in some parts of the country; and, again, though political platform and pulpit may utter their indignant protests, this great government looks on helplessly. You may attempt a journey in a palace car across the continent, or you may send a train with treasure across; but you do it with the liability that your train or car will be held up by banditti, and the treasure stolen and the passengers robbed. Or look at our latest anti-Chinese bill,— a piece of legislation which is both a perfidy and an atrocity, a violation of our own solemn treaties and an institution of legal measures against unoffending Chinamen, now for years resident in this country, which revives the spirit and some of the features of the fugitive slave law. Let there be needed restriction on immigration, applicable alike to all nationalities; but let, at least, the legislation be equitable and the laws humane. And the humiliating feature about it is that this legislation was adopted against the sober conscience of the country, and at the behest of party expediency. It was one of the things which neither party in Congress dared to oppose nor the President to veto, for fear of losing the support of the Pacific States in the coming campaign.

Noting all these things, are we, it may be well

asked, a nation of civilized men, or are we still in a semi-barbarous condition? And yet, remembering all these things, where, on the whole, shall we find a better country? where one with vaster possibilities for good and a more promising future? Taking things even at their worst among us, what is the duty, what the lesson, of our national birthday? Not to flee the country, not to fold our hands and leave it to be preyed on by the harpies of ruin. Here, rather, is our opportunity to show our patriotism,— the opportunity for that higher patriotism which would go to the rescue of a country in peril and save it, an opportunity for making a country which shall be worth living for and worth dying for. Our fathers were not dismayed when first, on these rugged New England shores, they had to fight for their very existence, as well as for their religious liberty, against climate, against the wilderness, against savage man and savage beast, against famine and disease. They did not succumb: they conquered. Our fathers of the Revolutionary epoch did not yield to the discouragements of their era. They did not sink in despair at the thought of their untrained militia meeting in armed conflict the veteran soldiers of Great Britain, of their poverty contending against England's wealth, of traitors at home ready to attack them in the rear. They had faith in the strength of their cause, in the strength of their hearts, in the strength of their right arms; and they conquered. And, when that more recent trial hour came,—the slaveholders' rebellion,—the country did not falter. At first, indeed, there was the discouraged cry, "Let the wayward sisters go!" But, when the flag was struck, the country's heart felt the blow, and was smitten with a righteous indignation. The country rose to the level of the need. Men, means, statesmanship, military leadership, all came amply adequate to the emergency; and the country was saved,—the whole country,—and rededicated entire to liberty. With such memories in our national history we ought to be shamed out of all half-faith in our republican institutions, out of all half-heartedness and cowardly discouragement in face of the evils that now seem to endanger them.

Yet we are not to close our eyes to these evils. We are not to trust in any principle of "manifest destiny" to save us from them. No doctrine of the old-fashioned optimistic fatalism, that, because we are the freest nation and have the best form of government on earth, therefore no evil can befall us, is going to meet present emergencies. We must meet them just as the country has always met the evils that have beset it hitherto,—by resolute vigilance and courage, by thoughtfulness, by boldly facing the evils and overcoming them, not necessarily by military power, but by steady application of the best intellect and conscience of the country to the devising of political, legal, and moral remedies. Most solemn duties rest upon the people of these States,—duties to be performed under a sense of religious obligation, duties to our country and duties to mankind, whose welfare is so closely involved in the success and prosperity of our free institutions, duties to liberty, to justice, to human rights. We justly honor those who have died for their country. But it is a harder and therefore a nobler task to live for one's country.

www.ingramcontent.com/pod-product-compliance
Lightning Source LLC
Chambersburg PA
CBHW032000300426
44117CB00008B/849